The Rhythm of Thought

The Rhythm
of Thought

Art, Literature, and Music after Merleau-Ponty

JESSICA WISKUS

The University of Chicago Press

Chicago and London

Jessica Wiskus is associate professor of musicianship and chair of the Department of Musicianship Studies at Duquesne University.

The University of Chicago Press, Chicago 60637
The University of Chicago Press, Ltd., London
© 2013 by The University of Chicago
All rights reserved. Published 2013.
Printed in the United States of America

22 21 20 19 18 17 16 15 14 13   1 2 3 4 5

ISBN-13: 978-0-226-03092-0 (cloth)
ISBN-13: 978-0-226-03108-8 (e-book)

Library of Congress Cataloging-in-Publication Data

Wiskus, Jessica, 1976–
    The rhythm of thought : art, literature, and music after Merleau-Ponty / Jessica Wiskus.
        pages : illustrations ; cm
    Includes bibliographical references and index.
    ISBN 978-0-226-03092-0 (cloth : alkaline paper) — ISBN 978-0-226-03108-8 (e-book)   1. Philosophy, French—20th century.   2. Art and music.   3. Music and literature.   4. Merleau-Ponty, Maurice, 1908–1961.   5. Cézanne, Paul, 1839–1906—Criticism and interpretation.   6. Debussy, Claude, 1862–1918—Criticism and interpretation.   7. Mallarmé, Stéphane, 1842–1898—Criticism and interpretation.   8. Proust, Marcel, 1871–1922—Criticism and interpretation.   I. Title.
    B2430.M3764W57 2013
    194—dc23

                                                                    2012037864

♾ This paper meets the requirements of ANSI/NISO z39.48-1992 (Permanence of Paper).

Contents

Illustrations

Figures

Musical Examples

Preface

In engaging with the philosophy of Maurice Merleau-Ponty, I take as inspiration the work of Stéphane Mallarmé, Paul Cézanne, Marcel Proust, and Claude Debussy. Chapters 1–4 explore the notion of noncoincidence (as silence, depth, mythical time, and rhythm), chapters 5–7 investigate the dynamic process of institution (through style, essence, and harmony), chapters 8–9 discuss the idea (as the "musical idea" and as form), and chapter 10 attends to the notion of transcendence.

The material informing chapters 1–3 will be familiar to Merleau-Ponty scholars, but chapter 4 (on Debussy's *Prélude à l'après-midi d'un faune*) explores new territory. Yet we see also that chapter 4 resonates with chapter 1 (through Mallarmé's poem), and that this resonance therefore inaugurates a certain depth: chapters 5, 6, and 7 relate, respectively, to chapters 2, 3, and 4 (through their focus upon the figures of Cézanne, Proust, and Debussy). These middle chapters serve as noncoincident layers, opening up an additional fold within the structure of the work. Chapters 8 and 9 (on Proust and Debussy) likewise intensify the explorations of chapters 3 and 6 and chapters 4 and 7, respectively. In chapter 10, prevalent themes of color, sound, movement, and emotion cohere (through synesthesia), finally returning to the question of dynamic expression from chapter 1.

Thus, the book has cast itself in a kind of musical form, where the individual chapters proceed not only linearly but through depth.

Acknowledgments

I am grateful to have received a fellowship from the Camargo Foundation in Cassis, France, in support of the early stages of research for this book. In the latter stages of my work, Duquesne University granted a Presidential Scholarship Award to help bring the project to completion. I especially wish to thank Dean Edward Kocher and Dean Jim Swindal at Duquesne University for their sustained and sustaining enthusiasm for interdisciplinary endeavors in music and philosophy.

I wish to acknowledge the kind permission of Ullrich Haase, editor of the *Journal of the British Society for Phenomenology*, to revise and reconfigure some material for chapters 1 and 9 that originally appeared in *JBSP* 43, no. 3 (2012) under the title "Merleau-Ponty through Mallarmé and Debussy: On Silence, Rhythm, and Expression."

This book could not have been written without the inspiration and encouragement that so many colleagues have shared with me over the years. I am particularly indebted to Leonard Lawlor and Galen Johnson, who graciously commented on an early manuscript version of the book, as well as Mauro Carbone, William Hamrick, Richard Kearney, Dennis Schmidt, Steve Watson, Jason Wirth, David Wood, and the wonderful members of the Merleau-Ponty Circle. I savor their conversations and treasure their work.

I wish also to thank Elizabeth Branch Dyson and her colleagues at the University of Chicago Press, and I am grateful for their commitment to music in its interdisciplinary possibility.

Finally, for the years of love, laughter and discovery that nourished me while writing this book, my heart is thankful to Larry Collins.

Mallarmé and a Proffer of Silence

The definition of philosophy would involve an elucidation of philosophical expression itself (therefore a becoming conscious of the procedure used in what precedes "naïvely," as though philosophy confined itself to reflecting what is) as the science of pre-science, as the expression of what is before expression *and sustains it from behind.*
MAURICE MERLEAU-PONTY, *The Visible and the Invisible*

In reading the philosophy of Maurice Merleau-Ponty, one must navigate both the opacity of his language and the incompleteness of his work. His penchant for holding in tension the relationship between oppositional pairs—visible and invisible, activity and passivity, sensible and ideal—as well as his development of a unique vocabulary nevertheless replete with traditional Christian terms—"chiasm," "advent," "flesh," "Word"—has led to more than one characterization of his work as something close to that of the mystic's vision.[1] Indeed, anyone who reads the final completed chapter, "The Intertwining: The Chiasm," of *The Visible and the Invisible* cannot help but note the changed tone of Merleau-Ponty's discourse.[2] His writing seems charged with philosophical revelation, and the unexpected tragedy of his death following so closely upon a claim of "ultimate truth" can tempt one to question fate.[3] Why should this philosophical voice have been wrested away so immediately after it had declared its aims? But better than succumb to such speculation, we might ask what has been left for us, now, to gather from his travail. For we have only this: a few books, a few essays. The greater portion of his work was never brought to complete expression; rather, it lies within pages upon pages of fragmentary notes.[4]

Yet it is perhaps appropriate that much of Merleau-Ponty's late work comes down to us not in the form of narrative, but in rough outline. For instead of offering us the sedimentation of a philosophy spoken from the *end* of thinking, his work promises an opening—an initiation to a philosophical discourse that by its very nature could be nothing other than ongoing and incomplete. In this sense, the course notes and working notes contribute to our understanding of his philosophy precisely in the degree to which they illustrate that philosophy in practice. When we read the notes, we participate in a movement of thought.

And so the difficulties that one encounters when engaging with these notes invite us to develop a sensitivity to his writing that would take into account not only the fixed meaning of each word or phrase, but also the process through which the word or phrase arrives at an original sense. We must turn to the viscous link that binds the words into meaning, for beneath the conceptual content of each word—beyond our everyday employment of language as representation—lies a dynamic and creative realm of expression. Thus Merleau-Ponty can write, "The words most charged with philosophy are not necessarily those that contain what they say, but rather those that most energetically open upon Being, because they more closely convey the life of the whole and make our habitual evidences vibrate until they disjoin."[5] It is the play of ideas across disjuncture that inspires the philosopher. Thus we begin to understand Merleau-Ponty's work toward crafting a specific language of oppositional pairs; the tension inherent to these oppositions allows them to "open upon Being" and offers a sort of philosophical energy not entirely unlike the aesthetic vibration of a green that calls for a red in Manet's *Le déjeuner sur l'herbe*.[6] Here, the power of the words or colors emerges from the space that is cleared between a contrast of elements. Yet even considered not in pairs but individually, terms like "chiasm," "advent," "flesh," and "Word" work in much the same way, insofar as Merleau-Ponty implicitly draws upon their own charged history as counterpoint to his realization of them. His use of these terms does not so much make ambiguous a vocabulary that would otherwise appear as transparent to our minds, but calls upon us to recognize a dimensional meaning. Only then might we see that "language in forming itself"—or, we might say, language in performing itself—expresses "an ontogenesis of which it is a part."[7]

It is in this sense that Merleau-Ponty's writing is poetic—poetic in the etymological sense—for it consistently works to disclose the creative generation of philosophical thinking as emerging from the depth between (or beneath, behind, or before) articulated words. In this way, it might seem that the thinking that remains for us, through Merleau-Ponty's late sketches of notes, stands close to the tradition of poetry. Indeed, the notes are significant not only with respect to their content but also in the way that they expose lacunae upon the printed page. It is as if the later Merleau-Ponty deliberately employs words in such a way that they work not so much to convey an explicit meaning as to articulate the empty space upon the page: as space—as an opening—for a continuous reinitiation to philosophical thought.

Thus the status of his written work as unfinished is in harmony with the nature of the work itself. Though we feel his death to be the tragic cause of its incompleteness, how, even if he had lived for many more decades, could we ever have called his work complete? Would not that work, from a Merleau-Ponty of 1971 or 1981, also have left us with more questions, more openings, if it were truly philosophical work? Philosophy lives precisely through its incompleteness, offering its richness according to the demand that it be taken up again.

As we grapple with the distinct difficulties (and, it should be noted, pleasures) of engaging with a dynamic work of this sort, it is not altogether unexpected that we should find ourselves in good company. Many of the challenges that confront us in taking up the "incomplete" work of Merleau-Ponty are similar to those that he himself encountered in his engagement with the writings of Edmund Husserl. Indeed, what better guide could we find, in facing these challenges, than Merleau-Ponty? With respect to Husserl's philosophy, Merleau-Ponty asks: "What if its conclusions are merely the results of a progression which was transformed into a 'work' by the interruption—an interruption which is always premature—of a life's work? Then we could not define a philosopher's thought solely in terms of what he had achieved; we would have to take account of what until the very end his thought was trying to think."[8]

Merleau-Ponty suggests that we would miss the import of the philosopher's work if we were to regard it as complete and finished. Above all, it is the very nature of Husserl's philosophy as irreducible to "a system of neatly defined concepts" that necessitates a dynamic and creative approach.[9] One can "take account of what until the very end his thought was trying to think" not by fleshing out a more thorough analysis of conclusions or concepts (as if Husserl's work offered a closed system that had only to be clarified), but by attending to the generative movement of that thought—by attending to what Merleau-Ponty describes as "the expression of what is before expression *and sustains it from behind.*"[10] For genuine philosophical inquiry does not complete itself first within the mind (fully formed and even clothed in an accessible style), only then to spring forth, Athenalike, into the world through language. Rather, it is through the process of expression that truly philosophical thought comes to be known. As Merleau-Ponty writes, "Speaking and writing is [*sic*] not a codification of an *available* piece of evidence. Speaking and writing make it exist."[11]

And herein lies the crux of our own difficulty in engaging with the work of Merleau-Ponty. We cannot presume to complete a life's work whose creative quality resonates with its incompleteness; we would be foolish, indeed, to think that our own "speaking and writing" could bring the unfinished manuscripts and course notes into a codified version of the whole of Merleau-Ponty's philosophy. "What until the very end his thought was trying to think" is not available to one who would analyze that thought through the language of concept; in aiming to coincide exactly with his conclusions, we would consistently miss the mark. What we seek, therefore, is not to think about the content of his thought, but to think according to the movement of his thought; we seek "participation in an operative thought."[12] Rather than codifying or completing his work, we recognize that the "miss"—the gap between a work and the engagement it inspires—in fact confirms the generative capacity of expression. And thus our very endeavor serves as an exemplar of a principle that, according to Merleau-Ponty, characterizes all philosophical reflection: that of noncoincidence.

*

Ordinarily, we may think of consciousness as the seat of a certain command center, as that power of organized mental and perceptual faculties which enables us to reflect upon the objects of the world absolutely, in their own place. We think that we meet the objects as they actually are, or as they would be if they were unobserved. But this notion of reflection as a hold upon the things of the world does not take into account the temporal dimension of perception.[13] Merleau-Ponty asks us to attend to this process as a kind of uncertainty principle of reflective thought: even at the moment that consciousness feels it has grasped the object, the original or "brute" perception of that object has already suffered a temporal dislocation. What consciousness grasps, therefore, is not the thing itself but the reflection—the image—of the initial perception of the thing. There exists always a lacuna, a gap, between reflection and the thing; consciousness does not obtain to the world directly but only, as it were, through a "cycle of duration that separates the brute perception from the reflective examination."[14] Thus, in describing this cycle, Merleau-Ponty characterizes our perception of the thing as consisting of a "thing-perceived-within-a-perception-reflected-on."[15] What we thought we could grasp—the thing itself—is not at all available to us. But how is it that we fail to notice this dislocation? How is it that we miss the lacuna? Reflection would propose to offer us the very thing—the very world; reflection would set itself up as a bulwark against discontinuity. Yet, according to Merleau-Ponty, in order to achieve this—in order to sustain the perception of the thing across a cycle of duration—reflection "presume[s] upon what it finds and condemn[s] itself to putting into the things what it will then pretend to find in them."[16] It constructs a sustained sense of the thing by retroactively identifying the reflection with the initial perception. In so doing, however, it operates according to a deception: it conflates the distinction between brute perception of the thing and reflection upon the perceived thing. And while that conflation enables consciousness to claim that it has grasped the thing and not a momentary image, it nevertheless exposes a limitation inherent to the structure of reflective consciousness: reflection is incapable of opening upon the world at the level of brute perception.

> But it is just as sure that the relation between a thought and its object, between the *cogito* and the *cogitatum*, contains neither the whole nor even the essential of our commerce with the world and that we have to situate that relation back within a more muted relationship with the world, within an initiation into the world upon which it rests and which is always already accomplished when the reflective return intervenes. We will miss that relationship—which we shall here call the openness upon the world (*ouverture au monde*)—the moment that the reflective effort tries to capture it, and we will then be able to catch sight of the reasons that prevent it from succeeding, and of the way through which we would reach it.[17]

By means of proposing a new understanding of the noncoincidence of reflective thought and the thing itself, Merleau-Ponty claims that "we are catching sight of the necessity of another operation besides the conversion to reflection, more fundamental than it, of a sort of *hyper-reflection* (*sur-réflexion*) that would also take itself and the changes it introduces into the spectacle into account."[18] This operation of hyperreflection would set itself up within the dynamic process of thought, attuned to noncoincidence. It would not, that is to say, utilize reflection to effect conflation, as the power of a *kosmotheoros* who looks out over the world and claims to see things "as they are" because, being pure mind, it has no contact with the things. Rather, philosophy would attend to the prereflective by investigating thought as a dynamic system involved in the world.

In *The Visible and the Invisible*, Merleau-Ponty initiates this investigation by turning toward dialectic thought. The process of dialectic thought, like that of reflection, manifests a temporal dislocation. The distinction between dialectic thought and reflection, however, hinges upon the way that the two operations meet this dislocation. Reflection works upon brute perception and, as Merleau-Ponty phrased it, "put[s] into the things what it will then pretend to find in them." That is to say, reflection circles around noncoincidence and, thanks to the temporal dislocation, projects backward into perception what it had already formulated. Thus it is that reflection deceives us into believing that we had grasped the thing, when in fact we are left with a reflective image and no contact with the thing at all. But the dialectic seizes upon the lacuna between brute perception and thought and, in contrast to reflection, operates from within its complex temporal structure. It seeks not to produce a single fixed image, but to return through a continuous cycle of perception and reflection. It owes its authenticity to this return—a return that does not seek only what it wishes to find, but develops according to the other-than-itself that is there: latent difference or possibility that is the expression of the lacuna. It is indeed only because of the lacuna that dialectic thought can be dynamic. As dialectic thought turns back toward the brute perception, it takes the measure of the separation between itself and the past perception now held within the present; rather than to effect a conflation, it can be said to embrace this difference, to reconfigure itself according to this difference, and to find within the difference the potential for movement and transformation. This is why Merleau-Ponty writes, of the dynamic stages of dialectic thought, "Hence there is a question here not of a thought that follows a pre-established route but of a thought that itself traces its own course, that finds itself by advancing, that makes its own way, and thus proves that the way is practicable."[19] *Practicable*: as operative thought—thought that works from within the relationship between our brute perception of the thing and the task of consciousness in arriving at the thing to be thought.

Therefore, this operative thought discloses a specific notion of the dialectic—a dialectic without synthesis. Merleau-Ponty writes: "In particular it does not formulate itself in successive statements which would have to be taken as they stand; each statement, in order to be true, must be referred, throughout the whole movement, to the stage from which it arises and has its full sense only if one takes into account not only what it says expressly but also its place within the whole which constitutes its latent content."[20] That is to say, dialectic thought continually goes back to take account of the noncoincident structure of reflection and advances according to this complex movement. It therefore does not arrive at a complete, fixed statement. "It has never been able to formulate itself into theses without denaturing itself," because to arrive at a fixed thought would be to betray the operative thought that lies at the heart of the dialectic.[21] By its very nature, it makes no claim toward disclosing a realm of the predetermined; rather, it consists in openness—openness to that which has never been formulated or spoken. And so Merleau-Ponty carefully distinguishes between his own understanding of the dialectic and what he terms the ordinary or "bad" dialectic (where "the thought ceases to accompany or to be the dialectical movement, converts it into signification, thesis, or things said").[22] Searching for a means to describe his dynamic notion of the dialectic, Merleau-Ponty adopts the term "hyper-dialectic" as an expression for the "good" dialectic: "What we call hyperdia-lectic is a thought that on the contrary is capable of reaching truth because it envisages without restriction the plurality of the relationships and what has been called ambiguity. The bad dialectic is that which thinks it recomposes being by a thetic thought, by an assemblage of statements, by thesis, antith-esis, and synthesis."[23]

And here, in reading Merleau-Ponty, we might pause. Hyperdialectic? Hyperreflection? What has become clear in Merleau-Ponty's search for a dy-namic process of thought is the inadequacy of ordinary language to the task. Merleau-Ponty seems to chafe at the language, stretching it, extending it, and returning to earlier statements as through a maze of difficulty. But this is not a fault of the author; it is a result of the noncoincidence itself. The only way to make this lacuna clear is to enter into it, from the very point at which things *not said* constitute the content. "Philosophy is the reconversion of si-lence and speech into one another," writes Merleau-Ponty.[24] The language through which one may express this dialectic thus cannot simply resort to words that bear a fully transparent relation to signification. The expression of dynamic thought must itself always take into account the principle of the lacuna, and just as philosophy seeks an operative thought that can work from the inside of noncoincidence, so must it also seek a language with the capac-ity to express that thought. Indeed, Merleau-Ponty writes that philosophy "must question the world, it must enter into the forest of references that our interrogation arouses in it, it must make it say, finally, what in its silence *it means to say*."[25] But how might one bring silence to speak without destroying the silence itself?

There would need to be an operative language—a language capable of set-ting itself up within the gap between sign and signification—a language that would turn back toward this noncoincidence for the movement of its mean-ing. Merleau-Ponty writes: "It would be a language of which he would not be the organizer, words he would not assemble, that would combine through him by virtue of a natural intertwining of their meaning, through the oc-cult trading of the metaphor—where what counts is no longer the manifest meaning of each word and of each image, but the lateral relations, the kin-ships that are implicated in their transfers and their exchanges."[26]

This operative language, it would seem, would be the language of poetry, the abode of metaphor.[27] Poetry and metaphoric language work precisely according to the principle of noncoincidence; they aim at "making silence speak, at saying what is not-said, at exploring language beyond its usual destination which lies (Mallarmé) in saying what is obvious, the familiar."[28]

Rather than employing language as a direct formulation of thought, poetry makes use of the clear space between sign and signification in order to allow meaning to be born in a fresh way, by taking into account all that is latent between the relations that words form through their interaction. Merleau-Ponty distinguishes between this poetic language (as that which constantly returns to the prearticulate for the generation of new meaning) and ordinary, empirical language (as that which is used in everyday speech):

> The empirical use of already established language should be distinguished from its creative use. Empirical language can only be the result of creative language. Speech in the sense of empirical language—that is, the opportune recollection of a preestablished sign—is not speech in respect to an authentic language. It is, as Mallarmé said, the worn coin placed silently in my hand. True speech, on the contrary—speech which signifies, which finally renders "l'absente de tous bouquets" present and frees the meaning captive in the thing—is only silence in respect to empirical usage, for it does not go so far as to become a common noun.[29]

Again, Merleau-Ponty points to the poet Mallarmé for the sense of this operative or creative language. It is to Mallarmé's essay "Crisis of Verse" that Merleau-Ponty refers. In this essay, Mallarmé writes:

> I say: a flower! And, out of the oblivion where my voice casts every contour, insofar as it is something other than the known bloom, there arises, musically, the very idea in its mellowness; in other words, what is absent from every bouquet.
>
> As opposed to a denominative and representative function, as the crowd first treats it, speech, which is primarily dream and song, recovers, in the Poet's hands, of necessity in an art devoted to fictions, its virtuality.[30]

The "virtuality" of which Mallarmé speaks—"what is absent from every bouquet"—is the very transcendence that distinguishes the use of language that articulates what is already known from the use of language that approaches depth or noncoincidence. Here lies the realm of creative thought. And the possibility of expressing this realm stands as the proper task of language.[31] Language cannot offer up merely "the material truth" (*matériellement la vérité*),[32] for it does not simply represent the world through a kind of onomatopoetic transference of essence into sound. Mallarmé notes that, if language worked solely through representative means, we would not have so many diverse languages upon the earth—one "absolute" (*suprême*) language would suffice for human expression.[33] But it is this lack of correspondence between the sound and the meaning of language that points to its creative potential, for in language there is always more than a mapping of thought to expression: there is something latent, something unaccounted for, that springs to life in the performance of language. The rift between meaning and sound means that language must always be renewed; it must turn back to itself, interrogate itself, in order to disclose a new sense from the transcendence that lies at the heart of the expressive process.

What therefore must also be underlined, as a theme consistent throughout his work, is Mallarmé's description of operative speech as arising "musically" (*musicalement*). What is musical about this speech—this speech that Mallarmé claims to be "primarily dream and song" (*rêve et chant*)? It is true that speech, even ordinary speech, routinely flirts with music through the use of vocal inflection. Yet it is especially through the repetition of speech or the establishment of a rhythm in the articulation of words that a phrase gains the capacity to lift itself out of ordinary discourse and establish the sense of a melody.[34] Indeed, we need not insert ourselves within a dream of ancient Greek life to realize that the poetic text beginning, "Sing, goddess,"[35] serves as the implicit opening of every poem, every creative use of language. Not without reason does Mallarmé emphasize the sonorous aspect of his language ("I say: a flower!"); by means of actual vocal performance is the idea brought forth in all of its musicality.[36] One could not only say that operative, poetic language distinguishes itself from empirical, everyday language (language "as the crowd first treats it") through its musicality but, more specifically, through its *rhythmicality*. Mallarmé writes that poets must "employ music in the Greek sense, at heart expressive Idea or rhythm between the relations."[37]

Indeed, rhythm is a notion that meets up with Merleau-Ponty's investigation of noncoincidence because rhythm consists precisely in what is not heard. Despite our common notion of rhythm as a series of definite, articulated sounds, the musician knows rhythm in quite a different way: as the interval *between* articulated sounds. It is the relationship of a second articulation to the first that creates a rhythm. This is why a conductor who leads an orchestra never begins a piece of music from the initial note; before the first sounded note, there must be a gesture (sometimes only a breath) that, when placed in relation to the first note, will initiate a rhythm or a pulse for the entirety of the musical movement or phrase. Rhythmically, the first gesture is never the beginning; it is the second gesture that initiates a beginning. Rhythm can be instituted only retroactively; it turns back from the second note to the first in order to recover the interval of silence between the two, even as it then lays forth a new structure that would support the articulation of an unfurling melody. Rhythm promises an ongoing, dynamic process that works by looking both forward and retrospectively, applying itself through the noncoincidence of each sound.[38] It is thus that language, too, utilizes a

rhythmic—that is to say, an essentially musical—process, with words turning back upon words to disclose what had remained silent between them. In
speech, it is arguably the rhythmic quality of language, more than its range of
vocal inflection, that offers the best possibility for leaping into song.

Certainly much of the history of poetry has maintained this close connection to music through the devising of poetic meters, but this surface manifestation of rhythm belies its structural significance. What is important about
rhythm is not the meter or the tempo, but the expression of silence that holds
each articulation together; what lies at the root of the work of rhythm within
a poem is the process of continually returning to the unheard interval or
unsaid lacuna of noncoincidence. And so, even when speech is formed into
words upon a page—when it ceases to be performed as speech and has been
fixed according to its graphical representation—it upholds a primary element of musicality through the dynamic development of expression.

In its most potent manifestation, writing maintains its musicality through
the use of metaphor. Indeed, as we have seen above, it is to metaphor ("the
occult trading of the metaphor") that Merleau-Ponty turns in searching for
an operative language.[39] He gives a hint of the power of metaphor in a description of Mallarmé's efforts:

> Many years have already elapsed since Mallarmé made a distinction between
> the poetic use of language and everyday chatter. The chatterer only names
> things sufficiently to point them out quickly, to indicate "what he is talking
> about." The poet, by contrast, according to Mallarmé, replaces the usual way
> of referring to things, which presents them as "well known," with a mode of
> expression that describes the essential structure of the thing and accordingly
> forces us to enter into that thing.[40]

The "essential structure of the thing"—not its "well known" surface—is
that very structure of noncoincidence brought forth through metaphor as a
unique "mode of expression." The metaphor, in language, works in a way
similar to rhythm in music; it can be said to reside not within the signification
of a single word, but within the hollow or relief formed by two or more words
in relation (or formed by the relationship between one word and its own history).[41] And through the metaphor, as through rhythm and as through the
dialectic, there is the recovery of the unsaid and the recasting of something
that is known and recognizable as having the potential to encompass, in fact
to adopt as essential to its nature, what is new, different, and other than itself.[42] The metaphor discloses the lacuna—the noncoincidence—as generative. This is the work, one could say, of all creative language. Notes Merleau-
Ponty: "As far as language is concerned, it is the lateral relation of one sign to

another which makes each of them significant, so that meaning appears only at the intersection of and as it were in the interval between words."[43]

As a poet, Mallarmé notably makes this lacuna principle visually clear upon the printed page as well. Here, his careful arrangement of the space through typesetting serves as another emblem of rhythmicality. The "interval between words"—the silent space of operative language—is presented literally on the page. The inspiration, as with Mallarmé's fastening upon the notion of poetry as "expressive Idea or rhythm between the relations," seems to come, once again, from music.[44] In "Un coup de dés," Mallarmé's approach to language and the appearance of words on the page results in what he describes in the *Preface* as "a musical score" (*une partition*).[45] Mallarmé continues: "The 'blanks,' in effect, assume importance and are what is immediately most striking; versification always demanded them as a surrounding silence, so that a lyric poem, or one with a few feet, generally occupies about a third of the leaf on which it is centered: I don't transgress against this order of things, I merely disperse its elements."[46]

Thus space, too, can be rhythmical, and Mallarmé's radical extension of space as silence holds particular significance for Merleau-Ponty. According to Merleau-Ponty, when it is clear that language consists of far more than an empirical formulation of preexisting thoughts—when it is clear that there is no absolute conflation of speech and meaning—then we understand that "the idea of *complete* expression is nonsensical, and that all language is indirect or allusive—that it is, if you wish, silence."[47] This silence, whether marked out upon the page for our eyes to acknowledge or suspended between the terms of a metaphor, stands as an entire field to which the poet turns his or her work:

> To speak of the world poetically is almost to remain silent, if speech is understood in everyday terms, and Mallarmé wrote notoriously little. Yet in the little he left us, we at least find the most acute sense of a poetry which is carried entirely by language and which refers neither directly to the world as such, nor to prosaic truth, nor to reason. This is consequently poetry as a creation of language, one which cannot be fully translated into ideas.[48]

Mallarmé's poetry is carried aesthetically and takes no part in subsumption under or imitation of the concept. As soon as it comes close to such formulation, it turns around once again to the opening of noncoincidence, from which springs its power and authenticity. It "catch[es] a meaning in its own mesh" through a (rhythmical) self-referential structure of dislocation.[49]

Yet, what must be the role of the philosopher who has uncovered the exigency of this silence? Having searched for an operative language as the only means by which to uncover the fundamental structure of the noncoincidence of thought, what is then to be done with this language, "which cannot be fully translated into ideas"? To speak in the ordinary sense is no longer to abide by the silence, but to speak according to the silence—through operative language—is to risk the end of philosophy and a fall into mysticism. "Is that still 'philosophy'?" Merleau-Ponty asks.[50] Yet he reassures us, "This reversal itself—*circulus vitiosus deus*—is not hesitation, bad faith and bad dialectic, but return to Σιγή the abyss. *One cannot make a direct ontology.* My 'indirect' method (being in the beings) is alone conformed with being."[51]

The "indirect" method that he adopts, as we have seen with the figure of Mallarmé, is navigated through an intensive investigation of the arts. Through the work not only of Mallarmé but also of certain painters, authors, and musicians, Merleau-Ponty discovers a path leading to a new ontology. And although his work was never completed, and although our best access is preserved, for the most part, only in the form of rough notes (leaving their traces of false starts, turns, and reconsiderations), the only way to understand this path is to travel anew upon it. "Nothing will remain without being proffered [*rien ne demeurera sans être proféré*]," writes Mallarmé in "Crisis of Verse."[52] And so we, too, must take up the work of this indirect ontology through the sole means available to us: by entering into it.

Cézanne: Depth in the World

The painter "takes his body with him," says Valéry.
MERLEAU-PONTY, *"Eye and Mind"*

Merleau-Ponty's engagement with the visual arts, and in particular with painting, spans the whole of his career. And, as is well-known, from *Phenomenology of Perception* through "Eye and Mind" Cézanne stands as a key figure in Merleau-Ponty's work.[1] However, if we are to enter into the development of his thought, we must apply ourselves not to his most well-known conclusions, but to the heart of the changes that his work underwent. This can be traced through the working notes, *The Visible and the Invisible*, and the course notes of "L'ontologie cartésienne et l'ontologie d'aujourd'hui" (1960–61). What one gathers from these notes is a subtle but important shift in emphasis, underlining *depth* as a philosophical notion. Depth, like the silent space of poetry, becomes in painting a means of expressing a fundamental structure of noncoincidence.

Merleau-Ponty takes up this theme by contrasting his own reading of depth with that of Descartes.[2] Indeed, for the Cartesian, a world of noncoincidence—of silence, of space, of depth—is only a world of illusion, for the truth is that of a world of positivity. In such a world, thought captures itself, and reflection, rather than suffering from a dislocation, directs its attention to the perceptual realm with exact coincidence. Thus perception is the domain of the mind, not the senses—"an inspection of the mind"—and, similarly, "reflection is only the perception returning to itself."[3] The Cartesian mind is flush with the world; there is no distance between thought and the world because thought *is* the world.

Or, rather, the modest Cartesian recognizes that his or her thought offers only a partial view of the world, like that seen through a window or in a painting. Although the Cartesian's thought recovers perception completely, perception itself is limited according to the position of his or her body within space. The Cartesian who stands at the foot of Montagne Sainte-Victoire cannot see to the other side of the Haut Var; the trees, rocks, and jutting cliffs conceal the hills that lie beyond. But our Cartesian knows that what he or she sees at that moment—the sense of the landscape that stands in front of him or her as a view of objects that block other objects—is not really how things are. The trees truly are never in front of or behind one another: standing from another position, this tree whose view is currently blocked by the foreground of shrubs and rocks would appear in its fullness; likewise, climbing from the foot of Montagne Sainte-Victoire to the summit would enable the Cartesian then to see the hills of the Haut Var stretching out beneath his or her gaze. And so the hiddenness of the Haut Var as experienced from the foot of the mountain in no way constitutes an aspect of its actual being. The truth would lie in going around the mountain, flattening the depth and bringing what was previously hidden into pure positivity. Our Cartesian would well appreciate the advances of the twentieth century, whereby he or she could confirm this hypothesis by looking over the landscape from the seat of an airplane, so that all that had blocked his or her view would appear flat, leading our Cartesian to see as width that which he or she had previously considered to be depth.

Merleau-Ponty writes that, according to the Cartesian system, "*space* remains absolutely in itself, everywhere equal to itself, homogeneous; its dimensions, for example, are by definition interchangeable."[4] What this means is that depth (and the apparent shrinking in size of objects that are far away) is only a sort of perceptual illusion, because at its root depth is equivalent to breadth and can be measured as a definite distance between things. According to this system,

> what I call depth is in reality a juxtaposition of points, making it comparable to breadth. I am simply badly placed to see it. I should see it if I were in the position of a spectator looking on from the side, who can take in at a glance the series of objects spread out in front of me, whereas for me they conceal each other—or see the distance from my body to the first object, whereas for me this distance is compressed into a point.[5]

The perception of depth can thus be thought of as the apprehending of an obstruction: things block the clear view of other things, effectively reducing the distance between them "into a point" (insofar as the shrubs and rocks that obscure the view appear to be right up against the edge of the tree that is blocked). For the Cartesian, it is thanks to this obstruction that we experience something like a dimension of depth. But depth as an obstruction is there to be overcome; simply by reorienting my position to take a view from the side, I realize that there is a distance to be measured between the shrubs and the tree, and that it can be measured as breadth. And so, for the observer who repositions him- or herself, depth is reduced to an illusion.

And it is precisely this that is the key to the Cartesian assessment of depth. Cartesian philosophy requires that the observer constantly reposition him- or herself, or at the very least imagine a repositioning. The Cartesian would like to overcome the limit that the body places upon him or her (that he or she is bound to a certain time and a certain place owing to the insertion of his or her body within the world). The Cartesian obtains to pure mind; indeed, he or she would like to view the world according to a Godlike perspective, whereby what was earlier perceived as depth would now be displayed as a broad plane of breadth. Better than our twentieth-century Cartesian flying above Montagne Sainte-Victoire in an airplane, the mind of God would see not only the whole of Provence, but the whole of the world laid out before it. Everything that had previously seemed obscure would become a completely transparent object; all would exist in positivity.

Therefore, what we begin to recognize in the Cartesian assessment of depth is the outline of an ontology, specifically a system of Being arranged according to a fundamental bifurcation of subject and object. If we wish to get at the truth, we must lift ourselves up above the world and view it from the mind of God. We must cast ourselves as a *kosmotheoros*. We must be pure subject, making no contact with the things but observing everything below our gaze exactly as it is, coincident with our thought. And such a gaze would never disturb or change the object of its attention because, as pure subject, it would make no contact with the things; it would simply observe from above.

While the Cartesian philosopher strives to install him- or herself at the "zero point of Being" of the *kosmotheoros*,[6] the closest that the artist might come to a vision of the pure subject is made possible through the Renaissance technique of perspective. Writes Merleau-Ponty, "Perspective is much more than a secret technique for imitating a reality given as such to all humanity. It is the invention of a world dominated and possessed through and through by an instantaneous synthesis."[7] This "instantaneous synthesis" discloses the totality that would be present to the mind of the *kosmotheoros*. Merleau-Ponty observes that, when I employ the technique of Renaissance perspective, "I think of and dominate my vision as God can."[8] That is to say, I do not succumb to the ceaseless change and flow of the phenomenal realm; I am not seduced by the calling of the sensible world of things—that which ever slips away when I attempt to seize it. Rather, knowing full well that I am not God—that I cannot see everything revealed to me all at once—my representation operates according to a certain ruse: *perspectiva artificialis*. How is it that the technique of Renaissance perspective constructs this knowable, coincident world?

According to Merleau-Ponty, perception operates through a certain principle of dislocation, for the more fixedly I stare at an object, the more it begins to vibrate—to lose its solidity. If I wish to grasp a sense of the object as stable, I must, paradoxically, keep my gaze in motion by, in effect, looking at the object in several different moments in time. Just as our Cartesian wished to annihilate depth by looking at the landscape before him or her from several different positions in space, the Renaissance painter must look at the object from several disconnected "positions" in time. And just as the Cartesian would aspire to a view from which no aspect of the landscape would be hidden—the view of God—the Renaissance painter would likewise try to reach a synthesis of various perceptions of the object across time, resulting in the representation of one solid object placed in relation to a single vanishing point, fixed within the constraints of the canvas. Therefore, what the technique of perspective achieves is not only to be regarded with respect to the realm of space; what it achieves is also a conflation of time. "The whole scene is in the mode of the completed or of eternity," writes Merleau-Ponty.[9] Contrary to the primary experience of perception, where the world offers up a depth of teeming, changing things (our access to which is mediated through noncoincidence), the scene that is represented in the Renaissance painting appears comprehensible and immediate, organized according to the positivity of geometric lines and planes: "Landscapes painted in this way have a peaceful look, an air of respectful decency, which comes of their being held beneath a gaze fixed at infinity. They remain at a distance and do not involve the viewer."[10]

But it is precisely this distance that calls our attention to the bifurcation of the subject and the object. From this distance, the subject has no access to the objects. The subject consists, rather, in an entirely different being from that of being object; the subject is not implicated in the realm of objects. For this world is not one in which the subject participates; instead, it is laid out before the subject, obedient to the laws of geometry—a "space without hiding places which in each of its points is only what it is, neither more nor less."[11] When the Renaissance technique of perspective organizes the depth of objects according to a dimension of breadth—a certain line that leads to the vanishing point—it effectively denies a subject's ability to enter into the teeming life of objects, for it is only from the "outside" of the world, from the view of the *kosmotheoros*, that depth appears as breadth. Therefore it is an "objectified depth detached from experience and transformed into breadth" that underlies the bifurcation.[12]

In contrast, Merleau-Ponty searches for a kind of "primordial depth" that could thematize a more profound relationship between subject and object.[13] For, according to Merleau-Ponty, it is this primordial depth that

> announces a certain indissoluble link between things and myself by which I am placed in front of them, whereas breadth can, at first sight, pass for a relationship between things themselves, in which the perceiving subject is not implied. By rediscovering the vision of depth, that is to say, of a depth which is not yet objectified and made up of mutually external points, we shall once more outrun the traditional alternatives and elucidate the relation between subject and object.[14]

It is his interest in depth as a theme of philosophical significance that leads Merleau-Ponty to engage with the works of Cézanne. In "Eye and Mind," Merleau-Ponty writes, "Four centuries after the 'solutions' of the Renaissance and three centuries after Descartes, depth is still new, and it insists on being sought."[15] But what was this particular depth that Cézanne was seeking?

Clearly, it is not the illusion of depth presented by the *perspectiva artificialis*; it is not a depth equated with breadth. Primordial depth does not consist in the measurable relationship between things: one could not, as a sovereign geometer, take a ruler to the landscape and calculate this dimension of depth. (What Merleau-Ponty describes as primordial depth is, in fact, quite difficult to comprehend, because of the influence that Cartesian geometry still holds over the everyday notion of points fixed within space.) He writes, rather, that depth is "a voluminosity we express in a word when we say that a thing is *there*."[16] That is to say, depth is not a dimension that presents itself to be seen in the way that a line is seen and measured; it is not, in this sense, merely a kind of object that one could grasp, look at from several points of view, or see openly deployed. Rather, it serves as that through which the measurable dimensions of breadth and height are seen: "a voluminosity." In this sense, it is an opening—"openness upon the world."[17] Moreover, Merleau-Ponty writes that there is a certain "enigma" associated with depth, which "consists in the fact that I see things, each one in its place, precisely because they eclipse one another, and that they are rivals before my sight precisely because each one is in its own place—in their exteriority, known through their envelopment, and their mutual dependence in their autonomy."[18] Therefore, depth is the "voluminosity" of space that not only allows for things to be seen (as "openness upon the world"), but allows for things to have an unseen side ("because they eclipse one another"); it is thanks to depth that the unseen side is constitutive of the things themselves. Like the work of rhythm in Mallarmé (through which a silent, past, or unheard relationship maintains expressive potency), the ontological significance of depth lies within its capacity to provide an expressive opening not only for the visible but also for the invisible, other side of objects. Indeed, Merleau-Ponty writes that depth "is pre-eminently the dimension of the hidden."[19]

It is this aspect of depth—that of the hidden or the absent—that Cézanne presents on his canvases. Cézanne abandons the technique of the *perspectiva artificialis* in order to explore a realm of depth that would not be measurable according to breadth. Some of the clearest indications of his experiments in this realm are to be found in his treatment of the still life, where, notoriously, he has a propensity to break apart the lines that would otherwise operate in measurement. For example, in *Still Life with Apples and Peaches*, the front aspect of the table makes an unpredictable shift in the lower left-hand corner of the canvas; the table that appeared slightly turned away from the viewer in the right half of the canvas suddenly becomes parallel to the viewer in the left half of the canvas. What is important is the principle of noncoincidence that works upon the canvas; it effects the distortion of the table's length, shattering the viewer's expectations of a space that would operate according to Cartesian principles.[20]

Yet we are perhaps better able to appreciate the process of Cézanne's painting, and specifically the process through which he creates a sense of depth, by looking at his landscapes of Provence. If we contemplate, for example, *Houses on a Hill, Provence*, an unfinished work, we find an entry into the way that Cézanne deploys color and texture—rather than linear perspective—as a technique of depth. In this work, there is no vanishing point to organize the landscape, nor does the apparent size of objects diminish according to their position relative to the horizon. (The brushstrokes present patches of color that are similar in size all across the canvas, from the bottom "foreground" to the upper "background.") In fact, aside from the two houses in the foreground that seem to provide the connection to the work's title, there are very few "objects" to be seen in this painting. Rather than objects, we seem to perceive movement of color and texture—movement evoked through the harmonization of blues (for the exact tone of the sky is woven throughout the assemblage of trees) and the broad horizontal brushstrokes that make up the distant ocher hill as well as the two houses in the foreground. And this constitutes a remarkable achievement in *Houses*: the landscape is presented as if within a temporal cycle of formation—it is dynamic (that is to say, not in the mode of "eternity"). That the blue in the distant sky is the same blue echoed throughout the trees, and that the texture of the distant hill is the same texture as the houses, make for a painting that does not freeze the representation of its objects. Through reconfiguration and resonance a harmony

FIGURE 2.1. Cézanne, *Still Life with Apples and Peaches*, c. 1905, oil on canvas, National Gallery of Art, Washington.

arises, and one is immersed within the assembling of the colors and textures. This is a painting that cannot be viewed coolly and from a distance.

Of the significance of Cézanne's style, Merleau-Ponty writes eloquently:

> If many painters since Cézanne have refused to follow the law of geometrical perspective, this is because they have sought to recapture and reproduce before our very eyes the birth of the landscape. They have been reluctant to settle for an analytical overview and have striven to recapture the feel of perceptual experience itself. Thus different areas of their paintings are seen from different points of view.[21] The lazy viewer will see "errors of perspective" here, while those who look closely will get the feel of a world in which no two objects are seen simultaneously, a world in which regions of space are separated by the time it takes to move our gaze from one to the other, a world in which being is not given but rather emerges over time.

Thus space is no longer a medium of simultaneous objects capable of being apprehended by an absolute observer who is equally close to them all, a

FIGURE 2.2. Cézanne, *Houses on a Hill, Provence*, 1904–6, oil on canvas, The White House.

medium without point of view, without body and without spatial position—in sum, the medium of pure intellect.[22]

Cézanne's refusal "to follow the law of geometrical perspective" in creating his landscapes represents a refusal as well of the *kosmotheoros*. There is no "absolute observer" at work upon *Houses on a Hill, Provence*. This canvas overcomes the convention of representing an object as if from eternity and without hiddenness, because the beauty of the canvas is to be appreciated in precisely what is not directly presented upon it, but instead in what arises through the (invisible) harmony of (visible) color and texture. The *unseen* forms the theme of the painting, and what Cézanne offers to his viewer is a canvas that teems with life because the viewer is implicated in the landscape. A viewer from above—a *kosmotheoros*, "without body and without spatial position"—could not perceive an unseen; he or she could only see the things completely displayed. And so what one can sense through the painting is the reinsertion of the viewer into the world. Merleau-Ponty writes, "Space is not what it was in the *Dioptrics*, a network of relations between objects such as would be seen by a third party, witnessing my vision, or by a geometer looking over it and reconstructing it from outside. It is, rather, a space reckoned starting from me as the null point or degree zero of spatiality. I do not see it according to its exterior envelope; I live it from the inside; I am immersed in it."[23]

Space unfolds from the viewer, who lives from within the world. That is to say, our experience of this space—the space of perceptual depth—arises through embodiment, and not by means of a reflection of the incorporeal mind. It is thus that Merleau-Ponty, who in his later works turns from phenomenology to ontology, emphasizes bodily structure as it relates to the visible: not because he reduces Being to the materiality of the body but because depth as experienced through the body serves as a "prototype of Being." Depth is an exemplar.

Merleau-Ponty's many investigations into the bodily experience of depth must be understood within this context; in particular, in a range of works from *Phenomenology of Perception* to *The Visible and the Invisible*, Merleau-Ponty investigates the significance of binocular vision. Why the extensive expositions on a phenomenon that, from a scientific perspective, is already well understood? It is thanks to these accounts of binocular vision that we may catch an analogue to the more ontological principle of depth for which Merleau-Ponty searches.

Thus I look out upon an object before me, perhaps an olive tree, and my body is immediately implicated in the look. For what I notice is that my vision does not give me one, single version of the tree revealed in its positivity. Rather, there are two versions, as in the double image of a stereoscope; the world before my left eye does not coincide exactly with the world before my right eye.[24] Moreover, like the two-dimensional pictures used in the stereoscope, what I see with each eye individually appears flat, lifeless. I may approximate a sense of depth by taking account of the relative size of objects that I see according to monocular perception and then calculating a certain distance between the objects. But clearly I am not able to see depth in itself; I employ a dimension of breadth in measuring the gap between objects. And all of this takes place under the careful attention of the mind: grasping, comparing, and calculating.

Yet, when I look at the olive tree with both eyes, I do not sense conflict between the image of the left eye and the image of the right eye. There is no need for consciousness to measure the difference between the two. In *Phenomenology of Perception*, Merleau-Ponty writes that "we pass from double vision to the single object, not through an inspection of the mind, but when the two eyes cease to function each on its own account and are used as a single organ by one single gaze."[25] Because the shift from monocular to binocular perception is a transformation rooted in the body, consciousness does not direct it. Consciousness might compare one image to another, but binocular perception is not the result of comparison; through it there is, indeed, a transformation of vision. It is this transformation that Merleau-Ponty emphasizes when he writes, in *The Visible and the Invisible*, that "binocular perception is not made up of two monocular perceptions surmounted; it is of another order."[26] Yet what is initiated is not an order that would exist parallel to or beyond the realm of experience. For it is the body alone—the body that has two eyes—that makes this possible.

In response to the function of my two eyes, the olive tree leaps into life, for now the tree and I inhabit the same world. And this counts as one of the great enigmas of our experience. When we mistakenly equate depth and breadth, we are measuring a distance that spreads out between our body and the object. This distance allows us to "objectify" our relationship with the object. But, paradoxically, primordial depth has the effect of making us feel close to the object. Only when the tree is laid out flat—without depth—is it inaccessible, held away as the limit of our vision. To view the tree in transparency is to view it from the perspective of the *kosmotheoros*—from the realm of the eternal and the omniscient. But binocular vision presupposes a kind of unity between the world of myself, as subject, and the world of the tree, as object. Merleau-Ponty writes, "The thickness of the body, far from rivaling that of the world, is on the contrary the sole means I have to go unto the heart of the things."[27] I see the tree in its depth because I, too, exist in depth; I see the world according to the insertion of my body into that world—according to the formula that binocular perception elucidates. The phenomenon of depth is the proof that I am not *kosmotheoros*.

Thus, because perceptual depth does not arise according to a vision that would see everything displayed in positivity, it is rooted within the body schema; it is visible, in particular, only because we have two eyes that see the same object differently. What we see, then, is not equivalent to one or another of the images that the left or right eye would offer; what we see is something else—something that the gaze of neither eye could confirm alone—something of another order that the total body effects.[28] Perceptual depth is, in a sense, the experiential space that unfolds from this noncoincidence. As such, it serves as an emblem of a more fundamental noncoincidence that is constitutive of Being. To think of the body as "sensible for itself" is to disclose a new type of relationship between the subject and the object: that of encroachment.[29] Recall that, in *Phenomenology of Perception*, Merleau-Ponty claimed that "by rediscovering the vision of depth, that is to say, of a depth which is not yet objectified and made up of mutually external points, we shall once more outrun the traditional alternatives and elucidate the relation between subject and object."[30] It is later, in *The Visible and the Invisible*, that he clarifies this remark:

> When I find again the actual world such as it is, under my hands, under my eyes, up against my body, I find much more than an object: a Being of which my vision is a part, a visibility older than my operations or my acts. But this does not mean that there was a fusion or coinciding of me with it: on the contrary, this occurs because a sort of dehiscence opens my body in two, and because between my body looked at and my body looking, my body touched and my body touching, there is overlapping or encroachment so that we must say that the things pass into us as well as we into the things.[31]

The dehiscence of which Merleau-Ponty speaks—when we think of it in terms of opening a space of difference and noncoincidence—is what makes the body schema so significant, as *flesh*. For our relationship to the world is never completely one-sided; literally, there is depth. We are not pure subjects before whom all things would appear in transparency, because we are also related to objects. We can be seen, as an object would be seen; we can be touched, as an object would be touched. So complex is this relationship that it also works upon our own body. In Merleau-Ponty's famous example, my left hand may reach out to touch the surface of this wooden desk. My hand is an extension of myself—myself as subject—and it feels the desk as an object. But at the same time, I may reach my right hand over to touch my left hand as it explores the surface of the desk. Now, my right hand is the extension of myself as subject, but what is the left hand? There is "a veritable touching of the touch, when my right hand touches my left hand while it is palpating the things, where the 'touching subject' passes over to the rank of the touched, [and] descends into the things."[32] That is to say, the left hand crosses over to the world of things even as it maintains its bond with me as a subject. It "opens finally upon a tangible being of which it is also a part."[33] Thus my body applies itself to the world, but it is also *of* the world. In an important passage from *The Visible and the Invisible*, Merleau-Ponty writes:

> The visible can thus fill me and occupy me only because I who see it do not see it from the depths of nothingness, but from the midst of itself; I the seer am also visible. What makes the weight, the thickness, the flesh of each color, of each sound, of each tactile texture, of the present, and of the world is the fact that he who grasps them feels himself emerge from them by a sort of coiling up or redoubling, fundamentally homogeneous with them; he feels that he is the sensible itself coming to itself and that in return the sensible is in his eyes as it were his double or an extension of his own flesh.[34]

This "coiling up" or "redoubling" articulates a more general intertwining that is characteristic of the sensible realm, as those who make a thorough study of it, particularly artists, have often expressed: "Inevitably the roles between the painter and the visible switch. That is why so many painters have said that things look at them. As André Marchand says, after Klee: 'In a forest, I have felt many times over that it was not I who looked at the forest. Some days I felt that the trees were looking at me, were speaking to me . . . I was there, listening.' "[35]

This beautiful passage is evocative in many ways, not the least of which is the way in which it describes the entering of the world into the body of the subject: through listening, because for the listener waves of sound enter the interior passage of the ear and are translated into "waves" or neural signals that the body itself generates. It is thus that the flesh responds: to an external stimulus that it transcribes internally. This transformation from the external world to an internal attitude of the subject, explored not only by the visual artist but by the poet as well (as in Paul Claudel's *The Eye Listens*), is readily understood in terms of sound but does not fail to provide a model for the visual as well. "Quality, light, color, depth, which are there before us, are there only because they awaken an echo in our bodies and because the body welcomes them."[36] This "echo" discloses our ultimate intimacy with the world that we see lying before us; for it is not simply the case that we, as subjects, are capable of being viewed—from the point of view of a stranger, for example—as objects. Our relationship to objects is much more profound. There is encroachment between subject and object because the world has a way of inhabiting us, through the flesh, as a vibration of air, of light—as a certain molecular pattern that inspires an interior response. And this phenomenon—that the world of objects inspires an internal response within the subject—must be emphasized. "We speak of 'inspiration,'" writes Merleau-Ponty, "and the word should be taken literally. There really is inspiration and expiration of Being."[37] There really is an exchange between the visible and vision, between the audible and hearing, between the touched and touching. This exchange, as an intertwining, necessitates a revision of the Cartesian notion of the bifurcation of subject and object, for it takes place precisely at the noncoincidence opened between the two, which, as we can now understand, functions at once as opening and as encroachment.

Thus the body, far from becoming an obstacle to our view of the world, proves itself as the very means through which we have access to that world. "It is the body and it alone," Merleau-Ponty writes,

> that can bring us to the things themselves, which are themselves not flat beings but beings in depth, inaccessible to a subject that would survey them

from above, open to him alone that, if it be possible, would coexist with them in the same world. When we speak of the flesh of the visible, we do not mean to do anthropology, to describe a world covered over with all our own projections, leaving aside what it can be under the human mask. Rather, we mean that carnal being, as a being of depths, of several leaves or several faces, a being in latency, and a presentation of a certain absence, is a prototype of Being, of which our body, the sensible sentient, is a very remarkable variant, but whose constitutive paradox already lies in every visible.[38]

This paradox is one of distance and proximity: there is always a noncoincidence between ourselves and the totality of the world, viewed as depth; yet, at the same time, we owe our remarkable contact with the world to the implication of our body within it—we are *of* the world. On the surface, the notion of "the sensible sentient" as articulated by Merleau-Ponty might appear to be somewhat simple—in fact, to amount to nothing more than a rather poetic description of our proprioceptive ability. Yet to think according to the flesh—according to "the sensible sentient"—is to necessitate the development of what Merleau-Ponty describes as an entirely "new ontology," calling for a remarkable transformation in Western philosophical thought.[39] Merleau-Ponty makes this clear when he writes, "It is imperative that we recognize that this description also overturns our idea of the thing and the world, and that it results in an ontological rehabilitation of the sensible."[40]

Indeed, the "rehabilitation" is what leads Merleau-Ponty to turn with particular interest to the work of Proust. For in Proust, the flesh occupies and secretes a depth not only of space, but of time as well.

Proust through the Fold of Memory

One turns toward that Being that doubles our thoughts along their whole extension.
MERLEAU-PONTY, *The Visible and the Invisible*

For the narrator of Proust's great work, *À la recherche du temps perdu*, the problem of depth is intimately connected with the question of artistic expression, just as for Cézanne. Yet Marcel, the narrator's youthful self, not only wonders at the visual depth of the realm in which he is immersed; his ability to imagine visual depth—"as though one had placed [an image] behind the lens of a stereoscope"[1]—serves throughout the novel as a metaphor for another (and, for Proust the writer, a more significant) capacity: a play of the mind as it strives to negotiate the depth between perception and memory. It is this latter capacity that must be developed for the writer, in contrast to the painter. And it is this realm of internal depth—a dimension revealed as if the mind itself operated as a kind of interior stereoscope—that serves as a principal theme throughout the *Recherche*.

Indeed, the entire project of the *Recherche*—as the title signals—is undertaken according to a depth structure. From the beginning, Proust presents his protagonist by means of two different aspects: as the young man (known as Marcel) for whom the events of the novel unfold, and as the older man (known as the narrator) who offers a written account of these events. Just as two photographs of the same scene, flat and out of phase, when viewed through a stereoscope, suddenly bind together in vivid dimension, the disjunction between Marcel and the narrator coheres, at the end of the novel, as a single, rich understanding. By means of this double aspect of character, the novel offers (as Merleau-Ponty might describe) "not only viewpoints of each, added up, but their articulation, their *Ineinander*, their alternating cohesion, their alternation which is a cohesion . . . the two viewpoints as *alternates* but the two viewpoints *together*."[2] We could therefore say that the novel is a novel of depth. Indeed, the theme of cohesive noncoincidence informs much more than its structure. Within the world of the novel itself, there are the two pathways that shape Marcel's childhood realm, the "Méséglise way" and the "Guermantes way." There are the two musical compositions of Vinteuil, the sonata in volume 1 and the septet in volume 3. There are the two loves in Marcel's life, Gilberte and Albertine (their essential relatedness indicated by their names). These doubles are not repetitions or variations on a theme. The initiation of each of these structural doubles secures for Marcel what Merleau-Ponty would describe as "the opening of a dimension that can never again be closed, the establishment of a level in terms of which every other experience will henceforth be situated."[3] That is to say, they offer to Marcel, by virtue of their depth, the possibility of developing a shape or a sense structure for his life—a means through which noncoincidence might cohere.

For example, the double structure of the Méséglise and Guermantes ways initiates not only a dimension of space—the geographical boundary within which Marcel's childhood days are played—but generates an opening for the interior landscape of Marcel's life. Along the Méséglise and Guermantes ways, Marcel will begin the labor of situating his experience, of laying the ground against which future experiences may gain a dimension of depth. Even as a young boy walking with his grandfather along the Guermantes way, Marcel seems to intuit a hidden presence—a "secret treasure"—embedded within the objects of the natural world before him.[4] Fascinated by this fecundity of the sensible, Marcel becomes something of a collector of mental images ("I would concentrate on recalling exactly the line of the roof, the color of the stone"), through which he hopes he might grasp the meaning of experience.[5] "Suddenly a roof, a gleam of sunlight on a stone, the smell of a path would make me stop still, to enjoy the special pleasure that each of them gave me, and also because they appeared to be concealing, beyond what my eyes could see, something which they invited me to come and take but which despite all my efforts I never managed to discover."[6] He cannot discern the meaning, the sense, that these perceptions seem at the same time to call for and conceal; for Marcel as a young boy, they remain flat, dimensionless—an accumulated "mass of disparate images," littering the interior landscape of his mind—since he is not able to see beyond or beneath their visible surface.[7]

Yet, what Marcel could not then know is that as an adult—as the narrator—these "disparate images" would take root, through memory, in the very soil of the Méséglise and Guermantes ways.[8] Every perception and every thought, even the most fleeting, would henceforth come to be situated along these two pathways according to the depth of experience that they initiated.[9]

The narrator writes, "It is pre-eminently as the deepest layer of my mental soil, as the firm ground on which I still stand, that I regard the Méséglise and Guermantes ways."[10] It is thanks to their capacity as structural doubles that the Méséglise and Guermantes ways open up a dimension through which the "disparate images" of Marcel's childhood might finally cohere. Thus, the narrator claims that the Méséglise and Guermantes ways succeed in "permanently and indissolubly unit[ing] so many different impressions in my mind"; the two ways allow him to experience these distinct and uncollected impressions "at the same time."[11] The depth that the two ways open up, therefore, is one not only of space, but also of time. This sense of the past as a temporal double—a past that operates in counterpoint with the present, like the two images of a stereoscope—plays out frequently throughout the novel, as when Marcel encounters a hedge of hawthorns later in life, at Balbec, that remind him of the flowers of his childhood. Here is a depth of vision and intensification that springs not from two views of what is immediately present, like binocular vision, but from two views that are temporally dislocated. Perhaps, the narrator speculates, "reality takes shape in the memory alone."[12]

In the *Recherche* it is undeniably memory—as disclosure of this realm of depth—that holds the greatest power of fascination for Marcel. In this context, the much-celebrated passage of the madeleine dipped in tea remains worth citing:

> No sooner had the warm liquid mixed with the crumbs touched my palate than a shudder ran through me and I stopped, intent upon the extraordinary thing that was happening to me. An exquisite pleasure had invaded my senses, something isolated, detached, with no suggestion of its origin. And at once the vicissitudes of life had become indifferent to me, its disasters innocuous, its brevity illusory—this new sensation having had on me the effect which love has of filling me with a precious essence; or rather this essence was not in me, it *was* me. I had ceased now to feel mediocre, contingent, mortal. Whence could it have come to me, this all-powerful joy? I sensed that it was connected with the taste of the tea and the cake, but that it infinitely transcended those savors, could not, indeed, be of the same nature. Whence did it come? What did it mean? How could I seize and apprehend it?[13]

This "exquisite pleasure" does not so much fill Marcel as define him: "This essence was not in me, it *was* me." Yet he cannot account for its existence: "Whence did it come? What did it mean? How could I seize and apprehend it?" Carefully Marcel retraces the thoughts and sensations of the moment:

> I place in position before my mind's eye the still recent taste of that first mouthful, and I feel something start within me, something that leaves its

resting-place and attempts to rise, something that has been embedded like an anchor at a great depth; I do not know yet what it is, but I can feel it mounting slowly; I can measure the resistance, I can hear the echo of great spaces traversed. Undoubtedly what is thus palpitating in the depths of my being must be the image, the visual memory which, being linked to that taste, is trying to follow it into my conscious mind.[14]

It is thus that Marcel finally discovers the memory that has been summoned by the taste of the madeleine: that of Sunday mornings in Combray. "The whole of Combray and its surroundings, taking shape and solidity, sprang into being, town and gardens alike, from my cup of tea."[15] The pleasure is not from the visual memory itself (because, as evidenced by Marcel's description, the visual memory is brought to clarity only after the feeling of joy), but from the sudden attunement to something like an "essence" of Combray, incited by sensual experience. There is a sudden upsurge of a structural double, in relation to which the whole of his experience takes on an altered aspect. And remarking upon this extraordinary blossoming of the world of his childhood, Marcel notes that it arose not from conscious retrieval or his visual imagination, but from the "lesser" senses of taste and smell. To these he ascribes an almost animate power; curiously, Marcel compares them to "souls." Taste and smell, he writes, "remain poised a long time, like souls, remembering, waiting, hoping, amid the ruins of all the rest; and bear unflinchingly, in the tiny and almost impalpable drop of their essence, the vast structure of recollection."[16]

Proust's theory of recollection—of accessing a moment of the past in all of its force, parallel to and pressing upon the present—has long invited comparison to Plato's notion of anamnesis (recollection), for where the work of Proust and Plato most strikingly harmonize is with respect to their insistence upon structural doubles. A single sense perception does not suffice to access reality; there must be a sort of operative double, or dimension of depth, that permits us to get at the truth. According to Plato, we access this dimension by recollecting our past life, and it is the eternal rebirth of the soul that allows for a double realm of knowledge and ideas. Declares Socrates in the *Meno*: "Seeing then that the soul is immortal and has been born many times, and has beheld all things both in this world and in the nether realms, she has acquired knowledge of all and everything; so that it is no wonder that she should be able to recollect all that she knew before."[17] To demonstrate, Socrates uses the example of Meno's own slave, who, by means of Socrates' questioning rather than dictating, seems to uncover a knowledge of geometric calculation. The slave develops this knowledge about geometry, "without anyone having taught him, and only through questions put to him, . . . recovering the knowledge out of himself."[18] And so, according to Socrates, if the slave, who has had no education in geometry, nevertheless is able to recollect geometrical knowledge, then it must be that that geometrical knowledge was acquired not during his present life, but during an earlier time—a "time when he was not a human being," as Socrates describes it.[19] The knowledge cannot be said to belong to the slave, then, but to the eternal soul that is but temporarily contained within the slave's body. What Plato advances in the *Meno*, therefore, is the determination of a kind of double between perception and recollection predicated on the eternity of the soul—a double consisting of a fold between the phenomenal (the slave's present self) and the eternal (knowledge that has come from the soul). This knowledge from the "nether realm" that the soul recollects, then, acts as a distinct counterpart to the kind of incomplete and untrustworthy knowledge that appears in the realm of the senses. The soul's knowledge would and indeed must exist without the body of the slave. Socrates holds that this knowledge existed all along without the slave as a slave—it existed even at a "time when he was not a human being." To access knowledge, then, the process of anamnesis carries one most decidedly away from the realm of the sensible.

But according to Proust's work, the double that generates depth cannot be formed of a "nether realm" beyond the sensible; the total structure of the double, and not simply the present side (that is to say, not simply the slave as a slave), must be rooted in the world of the senses. Whenever Marcel tries to understand perception in relation to a universal idea of the mind or soul (like the slave who, following the drawing of squares and triangles in the sand, discovers the universal laws of geometry), he fails to feel the depth that he seeks through experience. Indeed, the theme of Marcel's suffering due to the unbridgeable gap between ideal representation and perceptible manifestation is woven throughout the novel (as when, for example, he is disappointed while watching Berma at the theater for the first time, or visiting the Balbec Church, or participating in the social circle of the Guermantes).[20] Of the visit to the Balbec Church, for example, the narrator confesses:

> My mind, which had lifted the Virgin of the Porch far above the reproductions that I had had before my eyes, invulnerable to the vicissitudes which might threaten them, intact even if they were destroyed, ideal, endowed with a universal value, was astonished to see the statue which it had carved a thousand times, reduced now to its own stone semblance, occupying, in relation to the reach of my arm, a place in which it had for rivals an election poster and the point of my stick, fettered to the Square, inseparable from the opening of the main street . . . and it was she, finally, the immortal work of art so

long desired, whom I found transformed, as was the church itself, into a little old woman in stone whose height I could measure and whose wrinkles I could count.[21]

Marcel is sharply dismayed to find that the work of art that he had conceived in his mind as "endowed with a universal value" could be so paltry a thing as a stone object, subject to the wear of pollution and desecration by graffiti. (One thinks, likewise, of how the particular manifestation of so beautiful a concept as geometry could not but disappoint Meno, who seems quite stunned to see it arise through dialogue with his own slave.) At the Balbec Church, Marcel is confronted with "the tyranny of the Particular."[22] For Marcel, the sensible quality of the stone—its height and its wrinkles—casts it out from the "immortal" realm of art.

And so might we characterize this, in Proust, as the failure of the Platonic double? For the relationship between the particularity of the church and Marcel's notion of it as a universal artwork (a representation of the church that, like the idea of geometry for Meno's slave, would have existed before and apart from Marcel) does not secure depth. As a structural double, it fails. This is because, for Proust, it is always the sensible realm that is determinative. Only when the sensible has doubled up through the sensible—only when Marcel encounters something, within the world, for the second time—is the sense of depth achieved. The ideal of Berma, when compared to Marcel's first encounter with her, results in disappointment; the layer of ideal upon experience fails to function as a double. It is only when Marcel attends the theater for the second time—when his second encounter within the sensible realm has been brought into relation with his first—that the impact of Berma's art is realized. The work—the miracle—of memory always operates, for him, within the sensible. Thus even though, like anamnesis, it is memory that secures for Marcel a sense of life lived in rich dimension, it can never be a kind of memory before or beyond the sensible realm, never memory (as in anamnesis) as the mental representation of an intelligible ideal that would abide in a separate "nether" realm.[23] What is interesting in Proust, then, is the way that the operative double is always rooted in the sensible realm. It is the sensible, not the intelligible, that grounds Marcel's search for depth. This is why, when the narrator searches for a metaphor to describe the process of recollection, he situates the dwelling of the soul (the soul as memory, as animate past) not in the realm of the ideal, but "in some material object":

> I feel that there is much to be said for the Celtic belief that the souls of those whom we have lost are held captive in some inferior being, in an animal, in a plant, in some inanimate object, and thus effectively lost to us until the

day (which to many never comes) when we happen to pass by the tree or to obtain possession of the object which forms their prison. Then they start and tremble, they call us by our name, and as soon as we have recognized their voice the spell is broken. Delivered by us, they have overcome death and return to share our life.

And so it is with our own past. It is a labor in vain to attempt to recapture it: all the efforts of our intellect must prove futile. The past is hidden somewhere outside the realm, beyond the reach of intellect, in some material object (in the sensation which that material object will give us) of which we have no inkling. And it depends on chance whether or not we come upon this object before we ourselves must die.[24]

This past, evoked by means of a chance encounter, cannot become known through the exercise of the intellect, for it dwells here, within the realm of objects. And for Marcel, the famous episodes of involuntary memory—of Combray through the madeleine, of Venice upon the uneven steps of the Guermantes' courtyard, of Balbec in the stiffness of a napkin—arise through just such chance encounters with objects. There is no reaching back to the memory of a soul that would ever have been without a body. On the contrary, it is the memory of the body that secures this sudden recovery of the past as an open dimension—recollection through taste and smell (sensorial capacities that are "like souls"), motility and touch. "Our legs and our arms are full of torpid memories," writes Proust.[25]

Thus, for Proust, it is always the body—and not, as in anamnesis, the eternal soul—that remembers. Yet this remembering body is not merely a body in the sense of an object; the body that remembers consists in much more than a sum of experiences inscribed within its pulp, just as the sensible world consists in more than what is visible within it. What we must think through is the living body—the body that sees (as subject) and at the same time is seen (as object)—the body as a certain power of motility and desire—the body as animation—this body that would be the *"body of the spirit."*[26] For Merleau-Ponty, it is this that is the *flesh.*[27]

The flesh, that which shelters the bodily past within the present, is itself characterized as a "coiling over" and a "double relationship."[28] With the flesh, there is a doubling (of the sensible and the sentient) that at the same time exhibits an openness and differentiation—there is a transformation characteristic of depth. And so the flesh cannot be conceived of merely as a kind of additive layering of spirit upon body or of memory upon perception. More than a body, the "flesh," Merleau-Ponty writes, "is not matter, is not mind, is not substance."[29] He insists, "We must not think [of] the flesh [as] starting from substances, from body and spirit—for then it would be the union of contradictories."[30] It does not consist in two separate parts brought together (body and spirit); it is a double structure folded through itself (*"body of the spirit"*) by "invagination" that opens upon the richness of the world.[31] Rather than union, there is transformation, the launching of the depth dimension, the cohesion of noncoincidence. Merleau-Ponty writes:

> One should not even say, as we did a moment ago, that the body is made up of two leaves, of which the one, that of the "sensible," is bound up with the rest of the world. There are not in it two leaves or two layers; fundamentally it is neither things seen only nor seer only. . . . To speak of leaves or of layers is still to flatten and to juxtapose, under the reflective gaze, what coexists in the living and upright body. If one wants metaphors, it would be better to say that the body sensed and the body sentient are as the obverse and the reverse, or again, as two segments of one sole circular course which goes above from left to right and below from right to left, but which is but one sole movement in its two phases.[32]

The sentient is not layered upon the sensible; instead, through the flesh "there is reciprocal insertion and intertwining of one in the other,"[33] which generates a dimension of depth and movement ("as two segments of one sole circular course which goes above from left to right and below from right to left"). We are not speaking of an objective body that would exist only within the dimensions of space. It is important to underline that the flesh is not only in the world, but of the world—it is the condition of expressivity through which the world emerges.[34] "To designate it," writes Merleau-Ponty, "we should need the old term 'element,' in the sense [in which] it was used to speak of water, air, earth, and fire. . . . The flesh is in this sense an 'element' of Being. Not a fact or a sum of facts, and yet adherent to *location* and to the *now*. Much more: the inauguration of the *where* and the *when*, the possibility and exigency for the fact."[35] Through the flesh, then, the lived space (where) and time (when) within which and to which we apply ourselves are brought forth.[36]

Marcel exists, therefore, neither solely as body nor soul, nor as the simple layering of one upon another; he is not the layer of one upon the other because layers could be lifted apart (as, for example, the soul of Meno's slave is born apart from his body). For Marcel, there could be no separation of these layers, because it is thanks to their cohesion that he experiences the depth of the world. And so it is not that the soul recollects (as in anamnesis), nor even that bodily sensation, by itself, records and preserves the past. Rather, Marcel's extraordinary experience of the past—like that of Combray through the madeleine (with respect to which Marcel relates, as we have seen, that "this essence [of the past] was not in me, it *was* me")—discloses the "*body of the spirit*," for memory depends precisely upon the intertwining of the sentient and the sensible that is the flesh. Thus, this that Merleau-Ponty calls flesh cannot be only a flesh of space, but must be also a flesh of time. "Then past and present are *Ineinander*, each enveloping-enveloped—and that itself is the flesh," writes Merleau-Ponty.[37] Proust illustrates this most explicitly at the end of the novel, when the narrator relates: "And I felt, as I say, a sensation of weariness and almost of terror at the thought that all this length of Time had not only, without interruption, been lived, experienced, secreted by me, that it was my life, was in fact me, but also that I was compelled so long as I was alive to keep it attached to me, that it supported me and that, perched on its giddy summit, I could not myself make a movement without displacing it."[38] This flesh, "secreted by me" like a snail in his shell, is a flesh of time.[39]

This Marcel realizes, finally, through his introduction to Gilberte's daughter, Mlle de Saint-Loup. Mlle de Saint-Loup could be said to bear time quite literally within her flesh; she embodies, for Marcel, the whole of his life—the entire web of divergences and intersections, of loves and landscapes that make up the very matter of his existence. While Gilberte (Mme de Saint-Loup) fetches her daughter, Marcel reflects:

> My surprise at Gilberte's words and the pleasure that they caused me were soon replaced, while Mme de Saint-Loup left me and made her way into an-other drawing-room, by that idea of Time past which was brought home to me once again, in yet another fashion and without my even having seen her, by Mlle de Saint-Loup. Was she not—are not, indeed, the majority of human beings?—like one of those star-shaped cross-roads in a forest where roads converge that have come, in the forest as in our lives, from the most diverse quarters? Numerous for me were the roads which led to Mlle de Saint-Loup and which radiated around her. Firstly the two great "ways" themselves, where on my many walks I had dreamed so many dreams, both led to her: through her father Robert de Saint-Loup the Guermantes way; through Gilberte, her mother, the Méséglise way which was also "Swann's way." One of them took me, by way of this girl's mother and the Champs-Élysées, to Swann, to my evenings at Combray, to Méséglise itself; the other, by way of her father, to those afternoons at Balbec where even now I saw him again beside the sun-bright sea. And between these two high roads a network of transversals was set up.[40]

Through his encounter with Mlle de Saint-Loup, Marcel realizes not only the confluence of the Méséglise and Guermantes ways (and of Combray and Balbec) that form the landscape of his past, but even and especially the con-fluence of the people and expressions that form the interior landscape of his life—his passion, joy, and suffering. Through Mlle de Saint-Loup, Swann, Odette, Gilberte, and Albertine cohere, as well as the music of Vinteuil and the paintings of Elstir at Balbec. These cohesions make of his flesh not an object, but a lived, vital history. Mlle de Saint-Loup serves not only as the two ways incarnate; she is the flesh as dimension (space and time)—as the opening up of the double structure, through which life gains its intensity. Is Mlle de Saint-Loup not the inspiration that prompts Marcel, finally, to begin to write—to become the narrator? For in bringing about the cohesion of his past—his lost time—her presence releases Marcel to fill just this role. Through her, as the flesh (time and space) of the Méséglise and Guermantes ways, springs the entire notion of the double "I" (Marcel and the narrator); through her a depth structure is inaugurated that will generate the expression known as the novel itself. And so, after his encounter with Mlle de Saint-Loup, Marcel-as-narrator declares, "This notion of Time embodied, of years past but not separated from us, it was now my intention to emphasize as strongly as possible in my work."[41]

Likewise, in commenting upon the intention of his work *The Visible and the Invisible*, Merleau-Ponty writes:

> We shall render explicit the cohesion of time, of space, of space and time, the "simultaneity" of their parts (literal simultaneity in space, simultaneity in the figurative sense in time) and the intertwining (*entrelacs*) of space and time. And we shall render explicit the cohesion of the obverse and the reverse of my body which is responsible for the fact that my body—which is visible, tangible like a thing—acquires this view upon itself, this contact with itself, where it doubles itself up, unifies itself, in such a way that the objective body and the phenomenal body turn about one another or encroach upon one another.[42]

This cohesion of space and time, like that of the objective and phenomenal body, is to be understood precisely through the flesh. According to Merleau-Ponty, there is a flesh of time that would not be removed from space or the body, where the past would not be forgotten, dead, or nonpresent but would maintain efficacy in the world. As dimension, this flesh of time would set the condition for everything else to unfold and acquire meaning through depth. In the working notes of *The Visible and the Invisible*, Merleau-Ponty refers once again to the *Recherche*: "Proust: the *true* hawthorns are the hawthorns of the past."[43] For it is in recollecting flowers along the Méséglise and Guermantes ways that the narrator complains, "The flowers that people show me nowadays for the first time never seem to me to be true flowers. The Méséglise way, with its lilacs, its hawthorns, its cornflowers, its poppies, its apple-trees, the Guermantes way with its river full of tadpoles, its water-lilies

and its buttercups, constituted for me for all time the image of the landscape in which I should like to live."[44] What he experiences now, for the first
time—that is to say, what he experiences without a sense of cohesion with the
two ways of his childhood—lacks depth; new flowers that he encounters are
not, the narrator feels, "true flowers." The flowers of the past are true because
he has carried them, all along, inside himself—or rather, not inside him but
as himself. They too are of his flesh, and therefore they maintain a certain
efficacy. They inaugurate (but only in retrospect, only after having become
doubled) "a level in terms of which every other experience will henceforth be
situated."[45] Marcel could not be except as Marcel of the hawthorns. Indeed, it
is the past—that which he carries as himself—that redoubles the color, vitality, and power of the impressions of the present. The narrator writes, "The
cornflowers, the hawthorns, the apple-trees which I may still happen, when I
travel, to encounter in the fields, because they are situated at the same depth,
on the level of my past life, at once establish contact with my heart."[46] They
touch him to the quick, for their sense reverberates within the flesh of time
that is Marcel.

Thus the cohesion of time and space through the hawthorns—the "true"
hawthorns of the past—demonstrates the sense in which, as Merleau-Ponty
writes, "the visible landscape under my eyes is not exterior to, and bound
synthetically to . . . other moments of time and the past, but has them really *behind itself* in simultaneity, inside itself and not it and they side by side
'in' time."[47] For time as flesh overcomes the time of the series. "This 'past,'"
writes Merleau-Ponty, "belongs to a mythical time."[48]

It is thus that, following the final completed chapter of *The Visible and
the Invisible* ("The Intertwining—The Chiasm") in which Merleau-Ponty
develops the notion of flesh, the working notes of the manuscript look toward this "mythical time." Just as the depth of space would exceed the linear
dimensions of width and breadth as outlined by the *kosmotheoros*, the depth
of time would be that through which the separate realms of past, present,
and future might "take" as one whole, transformative dimension. Thus, "the
serial time, that of 'acts' and decisions, is overcome," writes Merleau-Ponty,
and "the mythical reintroduced."[49] He imagines this mythical time as a sort
of coiling up of the past and future into the present—a type of coiling that,
like all double structures, would not merely produce layers but inaugurate
depth. That is to say, for Merleau-Ponty, mythical time constitutes a realm
where the past lies not beyond the boundary of the present but stands as one
sole gesture *with* the present, as the obverse or unseen side of the present,
and therefore as a dimension of the depth of the present. Rather than experience this time as we do in ordinary life, "according to the dimensions of a

past that is no longer, a future that is not yet, and a present that alone fully is," mythical time offers a depth through which "certain events 'in the beginning' maintain a continued efficacity."[50] Past and present are not separated; rather, they are truly intertwined or encroach upon each other. Here "certain events" retain a degree of potency within the present, as we have seen with Proust's encounter with the hawthorns. But this is not to understand them through a causal, linear flow of time. Carefully does Merleau-Ponty call attention to the "beginning" of these events; it could never be an origin—an immutable beginning. It is not in time; it is of time—it *is* time. There is a mythical past that comes to be known through encroachment upon the present—a past not beside the present but beneath or behind it. Like the "true" hawthorns of the past, this "beginning" is instituted only in retrospect, by means of the double structure (the coiling up)—by means of the depth dimension of mythical time. This dynamicism Merleau-Ponty describes as the "retrograde movement of the true."[51]

Thus, there is no point of origin; there is, rather, movement. In correcting the implied spatiality of his notion of the flesh, we have already noted that Merleau-Ponty writes, "If one wants metaphors, it would be better to say that the body sensed and the body sentient are . . . as two segments of one sole circular course which goes above from left to right and below from right to left, but which is but one sole movement in its two phases."[52] The flesh of time offers a kind of operative noncoincidence, opening, or differentiation that is a setting into motion.[53] It is for this reason that Merleau-Ponty so often describes the flesh in active terms—through intertwining, reciprocity. And so, if Merleau-Ponty's philosophy is, as he declares, a philosophy of the flesh, we must take seriously his expressed desire to develop "an ontology which reveals in being itself an overlap or movement"—not simply as a double (of space) but as a rhythm (of time).[54] Merleau-Ponty writes:

> We are experiences, that is, thoughts that feel behind themselves the weight of the space, the time, the very Being they think, and which therefore do not hold under their gaze a serial space and time nor the pure idea of series, but have about themselves a time and a space that exist by piling up, by proliferation, by encroachment, by promiscuity—a perpetual pregnancy, perpetual parturition, generativity and generality, brute essence and brute existence, which are the nodes and antinodes of the same ontological vibration.[55]

This "ontological vibration," this movement of depth: what is it but rhythm? The "double formula"—the "double movement"—of the flesh of time: what is it but rhythm? For rhythm expresses the cohesion and encroachment of past, present, and future.

Is this not why music is so important in its role as a structural double throughout the *Recherche*? (And why it takes its place of honor in the final completed chapter of Merleau-Ponty's *The Visible and the Invisible*?) Music, Merleau-Ponty claims, gives us the flesh of time itself. "Like paintings without identifiable things, without the *skin* of things, but giving their *flesh*."[56]

4

Debussy: Silence and Resonance

Music as the model of meaning—of this silence from which language is made.
MERLEAU-PONTY, *"Two Unpublished Notes on Music"*

For Mallarmé, the expression of poetry lives through a fundamental musicality—through the "rhythm between the relations."[1] Thus Mallarmé objected when he learned of Debussy's intentions to set *L'après-midi d'un faune* to music, for he felt that he already had created the music through his poetry. Nevertheless, he accepted (by all accounts begrudgingly) Debussy's invitation to hear the first piano-reduction reading of *Prélude à l'après-midi d'un faune*, no doubt because he knew that Debussy shared with him a certain artistic sensibility, since the composer at that time frequented the circle of poets and artists known as Les Mardis, who convened regularly in Mallarmé's own home. There Debussy might, on any given Tuesday evening, have enjoyed the company of James Whistler, Claude Monet, Auguste Rodin, Oscar Wilde, or Paul Valéry, all the while that Mallarmé himself held court. Yet Debussy's own position within the circle was clearly deferential; twenty years younger than Mallarmé, Debussy was at that time a struggling musician with no significant achievement to his name.[2] Many years after the fateful reading of the piano reduction, Debussy described the "master's" reaction: "Mallarmé arrived looking like a soothsayer, with a Scotch plaid over his shoulders. He listened, and then there was a long silence before he said: 'I wasn't expecting anything like that! That music prolongs the emotion of my poem and conjures up the scenery more vividly than any color.' "[3]

And so, by Debussy's account, Mallarmé was surprisingly delighted with the piece. Indeed, after the premiere of *Prélude à l'après-midi d'un faune* with the full orchestra, Mallarmé sent to Debussy a signed copy of his poem, inscribed with a dedication:

Woodlander from when the world was young
If your flute was once inspired,
Listen to the radiance it acquired
When Debussy gave it tongue.[4]

Finally, in a letter to Debussy, Mallarmé wrote: "What a marvel! Your illustration of 'The Afternoon of a Faun' offers no dissonance with my text, except that it goes further, truly, in nostalgia and light, with finesse, uneasiness,
and richness."[5]

What is striking about Mallarmé's words to Debussy is the sense in which
they suggest depth—precisely the same kind of depth presented in not only
Mallarmé's work but also that of Proust and Cézanne. "Nostalgia and light"
make use of two structural doubles, one temporal (as Merleau-Ponty writes
of memory in Proust), the other spatial (as Merleau-Ponty writes of visible
light in Cézanne). The music's "finesse" and "uneasiness"—its movement
and change—as well as its "richness" conjure Merleau-Ponty's description of
the generative dimension that characterizes Mallarmé's own poetry. Indeed,
it is as if Debussy's music were able to give expression to exactly the musicality—the rhythmicality—that Merleau-Ponty identifies in the works of these
three artists, but especially in the poetry of Mallarmé.

In this respect, what is operative is Debussy's expressive use of silence.
The silence that precedes the piece becomes a part of the piece—it, and not
the sound of the flute, serves as the first event in the initiation of the rhythm.
Likewise Mallarmé had emphasized the role of silence in his work; as we saw
in chapter 1, this silence appears in printed form as the "white spaces" on
the page. In his preface to "Un coup de dés" (published in 1897, it should be
noted—three years after the premier of Debussy's Prélude), Mallarmé writes
that his poetry admits of "a strange influence, that of Music, as it is heard
at a concert; several of its methods, which seemed to me to apply to Literature, are to be found here."[6] What Mallarmé and Debussy share (and what
therefore manifests itself throughout their works, independently) is a similar
artistic receptivity to that very noncoincidence—that silence—from which
expression issues forth.

Indeed, it becomes impossible for one to say, as one would not hesitate to
say of other musical tone poems of the time (like those of Richard Strauss),
that Debussy's Prélude is an imitation or representation in sound. Debussy's
Prélude is not derivative—it "goes further" (as Mallarmé wrote to Debussy)
than the poem. It does not illustrate the words or narrative of the poem but
resonates with and amplifies the creative sense of poetry itself. "These nymphs
that I would perpetuate"—what are they but the artist's desire, the flesh of

expression itself?[7] Thus we could say that the *Prélude* serves less as an imitation and more as a double of the poem, and that from the depth between the poem and the *Prélude* spring the true dreams and desires of the faun.

This difference—this noncoincidence—between the poem and the *Prélude* highlights the contrast between an art (poetry) that had, by this time, succumbed to print, and the particular temporal movement that is music. Certainly time holds sovereignty over the way that we experience a musical piece. In listening to music, one cannot take a second look, reread, or go back over a line. The singularity of each moment—the past's inability to be reinstated—means that repetition within the flow of the music becomes essential to the unfolding of form. Indeed in music, form can only be said to exist to the extent that phrases and sections of music wrap around themselves in reference, thanks to the operation of memory. Music inscribes a certain temporal depth. It is not as if we might in our mind hear the second phrase at the same time as the first and thereby make a comparison between the two. Yet somehow we know the second phrase to be *second*, because the second, as a double, always gives birth to something more. It opens up a resonance of feeling that never characterizes the singular, the flat, or the linear. Like the two offset images of the stereoscope that initiate a vision of depth, two iterations of a melody "take" suddenly as the dimension of one whole phrase. Repetition in music, always noncoinciding because of the flow of time, inaugurates depth, and a great musical piece shapes this depth in multiple layers.[8] In this sense, "movement and meaning [are] indissociable."[9]

Indeed, it is in this way that music expresses the particular sense of "mythical time" that Merleau-Ponty describes in his work. And so, just as we questioned, with respect to Merleau-Ponty, the nature of a "beginning" that would serve as initiation in mythical time, we must ask of music, and of the *Prélude* specifically: when does the piece begin?

✶

Surely it does not begin with a C$\sharp$. The opening melody—a monophonic line in the flute—does unfold from that note, yet to identify that note as the beginning of the piece would be inadequate. On the one hand, it would be inadequate because that note is of the flute—is in fact of the breath. Before the sounding of the pitch, then, comes the breath, silently establishing a rhythm that will underlie the entire piece. This rhythm—the relationship between inhalation and exhalation—bears no resemblance yet to the meter or bar lines marked in the score. What one senses in the opening—in the silence that transitions to the motion of duple and triple divisions—is the life of the external world transformed, through breath, into the deep silver notes of the

EXAMPLE 4.1. Debussy, *Prélude à l'après-midi d'un faune*, mm. 1–4, flute.

flute; what one hears is the summoning and shaping of wind into columns of resonance, alignment, and amplification. It is as if the air itself had coalesced into a voice. Is not, then, this breath the beginning, as much as the sounding of the C♯? For it serves as the source of m. 1.

On the other hand, to identify the C♯ as the beginning of the piece would be inadequate because that note does not come from or go to anywhere at all in the musical phrase; it only arrives, unsteadily, at itself. One could hardly hear the C♯ as a beginning until there had already been reiteration—in this case, a chromatic descent to G♮ and return to C♯ in m. 2. This melody is an arabesque. There is already a process of looping back and thus a process of reinstitution that signals this gesture as opening. The subtle difference between m. 1 and m. 2 lies in the temporal gap between their sounding, such that m. 2 confirms the expression of m. 1; the subsequent melodic line in m. 3 can then expand via G♯ in the direction, however faint the implication, of E major—the overall tonality of the piece. (One hears the B♮ at the end of m. 3 as the dominant of E major—a sense quickly subverted, however, by the melodic arrival, in m. 4, on A♯.) Is not, then, the C♯ in m. 2 the beginning as much as the C♯ in m. 1? For it gives strength to m. 1, marking out its creative capacity for development.

And so the initial C♯ in the flute looks too much backward and forward simultaneously to constitute a positive beginning or sovereign point of origin. It is already a "beginning" like that of mythical time: "retrograde movement *in futuro*," as Merleau-Ponty writes.[10] The transformation, then, from silence to motion in the *Prélude* occurs through structural doubling. Sound is never the absolute negation of silence but emerges as a coiling up over silence— the blossoming of breath into song and of repetition into feeling. There is doubling of the external and internal world thanks to the silvery swirl of the breath through the flute, and this intertwining is that of the flesh. There is doubling of the past and the present thanks to the repetition of melodic lines, and this encroachment is that of rhythm. The vitality, the "motion" of music is rooted in the excess—the emotion—that springs from this intertwining and encroachment.

Debussy's entire *Prélude* unfolds as a series of doubles that open up multiple dimensions of expression. Many of these doubles disclose themselves within the first thirty measures of the piece, creating a "beginning" of depth—a beginning that folds through itself. The motion that these doubles generate does not pause until the cadence (in B major) at m. 30. Therefore, we will focus on these opening thirty measures: on the horn motif (mm. 4–10), the oboe and strings (mm. 17–20), and, finally, the flute melody itself. Perhaps, after thirty measures of analysis, we will better understand the nature of the "beginning" that Debussy offers to us.

In m. 4, we hear the first harmonic sonority of the piece, as the woodwinds and harp enter on the second beat. As nebulous in function (an A♯ half-diminished seventh chord) as the flute line and focused still upon the upper voices of the orchestra (oboes and clarinets), the entrance of the woodwinds and harp neither resolves the tension of the opening melody nor pushes to a new development. It is the first horn—an instrument that, like the flute, resonates by means of the human breath, but this time offering a rich timbre of gold—that lends pulse to the measure, with a soft, syncopated entrance leading to an expansive call (F–B♭–A♭) in m. 5, echoed by the syncopated dyad in the lower third horn. It is as if the idea of the flute melody—so concentrated in its half and whole steps and so tightly bound in register until the C♯ minor seventh outline in m. 3—combined with the woodwinds and harp in m. 4 could close into itself and disintegrate if not for the wide gesture in the horn at m. 5. Measure 5, too, expands in register through the B♭ seventh chord in the basses and muted lower strings (cellos and violas). This B♭ is connected, certainly, to the A♯ with which the flute melody ended (respelled enharmonically) but strikes the ear immediately as a new sound. It is an extraordinarily rich moment of color, this sonorous world of basses; it is a moment of B♭s and A♭s that rise out of the A♯s and G♯s of the previous measure (as enharmonic respellings that move from the sharp side to the flat side of the circle of fifths).[11] And then, in m. 6, there is silence—an entire measure of silence—written into the score.

At this moment, the music has shifted so much (as if, through the enharmonic accidentals, the piece had been rotated like a kaleidoscope), that it reveals a gap—a break in the movement of the arabesque. The motion must go back—it must return to itself—coil under itself—in order to continue. The silent m. 6, therefore, stands at the center of a double. The rupture is followed by resumption, in m. 7, of material from m. 4, but now with the muted violins and not the woodwinds sustaining the harmony. Again, the first horn, in a syncopated pulse, issues its expansive call, and the third horn echoes above the rich bass sonority of the B♭ seventh chord. The horns repeat their gesture through m. 9, sustaining a suspension and resolving quietly into the

EXAMPLE 4.2. Debussy, *Prélude à l'après-midi d'un faune*, mm. 4–11, orchestra.

D major triad at m. 11 (again, on the sharp side of the circle of fifths), where the flute melody returns.

It is this silent m. 6 (following the rupture of timbre, register, and harmony in m. 5) that demonstrates Debussy's achievement of the depth of noncoincidence through music. In a letter to a friend, Debussy comments

EXAMPLE 4.2. (*continued*)

upon this aspect of his compositional style: "I made use, quite spontaneously, moreover, of a means that seems to me fairly rare, I mean silence (don't laugh) as an agent of expression and perhaps the only way of making the emotion of a phrase gain its true weight."[12] Measure 6, therefore, is not actually an "empty" measure: it is an evocation of the silence from which expression emerges, the noncoincidence from which emotion is generated. Through these opening measures—and especially the silence of m. 6—the whole of the piece is conceived.

Of course, we hear all of this only in retrospect and, locally, only after the flute has reentered in m. 11 with the arabesque. This time, however, the melody is linked not with an expansive call of the horns (which instead move in conjunct chromatic steps) but with a transition, through the oboe, to a new melodic gesture in m. 17. Here the oboe shines brightly on the melody, ascending from the A$\sharp$ that it borrows from the flute. The harmony, no longer the B$\flat$ seventh chord of m. 5 (which had, in that context, seemed so dark and rich) but now an enharmonically respelled A$\sharp$ seventh chord, oscillates, by means of half-step movement from C$_\times$ up to D$\sharp$ and also A$\sharp$ up to B$\natural$, with an E$\sharp$ half-diminished seventh chord (confirmed in m. 19). It is as if, in m. 17, the idea of the B$\flat$ seventh chord from m. 5 had shifted from a cool to a bright timbre (i.e., from horn to oboe) and from a rich to a shining harmony (i.e., from the flat side of the circle of fifths in m. 5 to the sharp side in m. 17). This shift in harmony from an A$\sharp$ seventh chord to an E$\sharp$ half-diminished seventh chord occurs at the end of m. 17 and is repeated in m. 18. Measure 18, therefore, coils back to m. 17, emphasizing the oscillating harmonic motion but adding, as the excess of color that such reinstitution generates, muted violins to the oboe melody—the first melodic line to be heard in the violins. This has the effect of sweetening the reedy oboe sound, and the music reaches a *forte* dynamic level for the first time. It is here that the piece opens up, expands, and reverberates. The B$\flat$/A$\sharp$ sonority, as a double (from mm. 5 and 8, then 17 and 18), begins to realize the possibility of its generative power.

What then, of the flute arabesque that weaves itself through these full orchestral moments? As we have already noted, the opening flute melody contains its own, interior double (that is to say, according to the repetition between mm. 1 and 2), but it establishes its function as a structural double in its performance as a whole as well: its repetitions offer a kind of musical depth—new harmonies, timbres, and melodic figurations. Following the expansive horn call and B$\flat$ sonority of m. 5, the flute melody returns in m. 11 unmodified, except—because any "return" must encompass the excess that such a movement creates—for the new harmony (D major) in the accompanying strings and the clear sense of rhythmic pulse that the accompaniment provides. Measure 21, following the oscillating harmonies and bright oboe melody of mm. 17–19, marks another iteration of the flute arabesque, this time above the sonority of a C$\sharp$ minor seventh. Here the flute melody takes a new turn, fluttering through C$\sharp$ minor and landing upon the pitch A as the begin-

EXAMPLE 4.3. Debussy, *Prélude à l'après-midi d'un faune*, mm. 17–19, orchestra.

ning of a new melodic sequence that dips down a fourth before climbing up to a C♭, considered enharmonically to function as B♯ leading to C♯ on the downbeat of m. 26, which serves as yet another beginning of the arabesque.

The second measure of this final arabesque, m. 27, is transformed, swirling around the descending and ascending figure of the tritone in alternation between the first and second flutes until both flutes make a rapid ascent together to m. 28, where they languidly descend in triplet turns over an F♯ ninth chord, leading finally to the cadence, in m. 30, in B major. The descending

EXAMPLE 4.4. Debussy, *Prélude à l'après-midi d'un faune*, mm. 21–25, orchestra.

motion of the flutes along with the strong tonal relationship between F♯ and B (descent of a perfect fifth) contributes to the strength of this cadence—the first in the entire piece.

Certainly, we hear the arabesque differently in each of its entrances, not only because of the qualitative shift associated with the passage of time itself,

EXAMPLE 4.4. (*continued*)

but also because of the new musical material that intervenes. Yet the arabesque does not simply profit from a juxtaposition of different melodies and harmonies; instead, it is as if each iteration of the arabesque gives birth to another layer of depth and thus another layer of possible expression. Because the flute melody contains its own interior double, this double bears a capacity for inventiveness. In each of the returning arabesque statements, therefore, it

EXAMPLE 4.5. Debussy, *Prélude à l'après-midi d'un faune*, mm. 26–30, flutes and strings only (omitting other woodwinds and harp). Notice the descending triplet turns in the flutes in m. 28, which relate back to the accompaniment material in the violas and cellos at m. 22.

seems to be in the moment of the double that change springs forth, for just as the melody folds in upon itself does it open a new dimension. This is how we can understand the variations of the arabesque that occur in mm. 22 and 27 (as corresponding to the second measure or double of the initial melody). This repetition is productive, not merely reproductive, and leads each phrase into a structurally significant harmonic area: a B ninth chord in m. 23 leading to E in m. 26 (a movement accomplished by means of descending perfect fifth) and an F♯ ninth chord in m. 28 leading to B in m. 30 (as mentioned above, a movement of a descending perfect fifth).

And so in the *Prélude*, we begin to hear Merleau-Ponty's sense of mythical time, where, as we have seen, "certain events 'in the beginning' maintain a continued efficacy."[13] This "beginning" cannot be pinpointed to the opening of the flute solo, the harmony of m. 5, the silence of m. 6, the melody at m. 17, or the cadence in m. 30. Each of these moments serves as a beginning only in retrospect; their "continued efficacy" does not so much mark them out as causes as it underlines their operation as effects. In mythical time, the beginning comes through the middle; it does not initiate the events—it unfolds through them. Merleau-Ponty writes that "while listening to beautiful music," he has "the impression that this movement that starts up is already at its endpoint, which it is going to have been, or [that it is] sinking into the future that we have a hold of as well as the past."[14] This intertwining of past, present, and future opens up the expressive world of the *Prélude*.

Indeed, the flute arabesque is woven throughout the whole of the piece, not just the first thirty measures. It returns quite recognizably in m. 79 in the flute (transposed up a minor third to begin on E) and m. 86 in the oboe (transposed up a diminished third to begin on E♭). In m. 94, the melody appears in both flutes at its original pitch level (that is to say, on C♯). This signals an important structural event in the musical form. From that point to the end of the piece, the arabesque is almost constantly present: in m. 100 in the flute and cello through m. 102 (in repeated fragments), in the oboe in mm. 103 and 104, and finally, in m. 107, in the muted horns. The colors of these instruments—flute, oboe, horn—evoke the opening section of the piece (mm. 1–30) in which the arabesque was first heard. This expressive sense of repetition confirms the depths that the piece has traversed; the melody coils back to a reinitiation that is noncoincident.

In this way, the beginning and the end hold together. The final written measure of the piece, m. 110, offers an eighth-note pizzicato in the lower strings on the downbeat but otherwise sustains a motion of complete silence. It is a silence that returns to that of the very opening, the one that was transformed, through breath, into the silver notes of the flute. Indeed, in no way does the piece end with the last sounding pizzicatos in E major. Every live performance—even every recording—sustains a certain resonance through that final measure and beyond. It is not an audible so much as a felt resonance, an expressive silence.

EXAMPLE 4.6. Debussy, *Prélude à l'après-midi d'un faune*, mm. 107–10, orchestra.

The difference between the silence at the end and the silence at the beginning is this expression, this motion. Thus, if we ask once again where the
piece begins, it would not be preposterous to say that the beginning of the
Prélude comes only through the end—only through the expressive motion
that follows the final cadence. In this case, must we not (as passionate readers
of Proust are wont to do as well) then turn again to the opening measures—
to the silvery air of the flute—as soon as we have sensed the very last strains
of harmony die away?

Cézanne and the Institution of Style

For the artist, the work is always an attempt. And for history, painting in its entirety is
a beginning.

MERLEAU-PONTY, *Institution and Passivity*

We have heard, in Debussy, the line—in his case, the melodic line—initiate
movement, through silence. For musical motion springs from the noncoincidence of individual notes, phrases, and whole sections of a piece. In such
music, the line, though monophonic, could never be a flat one: it discloses,
through the dimension of mythical time, what one might call a depth of
expression.

Can the line accomplish as much in the visual arts? The traditional function of the line in a drawing or painting appears to be that of containment.
It works to keep an object within bounds, as if an outline were actually a
property of an object: the object's own fixed end or beginning. The line has
the effect of defining the edge between the object and the general volume of
space. Such an object, in this way, seems to be placed within space, but is not
of space. The line separates the object from the space that would threaten to
envelop it.

Yet, in the work of Cézanne (not unlike that of Debussy), there is no
hard edge, no finite boundary, no fixed outline. The line is freed. Its function
now is not to contain volume; rather, the line serves as a membrane through
which a certain depth or volume radiates. In *Four Bathers*, the deep blue lines
that stretch from chest to foot in the bather to the right, for example, seem
to press upon and open up the space toward which she is tending; a richness
of blues and greens swirls around, embracing the fullness of her thigh. Like
a creature of the water from which she has emerged, her body articulates a
fluid volume, and the sweeping lines of her left side and leg resonate through
the blue atmosphere of the shaded grove. It is as if, in order to bring forth
a certain depth, Cézanne must not impose strict separation between space
and the bather but must let them play—let them intertwine and *be of one*

FIGURE 5.1. Cézanne, *Four Bathers*, 1888–90, oil on canvas, Ny Carlsberg Glyptotek, Copenhagen.

another—as the bather herself inhales and exhales, breathing of the liquid substance of the air. The deep blue lines that reverberate against the flesh of the bather's body are thus like living tissue. These lines do not mark an "end" to space; rather, they evoke a certain promiscuity of flesh and space. The sense of the bather does not stop at an edge; it inhabits and lives as a dimension that spills over to the unseen vapors of the atmosphere. It is this—the line as an inauguration not of surface but of depth—that can be said to offer, in Cézanne's work, a power of expression.

In *Still Life with Milk Jug and Fruit*, for example, Cézanne traces not just one line that would circumscribe the plate and the fruit, but several lines of different shades of blue, as if each line were the string of a cello, vibrating. In this resonance of line, there is no edge and no beginning to the space; volume and shape form themselves—sing themselves, like the arabesque of Debussy's *Prélude*—through the objects on the canvas. And so, Merleau-Ponty writes, in Cézanne's paintings there is "the impression of an emerging order, [of] an object in the act of appearing, organizing itself before our eyes."[1] Like the

FIGURE 5.2. Cézanne, *Still Life with Milk Jug and Fruit*, c. 1900, oil on canvas, National Gallery of Art, Washington.

form of a musical work that does not proceed through absolute beginnings or endings but, as an expression of mythical time, creates itself through the fold of multiple layers, the repetition of the line in Cézanne participates in a particular kind of depth. Merleau-Ponty clarifies:

> In the same way, the contour of an object conceived as a line encircling the object belongs not to the visible world but to geometry. If one outlines the shape of an apple with a continuous line, one makes an object of the shape, whereas the contour is rather the ideal limit toward which the sides of the apple recede in depth. Not to indicate any shape would be to deprive the objects of their identity. To trace just a single outline sacrifices depth—that is the dimension in which the thing is presented not as spread out before us but as an inexhaustible reality full of reserves. That is why Cézanne follows the swelling of the object in modulated colors and indicates *several* outlines in blue.[2]

These "*several* outlines in blue" have the effect of generating a rhythm upon the canvas, through the heart of which springs the style of Cézanne's work. Do not these lines, and their rhythm, lend the fruit and especially the plate in *Still Life with Milk Jug and Fruit* a certain volume—a particular kind of movement? The lines seem to exert a force through which the colors and forms of the objects gather up the fullness of space. In Cézanne, therefore, the line inaugurates, once again, from the middle; it does not separate the depth of space from the object but serves as that through which they cohere. Like the interval of silence that binds together the articulated notes of a rhythm, the line on Cézanne's canvases is not "a positive attribute" or a "property of the object in itself."[3] It is a negative; it offers an opening through which space gathers and organizes itself.

Indeed, these "*several* outlines in blue" of Cézanne would not fascinate us were it not for their power to articulate the very question that the painter poses to the canvas: how to render the fecundity of a visible world that at every moment calls to us—that not only captivates our gaze but demands a complete response. For we, too, are the bather who inhales and exhales the liquid element of the space from which we have emerged; we, too, are the flutist who shapes a column of silence into a silvery-toned arabesque. For us, the strangeness and "inexhaustible reality" of the world is not out there, sepa-rate, as if we each guarded a firm division between our flesh and the flesh of the world. Our every gesture—our very breath—repeats the plenitude of this Earth. And so the artist creates not through imitation of this vital rhythm but through a certain resonance with it: a creative expression of the sensible that would be as the other side of the sensible. Art serves as a double—a measure of the depth of the world. Merleau-Ponty writes:

> Things have an internal equivalent in me; they arouse in me a carnal formula of their presence. Why shouldn't these correspondences in turn give rise to some tracing rendered visible again, in which the eyes of others could find an underlying motif to sustain their inspection of the world? Thus there appears a "visible" to the second power, a carnal essence or icon of the first. It is not a faded copy, a *trompe l'oeil*, or another *thing*. The animals painted on the walls of Lascaux are not there in the same way as are the fissures and limestone formations. Nor are they *elsewhere*. Pushed forward here, held back there, supported by the wall's mass they use so adroitly, they radiate about the wall without ever breaking their elusive moorings. I would be hard pressed to say *where* the painting is I am looking at. For I do not look at it as one looks at a thing, fixing it in its place. My gaze wanders within it as in the halos of Being. Rather than seeing it, I see according to, or with it.[4]

It is thus the performance of vision that the painter is called upon to repeat as art; and it is the sensible world, in all of its tangled, messy individuation, that calls for this double. Perhaps, in recounting the origin of painting,
Pliny the Elder was mistaken: perhaps the first painter did not trace out the
semblance of her present lover as he cast a shadow along the walls of her
home. The first painter, from the cave of Chauvet–Pont-d'Arc to the canvases of Cézanne, did not perform her gestures of line and form so as to
capture a mere silhouette—a mere echo of the real lover.[5] The first painter
brought forth something that was otherwise never there—a "carnal essence,"
or, as Merleau-Ponty writes in *The Visible and the Invisible*, "a possibility
that is not the shadow of the actual but is its principle, that is not the proper
contribution of a 'thought' but is its condition, a style."[6]

This style, not as a shadow or imitation of the world but as its very expressive principle, is exhibited through the seeming movement and vitality of the
horses, lions, and other creatures that populate the walls of the Chauvet–
Pont-d'Arc Cave. The Panel of the Horses in the Hillaire Chamber, which
features a bison sketched in multiple lines that trace out his hindquarters and
hooves, and the Panel of Rhinoceroses in the End Chamber, which includes
a rhinoceros whose single horn is indicated by multiple dashes, are extraordinary with respect to the way that their repetitive lines generate a sense of
animal movement. One has the feeling, as with Cézanne's outlines in blue,
of a visual space that secretes its own rhythms of space and time—and of an
artistry that seeks to express the wonder of dimension and overflow of the
sensible world. Likewise, when Cézanne follows the curve of the fruit or the
extension of the bather in not one but several lines of blue, his response is
not to a vision that only sets out objects before him, but to an intertwining
of vision and visibility, such that, through his brushstrokes, "there appears a
'visible' to the second power." He paints not shadows or imitations but the
whole of an artistic style. His radiant blue lines serve as gestures of resonance,
for their reinstatement—their repetition—opens up a realm of dimension, of
space as well as time. As we saw with the rhinoceros of the Chauvet Cave, we
perceive this repetition as a kind of vitality or movement, as the bather strides
through space or the plate of fruit tips toward the edge of the table. We see
something that is not there, yet precisely according to that which is there: the
pigment, proportions, and texture.

What is this motion, this movement of the line? The repetition of the
line—the "outlines in blue"—cannot effect an actual, physical dislocation
within space or time, not even if it were to inspire a movement of the eye
within the gaze of the viewer. Such movement would be purely mimetic, like

an eye that follows a sequence of lights appearing to move along a screen. This imitative movement is not the type of movement made present through the figures at the Chauvet Cave or the bathers of Cézanne. For, as Merleau-Ponty says, the work of art is not "there" in the same way that the walls of the cave or texture of the canvas are there; it is not a "faded copy" or imitation. The work of art elicits a specific kind of movement—a resounding movement—a depth of movement. It is not a matter of imitation but a question of the cohesion of the visible and invisible. The "mutual confrontation of incompossibles" (that is to say, of the seen and unseen or the present and past) gives rise to motion (in time and space).[7] In an important passage from "Eye and Mind," Merleau-Ponty writes:

> Movement is given, says Rodin, by an image in which the arms, the legs, the trunk, and the head are each taken at a different instant, an image which therefore portrays the body in an attitude which it never at any instant really held and which imposes fictive linkages between the parts, as if this mutual confrontation of incompossibles could—and alone could—cause transition and duration to arise in bronze and on canvas. The only successful instantaneous glimpses of movement are those which approach this paradoxical arrangement—when, for example, a walking man or woman is taken at the moment when both feet are touching the ground; for then we almost have the temporal ubiquity of the body which brings it about that the person *bestrides* space. The picture makes movement visible by its internal discordance. Each member's position, precisely by virtue of its incompatibility with that of the others (according to the body's logic), is dated differently or is not "in time" with the others; and since all of them remain visibly within the unity of one body, it is the body which comes to bestride duration.[8]

The body (as, in Rodin's sculptures, the work of art itself) bestrides space and time because it serves as that through which the "fictive linkages"—the "incompossibles"—cohere.[9] Thus, such a work appears to show movement; *movement is this very cohering of noncoincidence.* It is not a movement toward another position in space, nor toward another instant in time.[10] There is no external movement, no movement outside one thing and another. One must think of this movement through the flesh: movement "by a sort of folding back, invagination" (as we saw with depth).[11] Here there is a rendering visible that proceeds through the middle, as in the expression of the musical arabesque; it works through a principle not of revealing but of resounding.[12] Indeed, Merleau-Ponty writes, in "Eye and Mind," that painting makes "for itself a movement without displacement, a movement by vibration or radiation"[13]—a movement that arises through itself by means of the cohesion of noncoincidence. Like the resounding string of an instrument, all this is accomplished as resonance.[14] As Merleau-Ponty writes, "Painting searches not for the outside movement but for its secret ciphers, of which there are some still more subtle than those of which Rodin spoke. All flesh, and even that of the world, radiates beyond itself."[15]

As eloquently as Rodin speaks of movement in sculpture, Cézanne the painter turns to investigate what could not be of concern to a sculptor in marble and bronze: Cézanne turns to color.[16] "This inner animation, this radiation of the visible, is what the painter seeks beneath the words *depth, space*, and *color*."[17] And so all of this depth, space, and color must be understood as a kind of radiance—resonance—arising through the cohesion of incompossibles.[18] This is why, for Merleau-Ponty, color is so important in the work of Cézanne. Yet again, as with the question of movement, the canvas could never simply pose a problem of mimetic color; painting interrogates the depth of color. Merleau-Ponty writes: "Thus the question is not of colors, 'simulacra of the colors of nature.' The question, rather, concerns the dimension of color, that dimension which creates—from itself to itself—identities, differences, a texture, a materiality, a something."[19] That is to say, what Cézanne pursues is a style—a carnal essence—of color, not color merely as a property of an object. It is not an imitation of something else; it is, itself, a "something." It arises "from itself to itself," like the resounding of movement.[20]

In a curious way, then, operating through a cohesion of incompossibles, color serves as an emblem of what Merleau-Ponty describes as the "universality of the sensible"—a universality that would be not removed from the particularity of the world but would arise as a transformative dimension through that very particularity: universality as carnal essence or style.[21] Merleau-Ponty writes, "Now this particularity of the color, of the yellow, and this universality are not a *contradiction,* are *together* sensoriality itself: it is by the same virtue that the color, the yellow, at the same time gives itself as a *certain* being and as a *dimension,* the expression *of every possible being.*"[22] It is thanks to this cohesion of the particular ("as a *certain* being") and universal ("as a *dimension,* the expression *of every possible being*") that color, according to Merleau-Ponty, "can present us with things, forests, storms—in short the world."[23] And so we must not think of color—just as we must not think of the line—as an attribute of a thing; it arises as a radiance. In *The Visible and the Invisible*, Merleau-Ponty writes:

> A naked color, and in general a visible, is not a chunk of absolutely hard, indivisible being, offered all naked to a vision which could be only total or null,

but is rather a sort of straits between exterior horizons and interior horizons ever gaping open, something that comes to touch lightly and makes diverse regions of the colored or visible world resound at the distances, a certain differentiation, an ephemeral modulation of this world—less a color or a thing, therefore, than a difference between things and colors, a momentary crystallization of colored being or of visibility. Between the alleged colors and visibles, we would find anew the tissue that lines them, sustains them, nourishes them, and which for its part is not a thing, but a possibility, a latency, and a *flesh* of things.[24]

Color (like movement and like depth) effects a "momentary crystallization"—that is to say, a cohesion that works through the middle. It awakens a transformative view of the world; it "comes to touch lightly and makes diverse regions of the colored or visible world resound at the distances." What arises, then, through the colors of a canvas is something that would not belong solely to the canvas as a material object (for it is "a possibility, a latency, and a *flesh* of things"). What arises is a style of expression: a work of art. Certainly Cézanne's late paintings bear this out, and particularly those of Montagne Sainte-Victoire.

It is estimated that Cézanne painted a total of nine major oils and seventeen watercolors of Sainte-Victoire, most of them between 1902 and 1906.[25] Taken together, however, the canvases do not form a series that systematically explores a single subject within different parameters of daylight and season (like Monet's paintings of the Rouen Cathedral); such an approach, self-aware and carefully controlled, does not suggest the spirit of Cézanne's paintings. Rather, one has the sense that these paintings emerge from a compulsion on the part of the painter—a certain demand of the "carnal essence" of the landscape to which only Cézanne could respond.[26] An historical account of the old painter just weeks before his death, hampered by advanced diabetes, struggling up steep hillsides, and defying the fierce winds of an October mistral serves to weave a narrative around what it is that the works themselves show: a landscape of interrogation.[27] The vertical hatches of color—ocher, green, and rich violet—perform a rhythm, a style of space that forms itself.[28] There are no "objects" placed "within" spatial boundaries of the near and the far or the extensive and expansive; these landscapes, as we can observe particularly with respect to those canvases that appear to have been left unfinished by the painter, come together all at once. The trees, plains, houses, and mountain crystallize. The painting resounds; it composes its harmony through itself, not unlike the arabesque of a musical phrase. Merleau-Ponty writes:

Motivating all the movements from which a picture gradually emerges there can be only one thing: the landscape in its totality and in its absolute fullness, precisely what Cézanne called a "motif." . . . All the partial views one catches sight of must be welded together; all that the eye's versatility disperses must be reunited; one must, as Gasquet put it, "join the wandering hands of nature." "A minute of the world is going by which must be painted in its full reality." His meditation would suddenly be consummated: "I have a hold on my *motif*," Cézanne would say, and he would explain that the landscape had to be tackled neither too high nor too low, caught alive in a net which would let nothing escape. Then he began to paint all parts of the painting at the same time, using patches of color to surround his original charcoal sketch of the geological skeleton. The picture took on fullness and density; it grew in structure and balance; it came to maturity all at once.[29]

Like the movement of music itself, the motif that holds together the landscape as "a possibility, a latency," is not an object. For Cézanne in these later paintings, it is not the actual, physical limestone but the ungraspable, looming presence of Montagne Sainte-Victoire that, like the flute melody of Debussy's *Prélude*, orients the whole of the landscape.

Indeed, the way that Cézanne paints the mountain is extraordinary: on the one hand, it presides over the canvases in deep blues and purples. Of this choice of colors, Cézanne himself has said, "Nature for us men is more depth than surface, whence the need to introduce into our vibrations of light, represented by the reds and yellows, a sufficient amount of blueness to give the feeling of air."[30] And yet that blue—that depth and "feeling of air"—somehow does not make the mountain retreat into the background. Despite its distance, on the other hand, the mountain exerts a kind of gravitational pull over the landscape.[31] For Cézanne, Sainte-Victoire is a presence that more than beckons—it is a motif around which range not only the elements of the canvas but, it would seem, the entire question of painting. That is to say, in work after work, is it not the same mountain that asserts itself upon the canvas? Yet, for Cézanne, it must never have been the same; for Cézanne, the mountain calls for a reiteration—a renewed vision. It never could be exhausted by its representations; like the arabesque of Debussy's *Prélude*, there could be no absolute beginning or ending to this motif. Montagne Sainte-Victoire—that singular, "hard rock above Aix"—could not be sustained except via the middle: through resonance.[32] Writes Merleau-Ponty: "Art is not imitation, nor is it something manufactured according to the wishes of instinct or good taste. It is a process of expression."[33] It is this process that Montagne Sainte-Victoire demands of Cézanne—a process that

FIGURE 5.3. Cézanne, *Montagne Sainte-Victoire Seen from Les Lauves*, 1902–4, oil on canvas, Philadelphia Museum of Art.

emerges only through the many different canvases that the artist creates.[34] "What we call his work was, for him, only an attempt, an approach to painting," writes Merleau-Ponty.[35] What we call his work—the material production of paintings—was not, for Cézanne, an end; each work was formed as the momentary crystallization of a more total encounter with the sensible realm. The sum of this work, therefore, is not to be determined within any individual canvas or canvases. Rather, it is something that stretches across all canvases, as an orientation, a resonance, or a style. No more than music, then, is the expression of a painter contained within some material object; his work coheres through but in some way beyond these canvases, as a style that could only be determined in retrospect.[36]

And so the artist, like the musician who is ever compelled to perform a work through time, does not know what is or will be there, on the canvas, as expression—that is, until he paints. "The meaning of what the artist is going to say *does not exist* anywhere—not in things, which as yet have no meaning, nor in the artist himself, in his unformulated life."[37] Only in retrospect does it appear that the painter, at each moment, made the one choice necessary for the creation of a particular canvas.[38] In "Cézanne's Doubt," Merleau-Ponty writes, "Each brushstroke must satisfy an infinite number of conditions. Cézanne sometimes pondered hours at a time before putting down a certain stroke, for, as Bernard said, each stroke must 'contain the air, the light, the object, the composition, the character, the outline, and the style.' Expressing what *exists* is an endless task."[39] It is endless and difficult, for each stroke of the brush will not only articulate its own technical parameters—color, texture, form—but will alter the composition as a whole. Painting thus does not proceed linearly from conception to execution, as if it were merely a matter of filling in certain outlines with various shades of pigment. The work of art has not been determined in advance; the artist does not pursue a preformulated idea to the end of its technical manifestation.[40] On the contrary, it is only thanks to the "execution" that one could look back and begin to designate anything like a "conception" as confirmation that, through the "vague fever" of the artistic process, "there was *something* rather than *nothing* to be found there."[41] As with music, what we might call the beginning comes to be known through the end.[42] Therefore, each brushstroke that appears to the viewer in retrospect as a singular choice leading to the logical conclusion of a work, in fact indicates for the artist an ever-open process of initiation, since the end of the work was not, at the moment of the brushstroke, yet determined. Indeed, it is not that the "end" was merely hidden from the artist, waiting to be discovered; it is that an "end" could not evolve except through the creative recentering and surpassing of each reinitiation.[43] Art has always to be performed. Merleau-Ponty writes: "Each partial act reverberates upon the whole, provokes a deviation which is to be compensated by others. Rather than choice, it is necessary to say *labor*. The choices are the trace of this labor of 'germination' (Cézanne) (along with nature, along with other pictures). Each choice remakes painting by inheriting it. Each work re-creates the entire work of a painter by inheriting it if it is truly a work."[44]

Thus, what operates, for both the painter and the history of painting, is not a linear progression but a kind of "subterranean logic."[45] Merleau-Ponty describes this as *institution*[46]—as that which intends a sense "as open sense, which develops by means of proliferation, by curves, decentering and recentering, zigzag, ambiguous passage, with a sort of identity between the whole and parts, the beginning and end. A sort of existential eternity by means of self-interpretation."[47] Institution, therefore, works according to a temporal dimension of depth. It entails not an absolute identity of beginning and end—not an absolute coincidence—but rather, as we must emphasize, "a *sort of* identity . . . a *sort of* existential eternity." There is depth, an "open sense"—a transformation through difference. Institution is the process through which noncoincident hesitations, approaches, experiments, and productions cohere as a sense that exceeds every individual instant; it is a movement—a radiance—the reverberation of a call. It is through institution that artistic expression comes forth as style.

In the summary to his course on institution, Merleau-Ponty clarifies:

> Therefore by institution, we were intending here those events in an experi-
> ence which endow the experience with durable dimensions, in relation to
> which a whole series of other experiences will make sense, will form a think-
> able sequel or a history—or again the events which deposit a sense in me,
> not just as something surviving or as a residue, but as the call to follow, the
> demand of a future.[48]

What arises, then, through Cézanne's labor is not something that would be confined to a single canvas; it is a "call to follow" that resonates across the whole of his work. In this sense, Cézanne's reencounters with Montagne Sainte-Victoire serve as an emblem of his style. Insofar as what one no longer sees does not have to be taken up again, we might imagine a painter who ceases to paint, a lover who no longer feels, or a musician who no longer plays. Style, on the contrary, emerges through what must be reinitiated. Thus, there is no central point of origin in the institution of style; there is, rather, "a beginning *and a continuation*."[49] Style, Merleau-Ponty continues, is that which "exceeds its simple presence, and in this respect it is allied or implicated in advance with all other efforts of expression."[50] This style that is at once a beginning and a continuation—a retrospective movement "impli-cated in advance," a cohesion of depth—this style is rhythm.

And at the heart of rhythm, we know, is silence.

And yet, one might ask, through this notion of the institution of style are we condemned to view a life's work, or, indeed, a life, as necessarily incom-plete (that is to say, silent in a negative sense) or even meaningless, since any understanding of it could only be developed in retrospect—that is to say, only after it had ceased to be created? Is the value of work by Cézanne the artist or Merleau-Ponty the philosopher only determinable by some terrible, final event—only determinable by a death that, even if it retroactively secures a meaning, at the same time ensures the end of the expressive practice? Is this, moreover, how we must understand the process of institution in our own lives—in our work, our history, our loves? Are we always only operat-ing from a silent *hollow* of Being? Merleau-Ponty writes, "We are human precisely insofar as we always intend a singularity across the thickness of our lives, insofar as we are grouped around this unique interior *where* there is no one, which is latent, veiled, and escapes from us always leaving behind in our hands truths which are like traces of its absence."[51] Can we never grasp what would lie at the center? Is there not a center?

Proust: In Search of the *True* Albertine

That is going to require a total remanipulation of the distinction between fact and essence, *real and ideal.*

MERLEAU-PONTY, *Husserl at the Limits of Phenomenology*

When Marcel initially catches sight of Albertine, he sees only "a silhouette projected against the waves" at the seaside resort of Balbec.[1] Thus, from the very first moment, she has effectively been reduced to an entity without depth—a mere silhouette, such as one might frame and display in a drawing room. And perhaps it is through this original experience that Marcel formulates his desire for a relationship with Albertine, for he spends the next years of his life pursuing her in the belief that he might possess her (as one might possess an object). The increasing difficulty posed for Marcel, however, is that through every contact—and consequently, through every memory—he finds that she acquires an additional dimension of depth; there is "an increase of volume in the figure once simply outlined against the sea."[2] Proust describes the nature of this difficulty in a remarkable passage from "The Captive," where Marcel contemplates the expansion of Albertine's depth by comparing his first encounter with her at Balbec to his changing sense of her after a second sojourn at the seaside—just as one might attend to the different iterations of the flute arabesque:

> Between the two Balbec settings, so different one from the other, there was the interval of several years in Paris, the long expanse of which was dotted with all the visits that Albertine had paid me. I saw her in the different years of my life occupying, in relation to myself, different positions which made me feel the beauty of the intervening spaces, that long lapse of time during which I had remained without seeing her and in the diaphanous depths of which the roseate figure that I saw before me was carved with mysterious shadows and in bold relief. This was due also to the superimposition not merely of the successive images which Albertine had been for me, but also of the great qualities of intelligence and heart, and of the defects of character, all alike unsuspected

by me, which Albertine, in a germination, a multiplication of herself, a fleshy efflorescence in somber colors, had added to a nature that formerly could scarcely have been said to exist, but was now difficult to plumb.[3]

It is thus not without a sense of irony that Marcel registers the changing nature of his relationship to Albertine: the longer he knows her, the greater mystery she offers to him. No longer a silhouette, she is now perceived "in bold relief," complete with her "shadows"—the regions of her being that resist Marcel's knowledge. In the passage above, the narrator seizes immediately upon the reason for the existence of this structural double: the "interval" of years. For although these years add a crucial dimension to the development of Albertine's character, at the same time they present a formidable challenge to Marcel; their unfolding during a time of his absence means that he will never be able to grasp their significance to Albertine—nor to understand the effects that they wrought upon her.

But it is not only that he cannot possess the years of Albertine's life that passed during his absence; the notion of the "interval" or the lacuna extends to the core of his relationship with her even while they are together. Marcel constantly feels that she escapes him, and not simply because she lies to him and conceals certain facets of her life from him. As a creature of depth, Albertine's shadow side is constitutive of her being; some aspect of her remains always hidden from Marcel. It is not possible for him to see all sides of Albertine simultaneously, and thus he finds himself constantly confronted with the multiplicity of her being as she appears to him. He grasps only partial views of her—views that change according to aspect. One particular case of this difficulty is brilliantly described when Marcel, at long last, succeeds in winning from Albertine a first kiss:

> I can think of nothing that can to so great a degree as a kiss evoke out of what we believed to be a thing with one definite aspect, the hundred other things which it may equally well be, since each is related to a no less legitimate perspective. In short, just as at Balbec Albertine had often appeared different to me, so now—as if, prodigiously accelerating the speed of the changes of perspective and changes of coloring which a person presents to us in the course of our various encounters, I had sought to contain them all in the space of a few seconds so as to reproduce experimentally the phenomenon which diversifies the individuality of a fellow-creature, and to draw out one from another, like a nest of boxes, all the possibilities that it contains—so now, during this brief journey of my lips toward her cheek, it was ten Albertines that I saw; this one girl being like a many-headed goddess, the head I had seen last, when I tried to approach it, gave way to another.[4]

Thus the kiss that Marcel has desired does not deliver to him the possession of Albertine for which he longed; on the contrary, he hardly knows that he has kissed her at all. At the conclusion of the passage, Marcel tells us, "Without thereby gaining any clearer idea of the taste of the rose of my desire, I learned, from these obnoxious signs, that at last I was in the act of kissing Albertine's cheek."[5] His disappointment in the experience of the first kiss, its failure to deliver to him the "rose of [his] desire," is indicative of his more general failure to possess the multiplicity—of appearance, of action, of sentiment—that is Albertine's being. And each time he is initiated into a different view or aspect of Albertine, the stakes are raised; for Marcel clearly feels that, in order for his love for her to be real, he must know her completely. He must possess her; there must be no aspect of Albertine that is inaccessible or unknown to him. Proust writes:

> And I realized the impossibility which love comes up against. We imagine that it has as its object a being that can be laid down in front of us, enclosed within a body. Alas, it is the extension of that being to all the points in space and time that it has occupied and will occupy. If we do not possess its contact with this or that place, this or that hour, we do not possess that being. But we cannot touch all these points. If only they were indicated to us, we might perhaps contrive to reach out to them. But we grope for them without finding them. Hence mistrust, jealousy, persecutions.[6]

Thus, the lengths to which Marcel goes in attempting to possess Albertine could only be described as obsessive, as he strives to "touch all these points" of her life. He secretly keeps her at his house as his mistress, ensuring that she is financially dependent upon him; he does not marry her; and her position within his household effectively forestalls any real possibility of her being courted by any other man. Yet this is not enough to soothe Marcel's jealousy (for he suspects that Albertine is attracted not only to men but to women as well). In order to know her movements at all times throughout the day, he enlists the aid of a mutual friend, Andrée, who reports to him on Albertine's activities. Moreover, occasionally he cannot help but send Françoise or some other messenger to interrupt Albertine's plans (as a means of verifying her whereabouts) and call for her to return home. And Marcel incessantly questions Albertine herself—her actions, her motives, her desires. He cannot rest if he does not see all of Albertine's life arrayed in complete transparency before the power of his gaze, as if he were, indeed, the *kosmotheoros*.[7] He would thus like to reunite the multiple images of Albertine with one another, discerning a "pure essence" of Albertine.[8] But Marcel's work is exhausting, for each variation that he glimpses must be held up against yet another image of her. Moreover, in order to affirm the authenticity of Albertine's essence, Marcel himself would have to be of the order of essence. Yet, as an embodied subject, he cannot install himself as a figure of pure subjectivity before whom essence would be confirmed; he is not a *kosmotheoros*.[9] And so he admits that he is pursuing the impossible: "I could, if I chose, take Albertine on my knee, hold her head in my hands, I could caress her, run my hands slowly over her, but, just as if I had been handling a stone which encloses the salt of imme-morial oceans or the light of a star, I felt that I was touching no more than the sealed envelope of a person who inwardly reached to infinity."[10] Indeed, the only time that Marcel is able to feel possession of her is not when she is of the order of essence but when she has been reduced, in sleep, to a mere physical body.[11] This sense he pursues as an alternate means of possession, diametrically opposed to pure essence but just as flat and dimensionless. For then he studies her as he would an object; he equates her being, in fact, to that of a plant:

> By shutting her eyes, by losing consciousness, Albertine had stripped off, one after another, the different human personalities with which she had deceived me ever since the day when I had first made her acquaintance. She was ani-mated now only by the unconscious life of plants, of trees, a life more differ-ent from my own, more alien, and yet one that belonged more to me. Her personality was not constantly escaping, as when we talked, by the outlets of her unacknowledged thoughts and of her eyes. She had called back into her-self everything of her that lay outside, had withdrawn, enclosed, reabsorbed herself into her body. In keeping it in front of my eyes, in my hands, I had an impression of possessing her entirely which I never had when she was awake. Her life was submitted to me, exhaled towards me its gentle breath.[12]

Inspired by this vision of her as a plant—as "a long blossoming stem that had been laid there"[13]—Marcel would like to sustain this state of complete possession. Yet Albertine in her plantlike state (as he imagines her) is unable to reveal to Marcel anything about herself as a subject. When her personality retires into her body, she becomes nothing more than a mute object.

In response, a curious psychology comes into play for Marcel. It is as if Albertine vanishes; Marcel, gazing intently upon Albertine-the-object, makes her serve as a sort of mirror for himself. And what that mirror reveals is doubt. As Proust writes, there is a "binary rhythm which love adopts in all those who have too little confidence in themselves to believe that a woman can ever fall in love with them, and also that they themselves can genuinely fall in love with her."[14] It is a binary *rhythm* because it hinges always upon the unknowable—the silent or unseen depth—of the woman whom one loves, which the lover, working against the tenets of rhythm, always tries to fill with himself.[15] Thus Marcel's comportment toward Albertine as an object makes impossible an authentic love, for as object she serves only as a screen upon which he projects his own fears.[16] Merleau-Ponty writes, "[He] doubts Albertine's love, does not believe that he is loved, because he doubts his love, because he does not love."[17] Narcissism seems to make his love an illusion, for Marcel conflates himself with Albertine; the greater her depth and opacity, the more insistently does he fill the void with his own emotion. Indeed, it is only when Albertine leaves him—generating by her absence a chasm so deep that only the most significant of desires would suffice to fill it—that Marcel is inspired to marry her.[18] It is here in the novel, with the opening of "The Fugitive," that Marcel's narcissism seems nearly absolute.

Moreover, this narcissism, thanks to the conflation it effects, commits a double error: not only does it attempt to efface the depth of Albertine, but it likewise requires that Marcel himself be a creature without depth. What Marcel fails to recognize—and what dooms his project to possess Albertine—is that he, himself, is always implicated in narcissism. And this encroachment shows that the very depth of Albertine that he wishes to overcome can never be eliminated; it can only be amplified, for he necessarily tries to fill it with his own self—a self (not unlike Albertine) characterized by depth and movement. Thus, for Marcel, there could be no day when Albertine might lie fully disclosed before him, as for a scientist or researcher who might pin a specimen beneath the penetrating lens of a microscope. For at the very moment that Albertine might lie motionless beneath that lens (that is to say, in the period of time that follows her death, when she is truly an object—a corpse—without depth or movement), our researcher, Marcel, would already have changed, as would also his memory of her. This is why, even after her death, Marcel is confronted with a multiplicity of images—no longer images of an Albertine present to external phenomena, but images of an Albertine "*in him.*"[19] Marcel laments, "In order to be consoled I would have to forget, not one, but innumerable Albertines. When I had succeeded in bearing the grief of losing this Albertine, I must begin again with another, with a hundred others."[20] And so he is no better able to possess Albertine after her death than during her life; this is the double failure of narcissism. Even as Marcel continues to live, he augments his own multiplicity.

Thus, Marcel's obsession seems to have been rooted in error all along. He thought that the problem of possession resided solely within the nature of Albertine—within her depth and multiplicity—which he sought to reduce to a pure essence or, conversely, an object. But in fact the problem lay equally within himself—within his depth and multiplicity.

This he is able to understand only after Albertine's death, when he develops a series of new selves that replace the former Marcel who loved Albertine. And these new selves eventually bear no capacity for loving an Albertine whom they had never known: "It is not because other people are dead that our affection for them fades; it is because we ourselves are dying."[21] In this way, Marcel becomes aware of his own kind of internal process of death and birth:

> This process, as it happens, automatically occurs from time to time, like the decay and renewal of our tissues, but we notice it only if the former self contained a great grief, a painful foreign body, which we are surprised to find no longer there, in our amazement at having become another person to whom the sufferings of his predecessor are no more than the sufferings of a stranger, of which we can speak with compassion because we do not feel them.[22]

And so Marcel learns, eventually, no longer to feel desire for Albertine. What Marcel does feel, however, through his attention to this process, is an incredible sense of alienation. He realizes that, if it is inevitable that his desire for Albertine should be shed, as if it were nothing more than a layer of skin, then there could be no interior region of himself—no core—that might persist as meaningful:

> My life appeared to me—offering a succession of periods in which, after a certain interval, nothing of what had sustained the previous period survived in that which followed—as something utterly devoid of the support of an individual, identical and permanent self, something as useless in the future as it was protracted in the past, something that death might as well put an end to at this point or that, without in the least concluding it.[23]

Thus his alienation stems not only from his understanding that his hope for possessing Albertine is a false one; it comes, more painfully, from seeing this dispossession with respect to himself. Indeed, this failure—this divergence between Marcel and Albertine, as between Marcel and himself—permeates his life. It colors his relations with all those whom he has failed to love as a "law" of the human soul: that of "intermittence."[24] "But why do we not love?" asks Merleau-Ponty in his analysis of Proust. "Because of the intermittences of the heart."[25] Thus Marcel is unable to sustain his love—for Gilberte any more than for the Duchesse de Guermantes—not because of some flaw inherent to the object of his affection, but because of a fundamental discontinuity that characterizes his own self. In a particularly poignant episode of the novel, this law of intermittence manifests itself with respect to Marcel's love for his grandmother; it is disclosed by his inability sincerely to mourn her death until more than a year after her passing. Marcel is brought to register the profound difference between his former self (the one loved by his grandmother) and his present one (the one concerned, it seems, only with social conquest) when an involuntary recollection seems to bring his grandmother back to him as a "living reality."[26] Accompanying the recovery of his grandmother through memory is a parallel, and equally astonishing, recovery of his old self. Proust writes that "with the perturbations of memory are linked the intermittencies of the heart";[27] through this experience of involuntary recollection Marcel becomes aware of a former self so foreign to the present Marcel that its very existence casts into doubt any conviction he had held regarding his soul as unified. The narrator concludes, "At any given moment, our total soul has only a more or less fictitious value, in spite of the rich inventory of its assets, for now some, now others are unrealizable, whether they are real riches or those of the imagination."[28] Indeed, if it is impossible to realize the totality of the soul simultaneously (i.e., to live as the present self along with the complete array of former selves), then how can one grasp what the soul is?

For the law of intermittence characterizes an ontological divergence that serves to thwart Marcel precisely when he would attempt to extract an essence of Albertine and overcome her depth, or, significantly, when he would consider his own soul to be an unchangeable, pure essence. Regarding this constitutive noncoincidence, Merleau-Ponty asks, "Shall we say then that we *fall short of* the essence, that we have it only in principle, that it lies at the limit of an always imperfect idealization?"[29] Yet Merleau-Ponty goes further, providing a new assessment of the possibility of essence:

> It is on account of having begun with the antithesis of the fact and the essence, of what is individuated in a point of space and time and what is from forever and nowhere, that one is finally led to treat the essence as a limit idea, that is, to make it inaccessible. For this is what obliged us to seek the being of the essence in the form of a second positivity beyond the order of the "facts," to dream of a variation of the thing that would eliminate from it all that is not authentically itself and would make it appear all naked whereas it is always clothed—to dream of an impossible labor of experience on experience that would strip it of its facticity as if it were an impurity. Perhaps if we were to re-examine the anti-thesis of fact and essence, we would be able on the contrary to redefine the essence in a way that would give us access to it, because it would be not beyond but at the heart of that coiling up (*enroulement*) of experience over experience which a moment ago constituted the difficulty.[30]

Marcel has undertaken the task of eliminating all that is not authentically Albertine in order to make her "appear all naked" before him. But he fails:

he falls short of immobilizing a pure essence of Albertine. However, what is to be gained from this failure is disclosure of the need for a new way of approaching the essence. The problem is not that essence is absolutely inaccessible, but that it is made inaccessible if one attempts to conceive of it as inhabiting a realm of "second positivity." How, then, could essence be perceived within the world of phenomena without losing its potency as essence? Only as an essence that would be active—that would be operative.[31] Rather than continually attempt—and fail—to grasp an immobilized essence within an atemporal realm, we might search for the trace or reverberation of essence within our world, through the "coiling up (*enroulement*) of experience over experience." Via this indirect route might we confirm the institution of Marcel's love.[32]

For although Marcel can never directly possess a pure essence of Albertine, nevertheless he is directly affected by her essence, as a power that "animates and organizes" his emotional life.[33] "She was causing my troubles just like a divinity who remains invisible," Marcel says.[34] It is indeed because of these troubles—because of their effect upon him—and not because he sees her arrayed in positivity—that Marcel finally comes to know an operative essence: "Probing ever more deeply, through the intensity of one's pain one arrives at the mystery, the quintessence."[35] Such an essence emerges through the depths as the effect of an orientation, change, or movement. The *true* Albertine belongs to an order of essence that "is not above the sensible world, [that] is beneath, or in its depth, its thickness," like the *true* hawthorns of the past.[36] Thus, the existence of Albertine's essence can be determined only indirectly and in retrospect, through the pain that has lodged within Marcel's heart.[37] As Merleau-Ponty writes, "Grief teaches you how to see."[38] Indeed, Marcel laments:

> How many people, how many places (even places which did not concern her directly . . .) had Albertine—like a person who, shepherding all her escort, a whole crowd, past the barrier in front of her, secures their admission to the theatre—from the threshold of my imagination or of my memory, where I paid no attention to them, introduced into my heart! Now, the knowledge that I had of them was internal, immediate, spasmodic, painful. Love is space and time made perceptible to the heart.[39]

Thus, Albertine has ushered an entire world into the heart of Marcel, and it is through his initiation into this world—which no longer lies outside of him but has become internalized—that he is able to uphold the authenticity of his love for her. In this way Albertine is regarded no longer as a pure essence nor as an object, but as a force upon his life.[40] Love is a force of change, of movement, the effects of which can be registered within Marcel himself.

Indeed, there is a complex temporal structure associated with this love, for love, as the internal perception of "space and time," can be realized only retrospectively, through what Merleau-Ponty, as we have seen, describes in his notion of the essence as the "coiling up (*enroulement*) of experience over experience."[41] Indeed, it is only after Albertine's death that Marcel fathoms the existence of this force within himself, thanks to his experience of it as a specific and profound pain. While Albertine is alive, he does not believe in the reality of a love that seems too subject to chance circumstance, but after her departure the inimitability of his pain compels him to believe that he had been truly in love all along. With precise attention to this temporal structure, Merleau-Ponty writes, "I have not believed in my love because it was in 'the volatile state'; I had believed in it when it is *crystallized* by Albertine's departure."[42] It is the generality of his love—when it exists for him in a "volatile state"—that at first leads him to conclude that it is based upon mere contingency. Marcel feels that Albertine "is simply an accident placed in the path of [his] surging desires,"[43] and that he might as well have loved Gisèle, Andrée, or any of a number of other women. He doubts his love for Albertine (thus ensuring its narcissistic quality) because he seems to see within it the mark of arbitrariness. But after her death and the crystallization of his pain, his entire past becomes transformed, retroactively; all contingencies are reinterpreted as leading to his affair with Albertine. Just as the painter's brushstroke comes to be viewed, in retrospect, as the one and only choice he could have made to produce the work, Marcel's love for Albertine is seen no longer merely as one of many possible loves (none more authentic than another because each would owe its existence to an ephemeral chain of circumstances). Rather, it succeeds in reordering the sense of all of his previous loves; through the power of retrospection, they each appear to prefigure his relationship with Albertine.[44] The narrator says, "If I now considered not my love for Albertine but my whole life, my other loves too had been no more than slight and timid essays that were paving the way, appeals that were unconsciously clamoring, for this vaster love: my love for Albertine."[45] Indeed, Marcel comes to believe that his boyhood passion for Gilberte in particular leads to Albertine, but he marvels that the reverse is not true: Gilberte can be seen within Albertine, but Albertine cannot be seen within Gilberte. "The example of Gilberte would as little have enabled me to form an idea of Albertine and guess that I should fall in love with her, as the memory of Vinteuil's sonata would have enabled me to imagine his septet."[46] Thus, his love for Albertine achieves a singular status and overcomes all appearance of contingency; it serves as a keystone for all other past loves. It is therefore to be understood not as an effect of circumstances, a "sum of accidents," but, retrospectively, as their cause.[47] It is a cause to the extent that it shapes his understanding of the entirety of his life—not simply of the years that he actually spent with Albertine, but of a future that he faces in her absence as well as a past that had never known her presence but that, in retrospect, takes on the aspect of inevitability. Merleau-Ponty writes, "It is quite impossible to claim that the present love is nothing but an echo of the past. On the contrary, the past takes on the outline of a preparation or premeditation of a present that exceeds it in meaning although it recognizes itself in it."[48] This curious "subterranean logic"—the logic of depth—is the work of institution.[49]

And so, if Marcel fails to possess or control Albertine as he pursues her, it is through this failure that he is brought to experience something far richer, far deeper, than what he had sought in the first place. Merleau-Ponty writes, regarding the love between Marcel and Albertine:

> There is fullness when we think there is emptiness, the reality of what is not immediately sensed. In exchange for what we had imagined, life gives us something else, and something else that was secretly willed, not fortuitous. Realization is not what was foreseen, but nevertheless what was willed. We advance by recoiling, we do not choose directly, but obliquely, but we nevertheless do what we want. Love is clairvoyant.[50]

The clairvoyance of love: it discloses the fact that the invisible works upon the world. This is the clairvoyance not only of a seer, who looks to the future, but also of a poet, who reconfigures the past.[51] Love is instituted, both retrospectively and prospectively, as a force that guides one's life. Marcel's initial desire for Albertine as an object to be possessed was far too one-sided and in no way able to take into account the "proliferation" and the "decentering and recentering" effected by means of love.[52] He was, rather, eager to possess Albertine, and this was why he did not believe himself to love her. But genuine (i.e., nonnarcissistic) love emerges as a resonance between two people. It can be said, therefore, that Marcel comes to recognize the validity of love only when Albertine has entered his soul as an irrefutable presence, animating his life. It is then that his understanding of the past is reoriented so that he *had always loved her*. In this way, the *true* Albertine is disclosed to Marcel—because he then sees the world according to the deep emotion of his having loved Albertine. Every moment of his present, future, and past is touched by her, if only indirectly, not because he possessed her but because he was wounded by her.[53] No Marcel can exist except for the Marcel who has loved Albertine, because even after he forgets her—even after he no longer loves her—she, through the process of institution, has irrevocably changed him.

It is in this way that one can also understand the problem of Marcel's own depth and multiplicity. Marcel is both astute and mistaken when he says, "My life appeared to me—offering a succession of periods in which, after a certain interval, nothing of what had sustained the previous period survived in that which followed—as something utterly devoid of the support of an individual, identical and permanent self."[54] He is astute in his observation of the discontinuity of his self.[55] But he is mistaken with respect to the conclusion that he draws from this observation, for Marcel interprets this discontinuity as revealing the useless contingency of his life. Yet, what is made clear in the relationship between Marcel and Albertine—as the clairvoyance of love—is that orientation, movement, and change, through their institution as the cohering of discontinuity, offer "sense as open sense"—the very possibility of meaning.[56]

We will see this same notion of institution at work in the musical idea through the harmony in Debussy's *Prélude à l'après-midi d'un faune*.

Harmony and the Movement of Style in Debussy

Philosophy is nothing other than the unconcealment of the depth dimension of all
other activities.

MERLEAU-PONTY, *Husserl at the Limits of Phenomenology*

One could be deceived, as Marcel was deceived in first perceiving Albertine
as a silhouette against the sea, upon listening to the flute melody of Debussy's
Prélude à l'après-midi d'un faune. That is to say, one could hear this monophonic line as without dimension. Yet that would not be the most musical—
the most rhythmical—way to listen to the *Prélude*. In chapter 4, we understood how the melody coils around itself both internally (through mm. 1 and
2) and across the form of the piece by means of repetitions and variations.
In this way, it has disclosed itself to us already as much more than simply a
"line": it has disclosed itself as a structure of depth. What we must attend to,
therefore, is the nature of this depth, not only melodically but harmonically;
it is a question of how a harmony—a musical color—expresses a style.

We begin our analysis, once again, with the opening of the piece, for the
flute arabesque does not only offer to us a linear, melodic gesture; it initiates
the opening of a harmonic world that will serve as the inspiration for the
entire composition (see chapter 4, ex. 4.1). This world is evoked, first of all,
through the relationship of two tritones: C♯–G and E–A♯. The pitch boundary
of the opening two measures articulates the first of these tritones (with C♯
as the highest pitch and G as the lowest); mm. 3 and 4 emphasize the other.
Although the G♯ (not a G♮) at the apex of the melodic gesture in m. 3 seems to
imply a resolution of the tension created by the first tritone (C♯–G♮), the feeling of the E major tonality sustained in m. 3 through the arpeggio (G♯, E, and
B) is displaced in m. 4 by the final note of the melody, the A♯. The melody,
therefore, does not end with a resolution but, like its beginning, articulates
the dissonant interval of the tritone (E–A♯).

Just as the flute arabesque, a monophonic phrase, begins and ends by
articulating the tritones melodically, in m. 4 tritones come to govern the

EXAMPLE 7.1. Relationships between the opening fully diminished seventh, A♯ half-diminished seventh, and B♭ seventh chords. The fully diminished seventh chord is heard in the opening not as a vertical sonority, but as being comprised of the two tritones outlined melodically in the flute arabesque (from C♯ to G and E to A♯). The A♯ half-diminished seventh chord is sounded in the woodwinds and horns in m. 4, and the B♭ seventh chord follows in the harp, strings, and horns, in m. 5.

fully diminished
seventh chord
A♯ø7
B♭7

harmony as well. The first horn's entrance on E, sustained against the A♯ taken over from the flute by the oboe, immediately ensures that the tritone is sounded harmonically, within the context, here, of an A♯ half-diminished seventh chord. This chord maintains a close relationship, in terms of intervallic content, with the opening two tritones offered by the flute. The flute tritones, considered vertically, spell a fully diminished seventh chord with an ambiguous root (either C♯, E, G, or A♯).[1] When the G♮ of this fully diminished seventh chord is raised to become G♯ (just as in m. 3, at the apex of the flute melody), an A♯ half-diminished seventh chord is created. And so the transition between the implied harmony of the arabesque and the A♯ half-diminished seventh chord in m. 4 is quite smooth. What, then, of the stunning B♭ seventh chord that sounds on the downbeat of m. 5? This, too, is drawn through a close relationship: the A♯ is respelled enharmonically as B♭, the G♯ is retained and respelled enharmonically as A♭, and the C♯ and E of the half-diminished seventh chord move up by half step (similar to the movement from G♮ to G♯) to become D and F. This harmony sounds, momentarily, like a kind of resolution, because the E–A♯ tritone between the horn and oboe, respectively, of m. 4 has been dissolved through the movement of the horn to F and then B♭, and A♭, and through the shift from the oboe's A♯ to a respelled B♭ in the strings (see chapter 4, ex. 4.2). The measure of silence that follows, as discussed in chapter 4, amplifies the harmonic expressivity of mm. 4 and 5, as if the move from the G♮ of the opening flute arabesque to the G♯ and then A♭ within a B♭ seventh chord (m. 5) offers such significance that it bears repeating. And it does, for it is a gesture that resolves both of the initial tritones: it resolves the dissonance of C♯ against G when G♮ moves up by half step to G♯ (and then respelled as A♭), and it resolves the dissonance of A♯ against E when the E moves up by half step to F (and the A♯ is respelled as B♭). It resolves these tritones, however, only by opening up more tension; this resolution does not close up on itself but initiates a new layer of expression: the B♭ seventh chord, notably, is not a triad but contains its own tritone between the third and seventh of the chord (that is to say, the tritone D–A♭). The very pitch, G♯, that resolves the initial tritone (C♯–G♮) only opens up another tritone (G♯/A♭–D). And, in a more structural sense, this harmonic area of B♭ itself also serves in a tritone relationship to the key of E major—the key in which the piece eventually concludes.

Thus, it is no surprise, as we saw in chapter 4, that the beautiful melody in the oboes and first violins in mm. 17–19 explores the harmony of an A♯ (as the enharmonic respelling of B♭) seventh chord or that the return of the flute arabesque in m. 26 is harmonized above an E ninth chord (see chapter 4, exx. 4.3 and 4.5). These key areas (A♯/B♭ and E) draw their meaning from one of the tritones articulated through the original melody in the flute. Yet this first section of the piece eventually cadences, at m. 30, in B major—a tonal area quite distant from the B♭ seventh chord of m. 5. And though this area of B major is emphasized through the preceding harmony (mm. 28–29) of F♯ ninth chords, descending-fifth relationships otherwise do not dictate the general harmonic movement of the piece. Instead of the interval of the perfect fifth (an interval that can reasonably be considered indispensable in tonal music), it is the interval of the tritone (an inherently unstable sonority) that shapes the music of Debussy's *Prélude*.

The two tritones articulated in the flute melody (C♯–G and E–A♯) form a sonority (a fully diminished seventh chord) that is, as we said, ambiguous, because it is symmetrical: it replicates itself, since each interval within the sonority divides into three half steps, just as the tritones themselves divide evenly into six half steps or three whole steps. The interval of a perfect fifth, by contrast, is not symmetrical—that is to say, it cannot be internally divided into even whole steps. Due to its asymmetry, the perfect fifth has a certain power of linear motion and resolution within a tonal context, whereas tritones, as symmetrical structural sonorities, shift and flicker, replicate and double up. Melodically, tritones can be realized in two different ways (that is to say, they spawn two different pitch worlds): through symmetrical half steps or through symmetrical whole steps. Of the first way we find many examples in the *Prélude*: the saturation of half-step intervals in the opening measures of the flute melody, of course, but also the brief descending tail of the melodic line in the violas and cellos introduced as counterpoint in m. 22 (see chapter 4, ex. 4.4). This motif blossoms throughout the piece: in mm. 31 and 34 in the cellos (see ex. 7.2), in mm. 83–84 in the oboe (see chapter 9, ex. 9.3), in m. 102 in the flute (see ex. 7.6), and, finally, in m. 107 in the horns (see chapter 4, ex. 4.6).

Symmetrical whole steps, often described in terms of the whole-tone scale, also color the harmony of Debussy's *Prélude*. Following the cadence in B major at m. 30, the music, in the absence of the arabesque that had

EXAMPLE 7.2. Debussy, *Prélude à l'après-midi d'un faune*, mm. 31–36, orchestra.

structured the piece up to that moment, seems to turn toward a new direction. On the one hand, the clarinet introduces an energetic motif in m. 31 that emphasizes the note G♮, descending and rising through half steps across the span of a diminished fourth. On the other hand, this motif is released in m. 32, when the clarinet rises through a whole-tone scale from F to E♯ and back down, a passage then echoed in the flute.

The relationship of this "new" melody in m. 31 to the original flute arabesque, because of the symmetry evoked through the half steps, is clear. Yet what is interesting is that the clarinet inaugurates that other kind of symmetry—that of whole steps—in m. 32, to be confirmed immediately afterward by the flute.[2] It is as if the tritones in the opening of the piece show themselves

EXAMPLE 7.2. (*continued*)

here to break into two different sonic worlds, one of half steps and another of whole steps. Beneath this clarinet melody, the supporting harmony spells a French augmented sixth chord, a harmony that, like a fully diminished seventh chord, is built upon two tritones, but in such a way that the two tritones are not arranged three half steps or a minor third apart (like the fully diminished seventh chord), but interlocking through a whole step to imply the whole-tone scale. In mm. 31–33, these two tritones consist of C♯–G and F–B. They imply the whole-tone scale or pitch collection that includes C♯ and G (i.e., C♯–D♯–F–G–A–B).[3] They also provide a new dimension of meaning for the C♯–G tritone that we heard from the first measures of the piece. This is why the clarinet's sustained G♮ in m. 31 is filled with tension: it not only retreats from the earlier resolution of G♮ to G♯ (respelled enharmonically as A♭ in the B♭ seventh chord of m. 5, etc.) but also evokes the unstable

EXAMPLE 7.3. Symmetrical harmonies folded out from the fully diminished seventh chord. We see that the fully diminished seventh chord, as a symmetrical sonority, gives rise to two whole-tone scales (one related to the opening flute tritone of C♯–G, the other related to the opening flute tritone of B♭/A♯–E). From these whole-tone scales, additional harmonies unfold through different French augmented sixth chords.

Fr+6   whole-tone   fully diminished   whole-tone   Fr+6
                                             seventh chord

harmony of the whole-tone scale. It is a tension that Debussy emphasizes, reinstituting the whole of the clarinet motif again as a sequence in m. 34. This time, the pitch level is raised a minor third, so that the clarinet sustains a B♭ on the downbeat (again, one should underline, a structural pitch from the opening two tritones, considered enharmonically) before descending and rising through half steps into another whole-tone scale in m. 35 (subsequently passed, once again, to the flute in m. 36). This is harmonized by a different French augmented sixth chord, this one made up of the interlocking tritones B♭–E and D–A♭, which implies the whole-tone pitch collection that includes B♭/A♯ and E (i.e., B♭–C–D–E–G♭–A♭). What we see, therefore, is that the potential of the two tritones from the opening of the piece (that is to say, of C♯–G and B♭/A♯–E), owing to their symmetry, folds out in two different directions; there is a double movement that works through the two whole-tone pitch collections to the two French augmented sixth chords and, ultimately, to two sides of structural harmonies that operate throughout the piece. It is the ambiguity of the opening fully diminished seventh chord, then, that gives rise to the double fold.

The sense illustrated in example 7.3 is that of symmetry. Yet, if it were only symmetry that gave rise to the harmony of the *Prélude*, there would be no movement. Movement arises through differentiation—through contrast, reinitiation, and noncoincidence. The harmonic motion of the *Prélude*, therefore, arises not out of symmetry but through the introduction of a key element of disruption—that of the change from G♮ to G♯. It is this change that is heard already in m. 3, as the flute rises to the apex of the arabesque. And it is this change that initiates the A♯ half-diminished seventh chord of m. 4 (as opposed to the fully diminished seventh chord implied in the beginning), which then sets forth a harmonic world that works in the direction (according to ex. 7.3) of the pitch collection built on the B♭/A♯–E tritone. Tracing this collection as it unfolds by common-tone movement across various harmonies yields a sense of the key areas that operate in significant ways throughout the whole of the piece. Example 7.4 shows this movement as it leads through the B♭ seventh chord to the E seventh chord, A♯ half-diminished seventh chord,

EXAMPLE 7.4. Harmonic movement derived from the pitch collection built on B♭/A♯–E. The root of each of these chords (B♭, E, A♯, C, G♭/F♯, D, and A♭) belongs to the whole-tone collection related to the opening flute tritone of B♭/A♯–E, as do each of their internal tritones (e.g., D–G♯ in the E seventh chord, A♯–E in the A♯ half-diminished seventh chord, etc.). These sonorities encompass the significant harmonies in Debussy's piece.

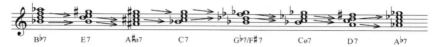

C seventh chord, etc. The root of each of these chords is related to the overall whole-tone collection born of the B♭/A♯–E tritone, as is each of their internal tritones.[4] A quick analysis confirms that the chords shown in example 7.4 represent almost all of the piece's important harmonic areas.

Although example 7.4 sets these chords out in a linear fashion to show their common-tone relationships, the way that these harmonies function cannot be thought of as restricted to a single plane. Rather, each of these harmonies connects not only with those situated, in example 7.4, to the right and the left, but through multiple levels. The C seventh chord and G♭ seventh chord share two common tones (with internal tritones between E/F♭ and B♭), as do the B♭ seventh and E seventh chords (with internal tritones between D and A♭/G♯), since their roots are a tritone apart. But additionally, both the C seventh chord and the G♭ seventh chord share three common tones with the sonority implied by the opening tritones of the piece, as a C♯ fully diminished seventh chord, and both the B♭ seventh chord and the E seventh chord share three common tones with the French augmented sixth chord; the C♯ fully diminished seventh and French augmented sixth chords themselves share two common tones; and, finally, the C seventh and B♭ seventh chords are linked through the A♯ half-diminished seventh chord, with which they each share two common tones. Figure 7.1 demonstrates these relationships. Debussy's harmony is in this sense a harmony of depth. It is liberated from the strictly linear motion associated with tonal hierarchies; instead, it at once folds back, forward, and through itself.

Once the general harmonic direction of the piece is established, as in example 7.4, what is also of interest are the harmonic areas that move in the opposite direction—those that spring not from the tritone relationship between B♭/A♯ and E, but from the tritone between C♯ and G. Indeed we must emphasize once again, the outline in example 7.4 cannot be interpreted unidirectionally. The harmony shown to the far right, an A♭ seventh chord, in fact wraps around quite smoothly to the B seventh chord of the C♯–G tritone collection, as the E♭ and G♭ can be respelled as D♯ and F♯, respectively, and

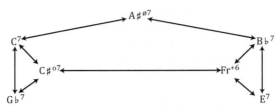

FIGURE 7.1. Web of multidirectional relationships between harmonies derived from the pitch collection built on B♭/A♯–E.

movement by half step from A♭ to A♮ and from C to B creates B, D♯, F♯, and A (the B seventh chord). This close relation, however, institutes a shift in the tritone: the tritone in the A♭ seventh chord (C–G♭) belongs to the whole-tone collection of B♭/A♯–E (i.e., B♭–C–D–E–G♭–A♭), while the tritone in the B seventh chord (D♯–A) belongs to the whole-tone collection of C♯–G (i.e., C♯–D♯–F–G–A–B). The same shift in implied whole-tone collections works in reverse: the B♭ seventh chord from the B♭/A♯–E collection can shift to the other side through a C♯ seventh chord (by respelling F as E♯ and A♭ as G♯ and moving B♭ to B♮ and D to C♯, yielding C♯, E♯, G♯, and B). This, in turn, can fold back to an E seventh chord (by retaining G♯ and B and moving C♯ to D and E♯ to E, yielding E, G♯, B, and D). Again, here the tritones have shifted from the whole-tone collection of B♭/A♯–E to the collection of C♯–G and back again. This kind of movement across the two collections happens throughout the piece, as in, for example, the French augmented sixth chord at the end of m. 16 (whose two tritones, F–B and D♯–A, come from the C♯–G collection) that leads to the A♯ seventh chord in m. 17 (whose tritone, C$_x$–G♯, comes from the B♭/A♯–E collection), or even the A♯ seventh chord in m. 18 that leads to the E♯ half-diminished seventh chord in m. 19 (whose tritone, E♯–B, comes from the C♯–G collection). Here, the shifting of tritones—their noncoincidence—generates a sense of motion, heard as a kind of undulating harmonic color (see chapter 4, ex. 4.3).

This harmony of depth—depth that is expressed as movement both within the B♭/A♯–E pitch collection and across the two collections—structures the overall shape of the piece and especially illuminates the function of the beautiful extended melodic section in D♭ major that begins in m. 55. This portion of the piece presents one of the few harmonic areas to be set up through a strong descending-fifth relationship (A♭–D♭, mm. 54–55), which has the effect of emphasizing its structural significance. It also features an unabashedly gorgeous melody, heard first in the woodwinds and then in the strings, over gently syncopated rhythms and lush orchestration. It is arguably the most extraordinary development of the piece, glorious and singing. But

EXAMPLE 7.5. Debussy, *Prélude à l'après-midi d'un faune*, mm. 55–62, orchestra.

why D♭ major? What is it about the harmonic color that contributes to the exquisite expression of this music?

The D♭, considered enharmonically, springs naturally from the very first note of the *Prélude* (C♯), and is thus connected to the initial harmonic world of the two tritones that form the fully diminished seventh chord. It bears a

EXAMPLE 7.5. (*continued*)

relationship to the C♯–G collection in that it serves as an important harmonic counterpart to the end of the piece (E major), which arises from the other collection, that of B♭/A♯–E. Figure 7.2 demonstrates the common-tone relationships between D♭ major and important harmonies derived from the contrasting B♭/A♯–E pitch collection: a B♭ seventh chord, an A♯ half-diminished

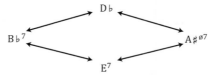

FIGURE 7.2. Relationship of D♭ major (from m. 55) to the harmonies derived from the pitch collection built on B♭/A♯–E.

seventh chord, and an E seventh chord. Thus, the D♭ functions as a double—a vibrant proliferation of color—against the predominant harmonic field of the piece (that of the B♭/A♯–E collection). Immediately the D♭ triad strikes the ear as a rich and shimmering gold shining forth from the deep blues and greens painted in so much of the rest of the piece. And its harmonic pedigree could not be more clear, because m. 56, following the D♭ major root-position triad of m. 55, features a shift in the bass line to G♮, above which the harmony sounds as a whole-tone scale: D♭, E♭, F, G, and A (from the enharmonically equivalent collection C♯–D♯–F–G–A–B). Here, at the midpoint or "fold" of the 110-measure piece, the tritone between C♯ and G finds its most powerful expression. The harmonic collection that springs from it, exemplified by the bass movement of D♭ to G♮, serves the greater part of this melodic section, confirmed by the extended cadence on D♭ in mm. 74–78.

Yet, even in this glorious section of unabashed, singing beauty, an internal tension is still operative: that of the unresolved conflict or energy that arises between G♮ and G♯ (a noncoincidence rooted in the opening flute arabesque). The stability of this D♭ major section is called into question in two ways.[5] In the first place, the D♭ major triad, the fifth of which is an A♭, is undermined by the movement in the bass to a G♮ in m. 56, generating a melodic tritone. This movement is emphasized by the whole-tone collection that sounds through the instruments of accompaniment in mm. 56 and 58—a whole-tone collection within which A♭ has no position. And so the strength of the perfect fifth (A♭–D♭) is undermined through the subverting of the A♭. In the second place, m. 62, which connects the woodwinds' initial melody in D♭ with its restatement (also in D♭) in the violins at m. 63, features a D♮ in the bass, plac-ing the A♭ (as G♯) in another tritone relationship and featuring, as articulated in the upper woodwind voices, the other whole-tone collection, that of B♭/A♯–E. And so the D♭ major triad—that stable and steady harmony built upon the essential partners of D♭ and A♭ (in the relationship of a perfect fifth)—is thwarted in two ways: through the G♮, which establishes a tritone with D♭ (of the C♯–G collection), and through the D♮, which establishes a tritone with A♭ (of the B♭/A♯–E collection). What the D♭ major section as a whole discloses, therefore, is yet another sense in which the tension of tritones is unresolved.

EXAMPLE 7.6. Debussy, *Prélude à l'après-midi d'un faune*, mm. 100–103, flute and oboe only.

It is unresolved, indeed, even at the recapitulation of the flute arabesque at m. 94, for the melody continues to utilize the original tritone, C♯–G♮, in an echo of the piece's opening. As if to restate one last time the source of the harmonic tension, the pickup to m. 100 in the flute offers E, G, and A♯ leading to C♯—that very same fully diminished seventh chord through which the entire harmonic world of the *Prélude* unfolds. Yet after this articulation of the governing source of harmonic tension (but played softly, monophonically, and in the flute's low register—lacking all emphasis that might make it explicit), we finally hear, in m. 100, the beginning of an arabesque that utilizes the interval of a perfect fourth, C♯–G♯ (not G♮). This special arabesque—this arabesque *without* the tritone—also features a solo cello that doubles the flute line. And so m. 100 initiates an extraordinary expression thanks to both the interval shift in the melody and the new color (solo cello) in the orchestration.

This is effective compositionally because it is here that the question of the opening measures—the tritone interval of C♯–G and the subsequent emphasis on G♯ at the apex of the melody in m. 3—is resolved. That is to say, the conclusion of the piece is built upon an accord between C♯ and G♯ such that the internal tension between G♮ and G♯ (from the beginning of the piece and especially developed through m. 55 ff.) dissipates. The oboe, entering as a reinforcement for the flute in m. 102, supports this interval of the perfect fourth (C♯–G♯) and in m. 103 additionally offers its own resolution to the G♮ that had been so conspicuously absent from mm. 100–102 by outlining a gesture of C♮ to G♮. Thus the original tritone, C♯–G♮, is resolved, as we would expect, in two ways: by descending perfect fourth (C♯–G♯ in the flute and cello in mm. 100–101, then in the flute and oboe in m. 102) and by ascending perfect fifth (C♮–G♮ in the oboe in m. 103).

Both ways, in the end, lead to the note E. In m. 107, the basses sustain E just as the final variation of this arabesque motif in the muted horns and violins—this time compressed still further to the interval of a major third (from G♯ down to E in the melody)—confirms the resolution to G♯ (see chapter 4, ex. 4.6). After a brief glimmer of G♮ (on the third beat of m. 107 in the first violins, sounding as C major like the oboe in m. 103, with E as the third), the final measures of the piece circle around $A_\sharp$ half-diminished seventh chords and E major triads in gentle eddies of sound, achieving a sense of relaxation and repose as the flute sustains a final $G_\sharp$ above the ringing pizzicato E in the basses.

*

How, then, does this music express a style? In the *Prélude*, not only the opening arabesque but also the two whole-tone collections that govern the harmonic color or movement of the piece unfold according to a depth initiated through the two tritones ($C_\sharp$–G and $B_\flat$/$A_\sharp$–E). Thus, the melodic contour, the intervallic content of the chords, and the linear relationships among the harmonies are all oriented by the interval of the tritone.[6] Yet if, as it seems, there is a unitary notion or essence (i.e., that of a tritone) operating throughout the piece, nevertheless it is a notion that does not exist outside of the piece, nor does it exist divested of the individual articulations of its musical character. For it is only through the performance of the whole of the *Prélude* that anything like a style comes to be disclosed. In this sense, there is less an essence behind the piece than an opening of expressive possibility through which, in Debussy, the double realm of whole-tone collections shines forth. Indeed, it could not be that we might simply hear the interval of a tritone in isolation, such as, for example, $C_\sharp$–G, and equate this with the sinuous lines and shades of Debussy's work. The harmony of a musical composition—like the rhythm—engages both prospectively and retrospectively across multiple sections of the piece. And so it is in all of its rich detail that the music speaks: as a timbre in the flute, a whole-tone scale in the clarinet, a sweeping $D_\flat$ major melody in the violins. Only in the specificity of the unfolding of time—only through "simultaneous decentering and recentering," that is to say, institution—do we come to understand musical harmony as an open and cohesive sense.[7]

In a similar way, then, we will investigate the institution of an idea: through the musical idea of Proust.

On the Musical Idea of Proust

Literature, music, the passions, but also the experience of the visible world are—no less than is the science of Lavoisier and Ampère—the exploration of an invisible and the disclosure of a universe of ideas.

MERLEAU-PONTY, *The Visible and the Invisible*

In Proust's *Recherche*, Marcel's path toward the achievement of his own literary vocation is occupied by his engagement with multiple arts, such as his reading of the works of Bergotte, his attendance at the performances of Berma, and the hours he spends in contemplation of the paintings of Elstir. Yet no artistic figure has a greater impact upon Marcel than that of the composer Vinteuil—a man whom Marcel never meets, and yet whose works inspire within him an extraordinary joy and feeling of hope.[1] Through Vinteuil's pieces—the sonata and the septet—Marcel is able to affirm the reality of the idea (as a bulwark against the meaninglessness of existence, the "dark night of the soul") as well as a means through which this idea might be accessed. And it is thus that Merleau-Ponty (better known, certainly, as a philosopher of painting) turns to the "musical idea"; the course notes ("L'ontologie cartésienne et l'ontologie d'aujourd'hui") and drafts (*The Visible and the Invisible*) on the "musical" or "sensible" idea are specifically inspired by Proust. For what Merleau-Ponty discloses through the musical idea is an ideality, like a style, that comes to be known according to the divergence, depth, and temporality of the flesh. Such an understanding of the musical idea is not immediately apparent in Proust. At first we catch only a glimmer of its ontological significance as we follow the musical idea—not yet even with Marcel— through the story of Swann and Odette.

Swann is a musical novice, and his great passion—aside from, of course, the pleasure that he takes in women—focuses upon the visual arts. Yet his work—his essay on Vermeer, incomplete and abandoned years ago—has ceased to find a place in his life. A gifted intellectual who travels in the highest realms of Parisian society, Swann had developed an acute awareness of the unbridgeable divide between the real and the ideal—as between the realm of experience and the realm of art—and despite or perhaps even because of his refined sensibilities had slipped into a dull period of resignation. His erudition in matters of art, for example, was applied in advising society ladies on their personal collections: "He had so long ceased to direct his life towards any ideal goal, confining himself to the pursuit of ephemeral satisfactions, that he had come to believe, without ever admitting it to himself in so many words, that he would remain in that condition for the rest of his days. More than this, since his mind no longer entertained any lofty ideas, he had ceased to believe in (although he could not have expressly denied) their reality."[2] Swann had ceased to believe in the reality of ideas, moreover, because he had always conceived of them as antithetical to the "ephemeral satisfactions" with which he presently occupied himself, as if they could exist only, if at all, on a "lofty" plane, beyond the perturbations of time. And so his brilliant social life had effectively swept away any desire to search out "any lofty ideas." Yet, it is precisely by means of such a social occasion—an evening party—that he is stirred from his lethargy, through an encounter with a "little phrase" of music:

> But now, like a confirmed invalid in whom, all of a sudden, a change of air and surroundings, or a new course of treatment, or sometimes an organic change in himself, spontaneous and unaccountable, seems to have brought about such an improvement in his health that he begins to envisage the possibility, hitherto beyond all hope, of starting to lead belatedly a wholly different life, Swann found in himself, in the memory of the phrase that he had heard, in certain other sonatas which he had made people play to him to see whether he might not perhaps discover his phrase therein, the presence of one of those invisible realities in which he had ceased to believe and to which, as though the music had had upon the moral barrenness from which he was suffering a sort of recreative influence, he was conscious once again of the desire and almost the strength to consecrate his life.[3]

What could be the nature of this "invisible reality," conveyed to him through music, such that it bears the power to elicit from him "the desire and almost the strength to consecrate his life"? Despite the force of its impression, it is not a reality that he is able to grasp; its invisibility or unknowability is constitutive. As revived as he feels by the "little phrase," as soon as the sound itself ceases to ring, he loses his sense of the idea. "An impression of this order," concludes Swann, "vanishing in an instant, is, so to speak, *sine materia*."[4] Indeed, Swann leaves the party unable to hum the melody, identify the title of the work, or learn the name of the composer. But even after he ascertains, upon hearing the piece on a later occasion at the Verdurins, that the "little phrase" is from the Andante of Vinteuil's Sonata for Piano and Violin—even after he obtains the score and is able to hear the phrase played over and over again on the piano—he is no better able than when he first heard it to isolate its "invisible reality." Indeed, throughout the first volume of the *Recherche*, Vinteuil's sonata seems to maintain its fascination for Swann precisely in the degree to which he fails to grasp its essence. His effort to study the phrase, in identifying characteristics of its range and rhythm and fixing a notation upon the musical staff, leads him to make certain conclusions about its affect; but these conclusions, he recognizes, are based "not upon the phrase itself, but merely upon certain equivalents, substituted (for his mind's convenience) for the mysterious entity of which he had become aware."[5]

And so the "mysterious entity" continues to haunt Swann; although he cannot grasp it, he does not doubt its significance. That his mind seizes upon a substitution—never the musical idea itself—is in no small part related to its very existence as an idea: though it speaks through sound, it cannot be reduced to the phenomenon of sound, for it is "of another world, of another order," as Proust writes:[6] "In [t]his little phrase, although it might present a clouded surface to the eye of reason, one sensed a content so solid, so consistent, so explicit, to which it gave so new, so original a force, that those who had once heard it preserved the memory of it on an equal footing with the ideas of the intellect."[7]

It is this notion of an idea—*sine materia*—that comes to be known thanks only to its unfolding within the sensible realm that informs the very last drafted effort of Merleau-Ponty's work. The final few pages from "The Intertwining—The Chiasm" in *The Visible and the Invisible* draw upon Proust's description of the "musical idea" as a model for the ontological shift that Merleau-Ponty seeks to articulate through his philosophy of the flesh. Indeed, it would have not been enough to simply advance and describe this notion of the flesh, as does the greater portion of the "Chiasm" chapter. Merleau-Ponty must show how this flesh—this depth dimension of being—shelters the emergence of the idea. He therefore needs to elucidate an idea that comes through the flesh and that is of the flesh—an idea expressed through the cohesion of incompossibles. And this is precisely what Merleau-Ponty discovers in Proust's account of the "little phrase" in Vinteuil's sonata. In *The Visible and the Invisible*, Merleau-Ponty claims, "No one has gone further than Proust in fixing the relations between the visible and the invisible, in describing an idea that is not the contrary of the sensible, that is its lining and its depth."[8] And in the late course notes on Proust and the musical idea, Merleau-Ponty asks, "Isn't it a general conception of ideas?"[9]

Indeed, Proust writes that Swann "regarded musical *motifs* as actual ideas, of another world, of another order, ideas veiled in shadow, unknown, impenetrable to the human mind, but none the less perfectly distinct from one another."[10] As ideas "veiled in shadow" and "impenetrable to the human mind" (a phrase that Merleau-Ponty underlines in his recounting of Proust's description),[11] these musical ideas are not to be regarded as intelligible ideas that have not yet achieved clarity, as if, in the end, the *kosmotheoros* could succeed in isolating and pinpointing their essence. Their shadow—their depth—is constitutive:

> For these truths are not only hidden like a physical reality which we have not been able to discover, invisible in fact but which we will one day be able to see facing us, which others, better situated, could already see, provided that the screen that masks it is lifted. Here, on the contrary, there is no vision without the screen: the ideas we are speaking of would not be better known to us if we had no body and no sensibility; it is then that they would be inaccessible to us. The "little phrase," the notion of the light, are [*sic*] not exhausted by their manifestations, any more than is an "idea of the intelligence"; they could not be given to us *as ideas* except in a carnal experience. It is not only that we would find in that carnal experience the *occasion* to think them; it is that they owe their authority, their fascinating, indestructible power, precisely to the fact that they are in transparency behind the sensible, or in its heart.[12]

These musical ideas cannot be separated from their resonant expression.[13] They work from the "heart" of the sensible not only because the realm of the senses offers the chance of their articulation, but because their very power of affectivity—a power that prompts Swann to change the trajectory of his entire life—springs from performative, dynamic realization. Indeed, the musical idea cannot be said to exist without the performance that calls it into being ("as though the musicians were not nearly so much playing the little phrase as performing the rites on which it insisted before it would consent to appear, and proceeding to utter the incantations necessary to procure, and to prolong for a few moments, the miracle of its apparition").[14] Merleau-Ponty writes: "[The musical idea] is therefore not a *de facto* invisible, like an object hidden behind another, and not an absolute invisible, which would have nothing to do with the visible. Rather it is the invisible *of* this world, that which inhabits this world, sustains it, and renders it visible, its own and interior possibility, the Being of this being."[15]

Thus, the musical idea cannot be reduced to a phenomenon nor to an intelligible idea. Rather, it is operative—it *sustains the world*. It illuminates

phenomena—it *renders visible*. The musical idea brings about transformation—it affects not just what but how we see; it manifests a power of orientation. The illuminating capacity of music explains why Swann feels such a
passionate awakening when he is stirred by the "little phrase." His life takes
on a completely new aspect, as if the contours of his soul had been altered.
Indeed, for Swann, the "little phrase" does not, as the "national anthem" of
his love for Odette, simply represent his great affection.[16] Rather, it could be
said that the musical idea expressed through the "little phrase" brings this
love into being. Thanks to Vinteuil's sonata, not only does Odette appear in
a new light; for Swann, the "little phrase" (through expressions "of tenderness, of passion, of courage, of serenity") makes possible his very ambition
to love.[17] Swann's character, actions, and desires are irrevocably cast under
the spell of the musical idea; the course of his life is changed: "We can no
more bring ourselves to a state in which we shall not have known [it] than
we can with regard to any material object, than we can, for example, doubt
the luminosity of a lamp that has just been lit, in view of the changed aspect
of everything in the room, from which even the memory of the darkness has
vanished."[18] Merleau-Ponty, too, compares the musical ideas, in this sense,
to light: "One has said Platonism, but these ideas are without an intelligible
sun, and related to the visible light: a membrane of the visible."[19] Unlike an
intelligible sun that would clear away all movement, all depth, all shadow (for
its penetrating force would offer up ideas as a totality known beyond time,
space, and the world), the visible light makes possible a world of shadow—a
world in which the unseen and the invisible are constitutive. It is in this sense
that the musical idea is like a "membrane" (like Cézanne's "*several* outlines
in blue" through which the flesh of objects and the flesh of the world are
permeable and intertwined): the musical idea is not a casing or a skin—not
a *thing*—but the adhesion through which noncoincidence coheres. Even as
it can be compared to the luminosity of visible light, the musical idea asserts
that *there is* the invisible—that there is an intertwining of the visible and the
invisible as flesh. Merleau-Ponty writes:

> There is a strict ideality in experiences that are experiences of the flesh:
> the moments of the sonata, the fragments of the luminous field, adhere to
> one another with a cohesion without concept, which is of the same type as
> the cohesion of the parts of my body, or the cohesion of my body with the
> world. . . . We will therefore have to recognize an ideality that is not alien to
> the flesh, that gives it its axes, its depth, its dimensions.[20]

This depth of ideality, through the musical idea, reveals yet another aspect of its nature: movement. This cohesion, "which is of the same type as

the cohesion of the parts of my body," articulates the sense of movement that, as we saw earlier, Merleau-Ponty found in Rodin: movement not toward another physical positioning, but movement through the cohering of noncoincidence. Indeed, one speaks more often of movement in music than in sculpture.[21] But how do the notes of a musical phrase move? It is not by a displacement of space. Merleau-Ponty writes, as we learned in chapter 4, that "while listening to beautiful music," he has "the impression that this movement that starts up is already at its endpoint, which it is going to have been, or [that it is] sinking into the future that we have a hold of as well as the past."[22] It is this cohesion of temporal incompossibles—of initiation and end, future and past—that creates, in music, the impression of movement: that which we understand as rhythm.

Yet as cohesion of noncoincidence—as depth, movement, or rhythm—the musical idea cannot be located within the musical notes (i.e., within the five audible tones of Swann's "little phrase"). As an idea, it exceeds its audible presentation; the musical idea "presents to us what is absent."[23] The idea itself manifests rhythm, for, as Merleau-Ponty describes, it haunts an ungraspable hollow "behind the sounds or between them,"[24] binding the present together with the past. In this sense we understand Merleau-Ponty's claim that the musical idea "is one of these entities which are not positives, but differences."[25] And because it is *behind* or *between* the sounds as rhythm, the musical idea itself is quite impossible to grasp directly. According to Merleau-Ponty, "We do not possess the musical or sensible ideas, precisely because they are negativity or absence circumscribed; they possess us."[26] He writes:

Each time we want to get at it immediately, or lay hands on it, or circumscribe it, or see it unveiled, we do in fact feel that the attempt is misconceived, that it retreats in the measure that we approach. The explicitation does not give us the idea itself; it is but a second version of it, a more manageable derivative. Swann can of course close in the "little phrase" between the marks of musical notation, ascribe the "withdrawn and chilly tenderness" that makes up its essence or its sense to the narrow range of the five notes that compose it and to the constant recurrence of two of them: while he is thinking of these signs and this sense, he no longer has the "little phrase" itself, he has only "bare values substituted for the mysterious entity he had perceived, for the convenience of his understanding."[27]

This "second version" of the musical idea points to the specific temporality that is characteristic of the musical idea—a temporality in accordance with the idea's intertwining with the sensible. The musical idea exhibits a temporality of the flesh—mythical time. As soon as active reflection attempts to raise the musical idea into a "positivity" (that is to say, as soon as reflection attempts to detemporalize the musical idea),[28] its essence slips away, leaving Swann with only "certain equivalents, substituted (for his mind's convenience) for the mysterious entity."[29] It is not only that the temporal quality of the musical idea ensures the impossibility, for Swann, of discerning a fixed essence; it is that the musical idea, as rhythm, comes to expression through a process of institution. In this sense, we can speak of the musical idea as "an ideality that has need of time."[30] The musical idea inhabits the depth dimension of the flesh—what Merleau-Ponty describes as that very "dimension between the series of events and intemporal sense, the third dimension of depth history or the genesis of ideality."[31]

And so, because the musical idea is born of such a generative dimension, the slipping away of its essence does not constitute a failure. Throughout Swann's love affair with Odette, it offers, rather, a possibility to institute and reinstitute a new sense, so that each encounter with Vinteuil's sonata circumscribes an open field of latent meaning. Just as, for Merleau-Ponty, Proust's musical idea discloses the membrane between the ideal and the sensible, so too does music provide the means for investigating the curious temporal structure that arises through this divergence, where the past and the present are intertwined. Merleau-Ponty writes:

> The melody gives us a particular consciousness of time. We think naturally that the past secretes the future ahead of it. But this notion of time is refuted by the melody. At the moment when the melody begins, the last note is there, in its own manner. In a melody, a reciprocal influence between the first and the last note takes place, and we have to say that the first note is possible only because of the last, and vice versa.[32]

There is encroachment between the first and last note, yet this intertwining never achieves a complete return through coincidence. The circularity revealed here is not one of identity between the first and last note, as if the experience of the melody were to remain the same when performed in retrograde. Rather, this "reciprocal influence" discloses not repetition but depth of the present. The melody "transcend[s] the past present distinction, realize[s] from within a passage from one into the other," as the flesh of time—as rhythm.[33] It is in this sense that Merleau-Ponty writes, in the *Notes de cours*, that the "consciousness of music is of 'always.' "[34] Elsewhere he claims, "Ideal being is omnitemporal";[35] and he writes again, "There is an intemporal which works on the inside of time, which is, rather, omnitemporal."[36] It is music that expresses the omnitemporal—the time "of 'always.' " Music discloses a time that flows forth as past, present, and future in depth, yet not a time that would be undifferentiated—not a time without or beyond time. Here, in music, the "instantaneousness"—the individuation of the temporal order—"which seemed to be obstacles to the permanence of ideal being, are on the contrary what founds it insofar as they are a call to reiteration."[37]

In the working notes of *The Visible and the Invisible*, Merleau-Ponty describes this expression of ideality as "the form that has arrived at itself, that is itself, that poses itself by its own means, is the equivalent of the cause of itself . . . auto-regulation, cohesion of self with self, identity in depth (dynamic identity), transcendence as being-at-a-distance, there is—."[38]

Such an "identity in depth" that participates in the temporal process of arriving at itself through institution "is the equivalent of the cause of itself" precisely because it does not imitate a preconceived model; its reiteration ensures its "dynamic identity" through the very lacuna that serves as the measure of its capacity for novel productivity.[39] The lacuna—the noncoincidence—in itself functions as an opening of continual regeneration and creative expression. This is why the musical idea springs from "behind the sounds or between them."[40] Thus, in the *Notes de cours*, Merleau-Ponty writes that what is radical about the musical idea is the notion that "the universe of knowledge is derived from this regulatory use, the idea (music generalized) that each music creates its own *Boden*."[41] That is to say, what is radical is that musical expression is achieved not by means of representation but through the genesis of an idea, "derived from this regulatory use"—from a process of departing and returning to itself (i.e., "that poses itself by its own means"), through the newness of time that never coincides absolutely with the past (i.e., "dynamic identity"). As an idea that participates in time, the musical idea retains the past not as a model but as a latency—as an open dimension, a possible productivity, a passivity flush with an activity—which, when taken up again, makes itself felt within the present.

Thus the musical idea consists precisely in what can be reinitiated; it achieves universality—its status as an idea—by means of institution within the sensible realm. Indeed, Merleau-Ponty writes that through the musical idea there is "initiation to a *world*, to a small eternity, to a dimension which is by now inalienable—Universality through singularity."[42] What is important to underline is that this process of repetition operates through initiation not along a series, but within depth. Truly, there is beginning each time—not *the* beginning (as origin), but the fact of a beginning announced retroactively, as a transformative remainder, excess, or dimension (exactly like the work of rhythm in a musical phrase or form).[43] That is to say, because the reinitiation of the idea cannot exactly coincide with an "original" (for its own temporal motion depends upon divergence, not origin), the idea does not operate through imitation; rather, the reinitiation is reproductive in the sense that it is in itself *again* productive: "pregnant" with the "power to break forth."[44] It is precisely this movement that enables passivity to be transformed as activity, like Rimbaud's "wood that becomes a violin."[45] This is the movement of expression. Thus, that which we can never grasp—the unpresentable—bears a certain potency, a "fascinating, indestructible power" that comes forth.[46]

In an important working note from *The Visible and the Invisible*, Merleau-Ponty emphasizes this movement—a movement through which the particular and the universal cohere—first by thinking in terms of color (in painting) and then by thinking of harmony (in music):

> It is precisely within its particularity as yellow and through it that the yellow becomes a universe or an *element*[47]—That a color can become a level, a fact become a category (exactly as in music: describe a note as particular, i.e. in the field of another *tone*—and "the same" note that has become that within whose key a music is written) = the veritable movement toward the universal. The universal is not above, it is beneath (Claudel),[48] it is not before, but *behind* us—atonal music = the equivalent of the philosophy of Being in indivision. Like paintings without identifiable things, without the *skin* of things, but giving their *flesh*—The *Transponierbarkeit* is a particular case of a more general transposition of which atonal music is the thematization.[49] All this implies the Being in indivision—
>
> This universality of the sensible = *Urpräsentation* of what is not *Urpräsentierbar* = the sensible hollowed out in the being without restriction, that Being which is *between* my perspective and that of the other, my past and my present.[50]

This flesh of the universal (as "element"—as "*originating presentation of the unpresentable*"[51]—as movement *between* the past and the present) is brought to presence through music. It is here, in the realm of the sensible, that we uncover the genesis of ideality itself, an ideality through the flesh that would not be separate from the world but would be affective.

Insofar as the movement or cohesion of the musical idea is of the present and past, equally, then, it is of one's own interior and expressive life—one's memories, hopes, and actions. For Proust, it is music more than any other art that bears the capacity to recompose—to join together—a coherent sense or movement of life: "This music seemed to me something truer than all known books. At moments I thought that this was due to the fact that, what we feel about life not being felt in the form of ideas, its literary, that is to say intellectual expression describes it, explains it, analyses it, but does not recompose it as does music, in which the sounds seem to follow the very movement of our being."[52] Here is a movement of being that leads through the depth of Being:

movement as the motion or emotion of being ("what we feel about life"). Movement arises through a cohesion of memory, attention, and anticipation that the performance or recomposition calls forth, such that we have not merely an imitation or description of life but a resonance with Being. Thus Merleau-Ponty writes that the musical idea "give[s] us the assurance that the 'great unpenetrated and discouraging night of our soul' is not empty, is not 'nothingness.'"[53] Merleau-Ponty's engagement is drawn from a passage by Proust:

> The field open to the musician is not a miserable stave of seven notes, but an immeasurable keyboard (still almost entirely unknown) on which, here and there only, separated by the thick darkness of its unexplored tracts, some few among the millions of keys of tenderness, of passion, of courage, of serenity, which compose it, each one differing from all the rest as one universe differs from another, have been discovered by a few great artists who do us the service, when they awaken in us the emotion corresponding to the theme they have discovered, of showing us what richness, what variety lies hidden, unknown to us, in that vast, unfathomed and forbidding night of our soul which we take to be an impenetrable void.[54]

The soul—"vast" and "unfathomed," but nevertheless not a "nothingness," nor a "void"—springs from the generative dimension of depth. And this is what Marcel, at the end of Proust's novel, comes to understand through music. Even as Swann might be said to fail in fulfilling the true measure of the call, issued by the "little phrase" of Vinteuil's sonata, to consecrate his life (Swann never becomes a writer—he never completes the essay on Vermeer), Marcel, on the other hand, is transformed.[55] The music elicits within him an extraordinary feeling of joy, such as he has experienced, and will experience, only very rarely over his lifetime. It leads him to believe that he, unlike Swann, will not fail to heed the summons to artistry—to a life of creativity and expression. The effect of the music upon Marcel is more profound precisely because Marcel is able to perceive through Vinteuil's compositions this generative dimension of depth; Marcel, unlike Swann, hears not one but two different works of Vinteuil—the sonata and septet—and is thus able to attend to the cohesion between them as Vinteuil's style.[56] For when Marcel begins to hear Vinteuil's music in depth—when, through the effort of memory in comparing one work with the other, the sonata and septet open up between them a dimension of expression—he identifies "an unmistakable voice" or style that discloses the fact of the "individual existence of the soul":

> When Vinteuil took up the same phrase again and again, diversified it, amused himself by altering its rhythm, by making it reappear in its original form, those

deliberate resemblances, the work of his intellect, necessarily superficial, never succeeded in being as striking as the disguised, involuntary resemblances, which broke out in different colors, between the two separate masterpieces; for then Vinteuil, striving to do something new, interrogated himself, with all the power of his creative energy, reached down to his essential self at those depths where, whatever be the questions asked, it is in the same accent, that is to say its own, that it replies . . . it is indeed a unique accent, an unmistakable voice, to which in spite of themselves those great singers that original composers are rise and return, and which is a proof of the irreducibly individual existence of the soul.[57]

What makes so profound an impression upon Marcel through Vinteuil's music is not a power of representation—of "deliberate resemblances"—but the institution of resonance. Moreover, it is in the context of Marcel's realization of the creative relationship between "those depths" (as arising through the noncoincidence "between the two separate masterpieces"), the "unmistakable voice" (as the notion of style), and "the soul" (as the unpresentable) that Merleau-Ponty's own engagement with music may be better understood. It is precisely as the summary to a section in the *Notes de cours* entitled "Music" that Merleau-Ponty writes, "Truth: there is an access to the exterior from the interior, there is a relationship to Being and beings which is absolute, on this side of the ambivalence and the thesis—Gesticulation of man who thinks and lives Being and beings, taken at its source: this is the very origin of music."[58]

This is truly one of the most remarkable notes composed by Merleau-Ponty.[59] He speaks of "access" to the openness upon the world from within the very "interior" or divergence (which is flesh, and neither mind nor body) itself; of a relationship to Being and the world that would be neither relative nor thetic; and of expression from the very source of expression. He continues, in the *Notes de cours*, "Music [is] an archaic axis"[60]—"archaic," we may read, in the sense of a dynamic *arche*, for music's movement discloses the existence of the originary unpresentable, the fact of which comes to presence retroactively. (Recall that he writes, in *The Visible and the Invisible*, "We will therefore have to recognize an ideality that is not alien to the flesh, that gives it its axes, its depth, its dimensions.")[61] Music, he writes, "reveals articulation before the articulation."[62] And we must take seriously the chiastic formulation that Merleau-Ponty explores in the *Notes de cours* on music, for in *The Visible and the Invisible* he very precisely describes the aim of his new ontology "as the expression of what is before expression *and sustains it from behind*."[63]

How can we, therefore, be surprised at the sudden and ecstatic tone of the final pages of "The Intertwining—The Chiasm"? For it is here that the philosopher of divergence, of noncoincidence, of "a reversibility always imminent and never realized in fact,"[64] writes, "At the moment one says 'light,' at the moment that the musicians reach the '*petite phrase*,' there is no lacuna in me; what I live is as 'substantial,' as 'explicit,' as a positive thought could be."[65] How could there be no lacuna? For one cannot say that the lacuna is no longer *there*. The lacuna is the *il y a*—the necessary "openness upon the thing itself [and] to the past itself."[66] As we have seen, the musical idea is a "negativity that is not nothing," for, through this divergence or negativity, the fact that *there is* an unpresentable comes to presence. We would have no world without the lacuna; thanks to the lacuna, there is a silence that fills me, through rhythm—a resonant silence that overflows as the cohesion of incompossibles. Here is the source ("the expression of what is before expression *and sustains it from behind*") of all movement and expression: "Gesticulation of man who thinks and lives Being and beings, taken at its source."[67] And the musical idea, springing from the depth "beyond the contradiction, without resistance and without 'grasps of position,'" takes hold of us within the divergence itself.[68] Inhabiting this dimension, we do not feel it to be a divergence; we do not approach it from the exterior, but live through it as "from the interior"—through the flesh. At the heart of this flesh of being— the heart of this chiasm—is not "nothing," but transcendence; and this is precisely what the musician feels.

At such a moment, Merleau-Ponty writes, "the performer is no longer producing or reproducing the sonata: he feels himself, and the others feel him to be at the service of the sonata; the sonata sings through him or cries out so suddenly that he must 'dash on his bow' to follow it."[69] Thus the violinist himself becomes the conduit for the encroachment, the coiling up, and the intertwining that opens the dimension of depth as the source—ever generative—of being. Merleau-Ponty concludes, "And these open vortexes in the sonorous world finally form one sole vortex in which the ideas fit in with one another."[70] Thus it is music that provides the model for Merleau-Ponty when, in one of the final working notes for *The Visible and the Invisible*, he says: "Fundamentally I bring the high-low distinction"—that is to say, the distinction of the intelligible and the sensible—"into the vortex where it rejoins the side–other side distinction"—that is to say, the distinction of presence (present) and absence (past)—"where the two distinctions are integrated into a *universal dimensionality* which is Being."[71]

Debussy: The Form That Has Arrived at Itself

Song is born of these divergences, these variations, the source of all music.

MARCEL PROUST, *Remembrance of Things Past*

It is in the *Prélude à l'après-midi d'un faune* that we may understand the institution of the musical idea: through musical form. A composition that, as we have seen, opens from silence and returns to silence, the *Prélude* has a form that proceeds not linearly but like a seashell, coiling around itself in successive variations of melody and harmony, articulated according to changing parameters of meter, orchestration, register, and dynamics. Does this shell—hollow and habitable—express an idea at all? It has no fixity—no possibility of intellectual possession; it is simply a secretion.

For Debussy, music in its essence "consists of colors and rhythmicized time."[1] The "colors" we may take to refer, as in chapter 7, to the depth expressed through harmony and timbre. But, for Debussy, what kind of rhythm is at work here? "Rhythmicized time" cannot refer simply to the use of musical meter—indeed, one of Debussy's most admired artistic achievements has to do with the way that he frees a phrase from the tyranny of the bar line.[2] The meter changes in the *Prélude* are flowing and unobtrusive; the sense of rhythmic pulse is less that of a metronome than of a shifting beam of light, like that which creates the dappled shade of the afternoon. When seeking to elucidate the particular kind of rhythm at work here, one must not consider rhythm simply as a durational measurement between two notes or two harmonies. "Rhythmicized time" operates across multiple layers: between the notes of a melody, yes; between the shifting of harmonies, yes; but also beneath the total unfolding of the piece, as what we call musical form.

The precise divisions of the form in the *Prélude* remain a subject of debate among contemporary music theorists. While most agree that, overall, the piece creates an arch shape—rising to the glorious theme in m. 55 and return-

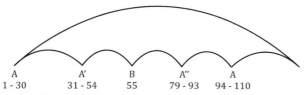

FIGURE 9.1. Diagram of a basic interpretation of the musical form (resembling an arch form, with B forming the center of the arch at m. 55).

ing, at the end, to the motif of the arabesque—analysis of the details of this shape has produced conflicting interpretations. William Austin observes:

> While we listen, the parts seem to overlap each other, so that the continuity of the whole work is extraordinarily smooth, and our recollection of it at the end is imprecise, though intense. We recognize similarities among many elusive parts, but unless we focus on very small parts we find no exact repetition and no conventional variation of whole phrases or motivic development of balancing phrases. At the end we know we have heard multiple versions of one principal melodic idea, but we suspect we may have missed the clearest statement of that idea. We recall the very beginning: should we call it an introduction? and if so, where does the main action begin? We know that somewhere in the middle of the piece the principal idea was either replaced by another one or vastly transformed, so that toward the end we could welcome its return in shapes nearly like those it had taken long before; but if we try, as many students of the piece have tried, to define three main divisions—beginning, middle, and end, or ABA'—we are likely to disagree with each other and fall into misunderstandings. In all this, incidentally, the music resembles the poem.[3]

Surely Austin provides one of the most honest and compelling descriptions of the challenges that we face in developing an understanding of the *Prélude.* Nevertheless, we can, for the most part, agree on the broad strokes of the form. There are certain points of articulation that can be clearly identified: the cadence at m. 30 (and new clarinet material into m. 31), the glorious melody in m. 55, the return of the arabesque at 79 (entering on E), and the recapitulation of the arabesque (moving from C♯ to G♮, like the opening) in m. 94.

It is in the judgment of sections internal to these articulations that a difference of interpretation is expressed.[4] One writer, for example, identifies mm. 1–10 as an introduction and locates the beginning of the B section at m. 37 (the oboe theme). Another writer specifies no such introduction and places the beginning of the B section at m. 55 (the glorious D♭ major melody).

EXAMPLE 9.1. Debussy, *Prélude à l'après-midi d'un faune*, oboe theme from mm. 37–39. Compare this to the melodic material of mm. 55–56 (chapter 7, ex. 7.5).

Yet the discrepancy between these two analyses tells us something about the musical material in the piece itself. That is to say, we may take their nonco-incidence as essential to understanding the form.

With respect to the beginning, one could hear the opening ten measures as so closely united with the following measures in terms of thematic and harmonic material that any labeling of those opening measures as "intro-duction" would be unnecessary; rather, we have the working out of one sole idea, and there is no need to specify a new section (A') until m. 31. (Compare, particularly, the statement of the flute arabesque in m. 1 to those in mm. 21 and 26. See exx. 4.1, 4.4, and 4.5 in chapter 4.) On the other hand, one might hear the oboe melody of m. 37 as distinct from the material of m. 31, yet so closely related to the woodwind melody in D♭ major that a B section would truly begin not at m. 55 but earlier, with the statement at m. 37 in the oboe. This interpretation would again point to a certain unity of musical material, but across different sections of the piece. Which interpretation is correct? Is it not thanks to their contrast that both ways of listening shed light upon the curious structure of the piece? For above all, what they disclose is a sense of the overall thematic integration across the *Prélude*'s various sections. Indeed, this integration is so characteristic of the piece that one could say that the *Prélude* is not only cast in some kind of an arch (ABA') form, but also utilizes the technique of theme and variations. It is as if only one idea informs the development of the piece.

Yet, if Debussy is using the technique of theme and variations to shape his piece, it is a theme and variations that does not unfold in an ordinary way. As Austin writes, "At the end we know we have heard multiple versions of one principal melodic idea, but we suspect we may have missed the clearest state-ment of that idea."[5] Indeed, if, as we explored in chapter 7, a fully diminished seventh chord comprised of two tritones (C♯–G and B♭/A♯–E) orients the un-folding of the entire piece, then it is fitting that this particular harmony is in fact *never* heard as a vertical sonority, and is heard horizontally only in the second half of m. 99—eleven measures before the end of the piece—where the flute leads melodically from E, G, and A♯ to a C♯ on the downbeat of

m. 100, which is precisely where the arabesque resolves the tritone by descending from C♯ to G♯. That is to say, if this sonority serves as a theme, we hear it only in the very moment that precedes its dissolution.[6] Indeed, this fully diminished seventh chord of m. 99 is not highlighted in any way compositionally; it sounds in one of the softest moments of the piece, diminished in sound as in quality. As a theme, therefore, it can be said to consist in a negative: it operates as the other, silent side of every audible variation.

In this way, the form of the *Prélude* deliberately undermines the classical model of theme and variations used throughout the eighteenth and nineteenth centuries, wherein a clearly delineated theme dictates the separate variations, which, being derived from the theme through resemblance, act as imitations. In the classical model, the theme is set forth as determining the variations. We might say, in the spirit of Merleau-Ponty, that this classical model already "is a metaphysics."[7] So different, however, is Debussy's approach that the listener cannot pinpoint the details of the structure. If the theme or idea is not the flute melody, but, rather, an operative set of intervals never presented as a theme—indeed, never audible as a set except in the last two beats of m. 99—then the ordinary relationship between a theme and its variations is here subverted.[8] Moreover, through the *Prélude*'s frequent use of phrase elision, deceptive resolutions, tritone relationships, and elongated harmonic pedals, the form seems to emerge not from a preinstituted model, but from a world that belongs entirely to the piece itself. In this sense, the musical form is autogenerative—it is "the form that has arrived at itself, that is itself, that poses itself by its own means"[9]—it "creates its own *Boden*,"[10] as we have seen Merleau-Ponty write.

And, as we have learned from Merleau-Ponty, the only way to know such a form is to enter into it. This is how we might understand form through rhythm.

*

We must, therefore, return to the beginning and follow the significant points of formal articulation. The flute arabesque, as we learned in chapter 4, initiates the movement of the entire *Prélude à l'après-midi d'un faune*. Yet the beginning itself goes back further than the opening C♯—it goes back to the breath and to the flesh: in this beginning is dimension folded through dimension—the noncoincidence of anticipation and retroactivity sustained in depth. How could we, then, label this as a mere introduction? It operates, rather, through institution. The "variations" that follow the initial arabesque, as well as the silence that precedes it, work to circumscribe the shadows—the hollow space—of the flute melody. They show what unarticulated theme there is behind the melody. Indeed, it is not through the repetition of the sounding notes of the melody but through the difference—the noncoincidence—between each iteration of the arabesque that new musical material springs forth: harmonies of a D major triad (m. 11), a C♯ minor seventh (m. 21), a B ninth chord (m. 23), and an E ninth chord (m. 26). Likewise, extensions of the arabesque (mm. 22, 24, and 27) open the possibility for contrapuntal material, and chromatic turns in the violas and cellos (in m. 22 and again in m. 27), introduced as accompaniment, blossom into the descending triplet turns in the melody of m. 28, leading to the cadence of m. 30 (see chapter 4, ex. 4.5).

Measure 31 features what might be described as a new, contrasting melody in the clarinet, set above harmony derived from tritone relationships (in this case, a French augmented sixth chord and whole-tone pitch collection, as explored in chapter 7). Yet this, too, coils back in reference to the arabesque (compare chapter 4, ex. 4.1, with chapter 7, ex. 7.2.) Here, the clarinet emphasizes the note G by sustaining it for three beats—G being, of course, the very pitch that set forth the initial tritone relationship in the arabesque (that of C♯–G). The clarinet's descent at the end of the measure from a sustained G to a D♯ compresses the tritone interval of the opening flute melody (that is to say, a diminished fourth rather than an augmented fourth), but the rise to an E♯ in m. 32 evokes a similar expansion of register (as in the flute in m. 3). Despite its immediate auditory impression as contrasting (in its change of orchestration, harmony, and rhythm), the clarinet offers yet another layer of the theme beneath the unfolding of the piece. Even the fact that there is a sequence (in mm. 34–36, this time emphasizing the note B♭—i.e., that other signal pitch of the thematic tritone relationship) evokes the work of the "double" (what Merleau-Ponty would describe as a coupling or a coiling up) that characterizes the internal repetition of the flute melody (mm. 1 and 2) and the restatement of the B♭ seventh chord in m. 7. And so, despite the formal delineation that occurs with the cadence of m. 30, nevertheless the musical material of mm. 1–30 and 31–36 springs forth as one organic gesture. Indeed, extending this notion, we see that the following oboe melody of m. 37—precisely that which one might be tempted to characterize as the beginning of the B section and therefore as distinct—recalls the arabesque, thanks once again to its expressive descent (this time not compressed, as in the clarinet, to the interval of a diminished fourth, but instead expanded to a perfect fifth). The oboe's next rising motif, in m. 39, outlines a tritone (G♯–D), further confirming a relationship with the opening flute arabesque by acting, at this moment, as a sort of mirror (insofar as the initial flute melody outlines a tritone and then, in m. 3, emphasizes a perfect fifth between C♯ and G♯, while the oboe in m. 37 outlines a perfect fifth but then, in m. 39, emphasizes a tritone). This oboe melody—the mirror of the flute arabesque—leads, through a transformation of the rising motif from m. 39, to the gorgeous melody in D♭ major of m. 55, which, like the motion of m. 37, descends by perfect fifth. So closely are these two melodies related that one can understand an inclination to consider them part of the same formal section.

Here, however, at the center of the piece—that which many listeners describe as the B section—the play between perfect fifths and tritones, which had always unfolded as a melodic relationship throughout the statements of the variations, is heard as a simultaneity: the melodic motion descending by fifth in the woodwinds (from A♭ in m. 55 to D♭ in m. 56) is coupled with a harmonic motion based on tritones in the basses (as D♭–G in m. 56, evoking the whole-tone pitch collection). What was horizontal meets up with the vertical (see chapter 7, ex. 7.5). And yet this conflict between fifths and tritones soars in its beauty. Soft, sustained, and expressive, the A♭ in the woodwinds—the very pitch that serves (enharmonically as a G♯) as a resolution to the opening C♯–G tritone—is magical. Reaching to the upper register, the woodwinds—flute, oboe, English horn, and clarinet in unison—describe a sequence of sweeping descents that build dynamically to a triumphant declaration of the triplet turns (i.e., the melodic turns that we heard first in m. 28). This material again spawns its own double, reorchestrated with the melody in the strings and enriched with more active accompaniment, and extends across mm. 63–73, giving passionate release to the rising motif (of m. 39) and triplet turns (of m. 28), reaching a climax at m. 70 (the only *fortissimo* in a piece that is predominantly marked *piano* or *pianissimo*), and finally swirling round to a slow eddy of melodic fragments through mm. 74–78.

Measure 79, then, marks the return of material from the A section, as the flute arabesque, unstated since m. 26, reenters (although in E major and metrically displaced). Interrupted by a lively oboe melody in m. 83, which, like the clarinet melody of m. 31, features compressed descending motion (but in the interval of a minor third), the arabesque returns in m. 86 (in E♭ major), succumbs to another iteration of the lively material (this time, in the English horn) at m. 90, and makes a true recapitulation in m. 94. Here, above an E seventh chord—the very root of which will serve as the resolution of the piece—the arabesque is presented in its original guise, featuring the tritone interval of C♯–G. As the energy of the piece dissipates, however, the triplet turns that had shaped m. 28 and led to the cadence in m. 30 are augmented rhythmically in mm. 96–99. The effect is a sudden elongation of the woodwinds' descent. Their languid melody over a texture of shimmering tremolo strings (performed *pianissimo* and on the fingerboard) prolongs anticipation for the final flute statement of the arabesque, at m. 100, that resolves the

EXAMPLE 9.2. Debussy, *Prélude à l'après-midi d'un faune*, mm. 79–82, flute. This arabesque marks the return of material from the A section.

EXAMPLE 9.3. Debussy, *Prélude à l'après-midi d'un faune*, mm. 83–84, oboe. This lively melody employs a range of a minor third (compressed from the opening flute tritone in the arabesque).

tritone to a perfect fourth (C♯–G♯) (see chapter 7, ex. 7.6). That perfect fourth coils around itself through a rising chromatic scale three times (in m. 102) before the melody shifts to the oboe (in m. 103). Here, the oboe rises (like the motif of m. 3) through a perfect fifth (from C up to G, thus offering contrast to the G♯ of the flute) but then slowly and sequentially descends to the note of resolution, E, in m. 106. Thus, as we saw in chapter 7, the initial tritone from which the piece as a whole was generated is resolved in two ways: as a descending perfect fourth in the flute (m. 102) and as an ascending perfect fifth in the oboe (m. 103). From here, only echoes—muted horns and low violins—repeat the murmur of the arabesque, as the piece slows, quiets and comes to rest.

*

Where does such an analysis leave us? One could—and should—caution that the analysis leaves us not with the music itself but, as Proust wrote of Vinteuil's sonata, merely with "certain equivalents, substituted (for his mind's convenience) for the mysterious entity."[11] Yet the endeavor is not entirely without merit, for it offers us a way, through language, of circling around a center. We can only think of this center as a hollow, and perhaps the inadequacy of language thus serves well by requiring that we continually point to that hollow. The music can and should never be captured. But an interesting structure emerges—a formal structure characterized as much by its silence and space as its eloquence. If it is sufficient neither to describe the *Prélude* as an arch form (ABA') nor to call it a theme and variations, then it would be best to describe the form as generated according to the noncoincidence between the two. For the form of the *Prélude* is to be understood not as any single model would propose: what our analysis discloses—through the harmonies, the melodies, the timbres—is a sense of form that gathers or arrives at itself or that, conversely, proliferates through "a sort of folding back."[12] The series of arabesque statements in the A section, for example, wrap through to the arabesque at m. 79 and recapitulation at m. 94. Also in the A section, the oboe melody in m. 37, descending by perfect fifth, carries forward to the gorgeous woodwind melody, also descending by fifth, at m. 55 of the B section. The two sections unfold according to a connection—a "membrane"[13]—that is traced between them through melodic variation, coiling about each other. Yet they also participate in the more broadly floating resonance between the arabesque statements of the opening and return of m. 79, since the motif of the descending tritone of the arabesque can be said to generate the descending fifth in mm. 37 and 55 of the B section. What we understand through these relationships is that even when the arabesque is not heard—even when it is not present—its absence is active. But just as the sense of the arabesque gathers itself inward across the variations, it moves outward as well, proliferating through differentiation (melodic, harmonic, metric, and dynamic) in the B section. It is this interaction between the unity of the variations and the differentiation of the arch form that makes possible the free and flowing expression of the music. Thus, what we hear as the form is not linear; it moves too deeply to be described as a line, for it is dimensional. There is always a gentle kind of divergence or dissonance at work in the form of the *Prélude*, a layering of sense and the institution of depth. From this depth springs the idea of the form itself.

As we have seen Merleau-Ponty write, with the musical idea there is "not the positing of a content, but the opening of a dimension that can never again be closed."[14] The musical idea is not a "positive thought," he continues, but "negativity or absence circumscribed."[15] We can never know it or grasp it directly, yet it generates the expressive gestures of the piece. The *Prélude* never presents an idea all at once, complete and set apart. Rather, it is only thanks to the succession of musical motifs that an idea arises at all. Variations do not, in this sense, come from the theme; as Merleau-Ponty likewise says of the institution of a philosophical idea, these variations rather serve "to make it say what at first it had not quite said."[16] They are productive, not imitative. Always they turn back to perform an idea that had never been completely present, through musical gestures of both extension and gathering. The flute arabesque of m. 94, for example, does not merely echo what has already been expressed; there is noncoincidence. In this sense, the musical idea cannot imitate or repeat, because the movement of expression comes to be instituted retrospectively. Already the idea—"the tie that secretly connects an experience to its variants"[17]—shifts the effect of repetition; repetition is transformed into resonance.

And this is the sense in which rhythm is significant. Indeed, Merleau-Ponty invokes this sense of rhythm in one of his earliest descriptions of music: "While the notes taken separately have an equivocal signification, being capable of entering into an infinity of possible ensembles, in the melody each one is demanded by the context and contributes its part in expressing something which is not contained in any one of them and which binds them together internally."[18] This "something" not contained in individual notes but capable of "bind[ing] them together internally" is, of course, rhythm. And rhythm—that which itself is unheard and unseen, which, as a membrane, holds together all sensation through prospective and retrospective resonance—expresses the idea; it expresses the idea not merely in time nor through time, but as the flesh of time itself. In describing the institution of an idea, therefore, Merleau-Ponty writes that there is a "double movement: the past recuperated by the present and contracted in it, but also the present anticipated by the past which remains operative in the present."[19] Like the musical phrase (on a local level), which flows according to a pattern of notes held in relation, or like the musical form (on a broader level), which evokes repetition, variation, and development, this "double movement" is the work of rhythm. Thus, music models most directly an opening through which the idea emerges; it offers the rhythm of thought.

We must emphasize that this rhythmic structure operates not only horizontally (that is to say, as a bond between a series of events), but on multiple levels, vertically. "Each present is dimensional," Merleau-Ponty writes.[20] Therefore, there is a "'deep' present"—a "'vertical' thought."[21] Merleau-Ponty speaks of this thickness of the present as "the *transgression of Ineinander* [in one another]. That is not a mixture of immanence and causality. It is the discovery of the third dimension, that of [philosophy], that of Being—the *living present* as the connection of the present and past of an invisible, therefore as nonenveloping unity . . . vertical."[22]

Thus, we should not imagine the "*transgression of Ineinander*" as a two-dimensional mixture; rather, it involves "the discovery of the third dimension"—depth. The dimensional present, Merleau-Ponty claims, "designates a presence that is richer than what is visible of it."[23] There is transcendence. Indeed, through rhythm, what is "invisible" coheres with the present: the invisibility of the past and the invisibility of the future. This "unity," however, is never a possession, constituted and determined in advance. I can no more see the whole of the past than I can predict the future; yet, in a moment of realization, they both appear as if they had been there, in the present, all along. A clairvoyance is at work. This dimensional present offers a sort of resonance through which certain events dissipate and others are brought into accord, amplified. It is a "rhythmicized time" that achieves a certain depth of simultaneity.[24]

Indeed, in the *Notes de cours*, precisely following his investigation of the musical idea of Proust, Merleau-Ponty explores this notion of simultaneity by turning to the poet, Claudel.[25] Merleau-Ponty describes simultaneity, in terms evoking both movement and rhythm, as "cohesion of space; cohesion of time; cohesion of space and of time . . . but cohesion that is not indistinction, that is of the incompossibles, that is encroachment, absence."[26] Simultaneity is considered, then, not to be a total presence or synthesis. As with movement and rhythm, absence or noncoincidence is operative. Merleau-Ponty cites the following passage of Claudel's:

> At each hour of the Earth, however, all hours exist at once; no matter what the season, all seasons live at once. While the seamstress sees noon on the dial of the Tower of Saint Eustache, the first low rays of the sun pierce the Virginian leaf; squadrons of cachalots frolic under the southern moon. It rains in London, it snows over Pomerania, while Paraguay is all roses, while Melbourne roasts. It seems that whatever exists can never cease existing, and that even time, meant to express existence under its fleeting aspect, implies a permanent, irresistible necessity.[27]

The cohesion of time "under its fleeting aspect" is, for Merleau-Ponty, simultaneity (simultaneity considered here, as we notice from the citing of Virginia, London, Pomerania, and so on, through the differentiation of both time and space). In the course notes, Merleau-Ponty writes, "I am there (past), there (spatial) and here, at each hour are all the hours, each season all the seasons. Not by reference to an essence or idea, but through differentiation in the flesh of Being."[28] And so Claudel's simultaneity is neither atemporal nor aspatial.[29] It is expressed not by the effacement of difference; on the contrary, there could be no cohesion without divergence. It is at the heart of this divergence—at the heart of each hour, each season—that simultaneity emerges. There is a "generating fundamental difference," as Claudel writes.[30] There is an "effective harmony"[31]—a "proportion"[32]—"the composition of an accord."[33] (There is, one could say, a music in Claudel's words.) He offers, "To be is to create. All things living in time listen, concert and compose."[34] Claudel continues:

And thus, Time is not merely the perpetual renewal of days, of months and years; it is the artisan of something real, which grows with every second, the *Past*, that which has once been given life. All things have to exist, in order to cease existing, in order to make room for the subsequent which they call forth. The past is an incantation of things to come, the generating difference they need, the forever growing sum of future conditions.[35]

There is a dynamic sort of simultaneity at work through time—that of the "omnitemporal"[36]—through which the past, as "incantation of things to come," maintains efficacy by reorienting every moment of the present. It is through this depth of time—mythical time—that everything decays and is renewed; it harbors the "generating difference": creativity. "At every breath, the world remains as new as it was at the first gulp of air out of which the first man made his first expiration," writes Claudel.[37]

It is this rhythmicized time, as a cohesion or simultaneity of difference or proliferation, that we hear in the *Prélude*. We feel the vertical depth of the form at moments when the variations and the ABA′ structure are aligned (such as the extraordinarily beautiful passage that begins at m. 55), and we feel it when the noncoincidence between them coheres as a deep silence, so deep that past and future resonate within the realm of the dimensional present. And it is this principle of resonance, finally, that leads one to hear silence through the *Prélude* as much more than mere lack of sound. Silence—as "Σιγή the abyss"—stands at the heart of an upsurge of movement.[38] It is the generative source of form.

Perhaps it is with this sense—this musical sense—after all, that Merleau-Ponty shapes his ontology, as the only way to express his ideas. For, as we saw in chapter 1, in sketching the notes for his final philosophical project, Merleau-Ponty seeks a means of writing from this source of silence. Yet to possess the silence—to force it into explicit speech—would be to betray that silence. "Can this rending characteristic of reflection (which, wishing to return to itself, *leaves itself*) come to an end? There would be needed a silence that envelops the speech anew," he writes in a working note of *The Visible and the Invisible*.[39] "What will this silence be?" And this is where Merleau-Ponty concludes:

> I will finally be able to take a position in ontology, as the introduction [to my book] demands, and specify its theses exactly, only after the series of reductions the book develops and which are all in the first one, but also are really accomplished only in the last one. This reversal itself—*circulus vitiosus deus*—is not hesitation, bad faith and bad dialectic, but return to Σιγή the

abyss.[40] *One cannot make a direct ontology.* My "indirect" method (being in the beings) is alone conformed with being.[41]

Is his "'indirect' method" not akin to the musical form of the *Prélude*? As a "series of reductions"—a series of variations—"which are all in the first one, but also are really accomplished only in the last one"? That would require a philosophy that could perform this silence—"in the same sense of music, that, speaking not at all, says everything."[42] This is what Merleau-Ponty is proposing as "alone conformed with being." With the "reversal" one understands the depth of time as institution, simultaneity, and concordance—not the making of "a direct ontology" but a resonant movement like that of "the string on which the bow starts and ends its play," as Claudel describes.[43] Indeed, in the *Poetic Art* (once again, Merleau-Ponty's source of inspiration), Claudel writes what one could take as a veritable description of the *Prélude* itself:

> May this discourse emerge in silence and on a blank page! Where only this last question remains unanswered: but, after all, the sense and direction, this *sense and direction* of life we call time, what is it? All movement, we have stated, is *from* and not *toward* a point. There starts the trace. This is the point to which clings all life unfolded by time: it is the string on which the bow starts and ends its play. Time is the means offered to all that which will be to be, in order to be no more. It is the *Invitation to Death* extended to each sentence, to decay in the explanatory and total harmony, to consummate the word of adoration, whispered in the ear of *Sigè*, the Abyss.[44]

Synesthesia, Recollection, Resurrection

The invisible is *there* without being an *object*, it is pure transcendence, without an ontic mask.

MERLEAU-PONTY, The Visible and the Invisible

I remember an afternoon in Vienna, springtime, in the Michaelerplatz. A bell begin to ring in a tower above the square and I paused, embraced by the sound as if it were a warm ray of sunlight. A second bell joined—a companion to the first, but lower, deeper, and more sonorous. And as I stood, transfixed by this beauty, I began to sense the materiality of the sound. It streamed out from the tower into a small clutch of sky above the plaza, and there it rested, suspended, having become not only sound but now color—particles of color shimmering like a mist thrown against the sky. The lower bell was dark cobalt, the color of ancient Chinese porcelain. But the first bell shone clearly as gold, the sound sparkling like a fireworks display.

I could not take my eyes off the colors in the sky; I felt myself to be immersed within the waves of the sound and color. And then, to my amazement, I began to hear, above the two tones of the pealing bells, a third tone—not the product of another bell, but a tone instituted through the resonance of the sound waves of the original two. It was a sort of phantom tone, but so clearly audible that, indeed, another color swept across my patch of sky—an emerald green. And the third tone now initiated a remarkable birth of tones; interactions between the original pealing of the two bells and the phantom tone produced another, and another, and another tone, so that one could identify intervals of the octave, the perfect fifth, the major third, the major sixth, the minor seventh, and the major ninth. Each new tone burst into its own color; I could see the shimmering sounds of the acoustic scale as clearly as a rainbow across the sky, but more brilliant and more palpable than any trick of sun and vapor. The colors were magnificent, like sonorous gemstones, and I felt that if I were to extend my arm toward them I might catch a bit of their substance. But I could not move; I felt myself to have become nothing other than a second bell tower—the excess of waves from the tones and colors transposed to an excess of emotion, an ecstatic expression.

After a time, the pealing began to slow and the volume of the bells to diminish, and one by one the phantom tones flickered and disappeared. The colors dissipated and vanished; even the original bell came to stillness and was silent. I became again aware of the street in front of me—of the people passing by in a hurry.

*

I understand the acoustic basis for the phantom tones, although I know that it is rare to hear them so clearly as I did on that afternoon in Vienna. Yet I may never find a satisfactory scientific explanation for the synesthetic dimension of the experience.[1] Those who theorize about synesthesia but have not experienced it may imagine it as a sort of layering or blending of two different sensations: simply a color within a sound.[2] But an additive notion does not suffice in describing the phenomenon; like the experience of depth, in which two different images offer more than a sum of breadth and width—an experience that opens an entirely new dimension—synesthesia is transformative. If one thinks of it simply as the synthesis or blending of two sense perceptions, it is difficult to explain the overwhelming power of emotion that it arouses. And, for me, it is the emotion of the synesthetic experience that serves as a marker of its significance. Synesthesia shows itself to be an inspired moment of Rimbaud: to perceive the phantom tones is to "hear the unheard," and to perceive the shimmering colors is to "see the unseen." There, before the witness of one's senses, is transcendence. How astonishing—how terrible—is this force of transcendence upon the order of one's body, this transgression of the interior and the exterior. As if he were a synesthete himself, Rimbaud writes, "The Poet makes himself into a *seer* by a long, involved and logical *derangement of all the senses*. . . . He arrives at the unknown, and when, bewildered, he ends up losing his understanding of his visions, he has, at least, seen them!"[3]

How can one "arrive at the unknown"? Rimbaud offers the poet as seer.[4] Also for the early Greeks, the poet and the soothsayer worked in association, owing precisely to their complementary roles of looking toward the invisible: the poet looks toward the past, and the soothsayer toward the future.[5] What does the seer see? It could not simply be an image in the ordinary sense—not a visible thing; one could be no closer to or farther from this unknown. What the seer sees must be this: the fact of transcendence. It is, as Merleau-Ponty tells us, "the transcendence of the present [that] makes it precisely able to connect up with a past and a future."[6]

In a working note from *The Visible and the Invisible* entitled "The Invisible, the negative, vertical Being," Merleau-Ponty writes that there is

> a certain relation between the visible and the invisible, where the invisible is not only non-visible[7] (what has been or will be seen and is not seen, or what is seen by an other than me, not by me), but where its absence counts in the world (it is "behind" the visible, imminent or eminent visibility, it is *Urpräsentiert* precisely as *Nichturpräsentierbar*, as another dimension) where the lacuna that marks its place is one of the points of passage of the "world." It is this negative that makes possible the *vertical* world, the union of the incompossibles, the being in transcendence.[8]

To think of "this negative" as the binding together through relationship of that which can in no way coincide is to think of it as a rhythm—"where its absence counts in the world." It is this bond that thematizes the very condition of presentability itself: as holding the sensible together with that which always exceeds what is able to be presented (i.e., "it is *Urpräsentiert* precisely as *Nichturpräsentierbar*, as another dimension"). Therefore, what is important is that this negative makes possible transcendence not only in the realm of space (as with synesthesia, in "seeing" transcendence), but also in that of time, where the past would lie not beyond the boundary of the present but in one sole gesture with the present, as the obverse or unseen side of the present, and therefore as a dimension of the depth of the present. That is to say, the intertwining of the interior and exterior regions of space as well as the past and present moments of time must be thought as the same negative structure—a negative in the sense of the other side of a sculptural relief.

*

One might immediately think here of Proust's *À la recherche du temps perdu*, perhaps not so much because the protagonist, Marcel, searches for "lost time," but because he seeks to understand a transcendent realm of time—a mythical time—where the "past and present are *Ineinander*, each enveloping-enveloped," like obverse sides of a temporal fold.[9] The experience of this depth of time comes to Marcel, unbidden, through the "resurrections"—the sudden swelling of the present through involuntary memory: the taste of a madeleine dipped in tea, for example, which elicits for Marcel a flood of the childhood essence of Combray, or his stumbling over uneven paving stones on the way to the Guermantes' party, which inspires within him a vision of the Venice sky. Marcel claims that these experiences "resurrect" an entire sensation from the past—a past that he had not consciously recalled through memory but that appeared, suddenly, as a vision. It seems to him that the past never ceased to exist but was preserved, somehow intact, within a timeless realm. And this conviction—that of the existence of a timeless realm—leads him to be unafraid of death. Thus, Marcel's first analysis seems to describe, in terms not too distant from the concept of anamnesis (or recollection) in Plato's *Meno* (as we saw in chapter 3), the past as fixed and the soul—the "being within"—as eternal. In a key passage of the *Recherche*, Marcel begins his analysis after he has stumbled upon the uneven paving stones:

> Another inquiry demanded my attention more imperiously, the inquiry, which on previous occasions I had postponed, into the cause of this felicity which I had just experienced, into the character of the certitude with which it imposed itself. And this cause I began to divine as I compared these diverse happy impressions, diverse yet with this in common, that I experienced them at the present moment and at the same time in the context of a distant moment, so that the past was made to encroach upon the present and I was made to doubt whether I was in the one or the other. The truth surely was that the being within me which had enjoyed these impressions had enjoyed them because they had in them something that was common to a day long past and to the present, because in some way they were extra-temporal, and this being made its appearance only when, through one of these identifications of the present with the past, it was likely to find itself in the one and only medium in which it could exist and enjoy the essence of things, that is to say: outside time. This explained why it was that my anxiety on the subject of my death had ceased at the moment when I had unconsciously recognized the taste of the little madeleine, since the being which at that moment I had been was an extra-temporal being and therefore unalarmed by the vicissitudes of the future. This being had only come to me, only manifested itself outside of activity and immediate enjoyment, on those rare occasions when the miracle of an analogy had made me escape from the present. And only this being had the power to perform that task which had always defeated the efforts of my memory and my intellect, the power to make me rediscover days that were long past, the Time that was Lost.[10]

Thus, for Marcel, resurrection seems to depend upon a recovery of the past itself—a past that he had not consciously recalled through memory but that appeared, suddenly, as a frozen image "outside time."[11] By accessing this lost time, he believes himself to have accessed a realm of eternity—the abode of the "being within" that would be the eternal soul.

As we know, Marcel's account can be seen to parallel that of Socrates' description of anamnesis in *Meno*.[12] Yet, once again, the general profile of Proust's Platonism falls apart upon closer inspection. This begins when we attend to Marcel's actual experience of the resurrections. They are not felt as intellectual reconstructions of memory; rather, they elicit an extraordinary feeling of joy—a joy of singular intensity. (A joy that Meno's slave boy, in completing his geometry problem, most decidedly does not share.) In the final book of the *Recherche*, Proust writes of the "resurrection" of Venice:

> The happiness which I had just felt was unquestionably the same as that which I had felt when I tasted the madeleine soaked in tea. But if on that occasion I had put off the task of searching for the profounder causes of my emotion, this time I was determined not to resign myself to a failure to understand them. The emotion was the same; the difference, purely material, lay in the images evoked: a profound azure intoxicated my eyes, impressions of coolness, of dazzling light, swirled round me and in my desire to seize them—as afraid to move as I had been on the earlier occasion when I had continued to savor the taste of the madeleine while I tried to draw into my consciousness whatever it was that it recalled to me—I continued, ignoring the evident amusement of the great crowd of chauffeurs, to stagger as I had staggered a few seconds ago, with one foot on the higher paving-stone and the other on the lower. Every time that I merely repeated this physical movement, I achieved nothing; but if I succeeded, forgetting the Guermantes party, in recapturing what I had felt when I first placed my feet on the ground in this way, again the dazzling and indistinct vision fluttered near me, as if to say: "Seize me as I pass if you can, and try to solve the riddle of happiness which I set you." And almost at once I recognized the vision: it was Venice, of which my efforts to describe it and the supposed snapshots taken by my memory had never told me anything, but which the sensation which I had once experienced as I stood upon two uneven stones in the baptistery of St Mark's had, recurring a moment ago, restored to me complete with all the other sensations linked on that day to that particular sensation, all of which had been waiting in their place—from which with imperious suddenness a chance happening had caused them to emerge—in the series of forgotten days. In the same way the taste of the little madeleine had recalled Combray to me.[13]

The event of this vision—so dazzling and indistinct—does not resonate with Plato's account of anamnesis. In many ways, it resembles the experience of synesthesia. Before Marcel as well as before the synesthete, what shines forth in this vision is Rimbaud's "unknown," something that could not be of the visible world; what shines forth is an evocation through sensible appearance of what could never serve as an object of vision in the ordinary sense. For one could say (with Merleau-Ponty) that when I stood in Vienna, captivated by the phantom tones and the appearance of the colors, "The invisible [was] *there* without being an *object*, it [was] pure transcendence."[14] And was this not also the case for Marcel when, stumbling over uneven paving stones, he suddenly saw the blue sky of Venice appearing above him? For he does not simply imagine a scene of Venice as reconstructed from his memory; he does not think it through, like Meno's slave who works on his geometry problem. Rather, he is captivated by what seems to be an external vision: "a profound azure intoxicated my eyes, impressions of coolness, of dazzling light, swirled round me."[15] He senses—with all the intensity and vitality that such an experience brings to us—the appearance of transcendence. He does not calculate it internally, like the slave boy, but sees it before him. How strange and how powerful, this "derangement of the senses"! The vision of Venice seems so real to Marcel that he would like to "seize" it—in much the same way that I wished to reach out toward the colors in Vienna and grasp them in my hand. Likewise, both synesthesia and resurrection are triggered not through an effort of consciousness, but as a response to a sensory stimulus: for me, through the ringing of the bells, and for Marcel, through the taste of the madeleine and the feeling of the uneven paving stones. Thus, the space of these visions—whether resurrection or synesthesia—is not that of interior image or visualization; they could in no way be confused with internal representations of the mind, for they offer the palpable materiality of the exterior world. They proceed not simply from the inside of the subject as an ordinary memory or recollection would; yet neither are they completely external to the subject, for their sensibility belongs to the subject alone. The inside and the outside intertwine, and this intertwining—as the sensing of an invisible that comes through the visible—gives rise to the emotion, to the wonderment.[16] Proust describes this as "a sudden shudder of happiness"—"a state of ecstasy . . . the only genuine and fruitful pleasure that I had known."[17] The intensity of this ecstatic joy exceeds that which might be evoked by ordinary sensory or imaginative experience. It is the ecstasy of the seer—perhaps, of the saint; for Marcel, it is so powerful "that the word 'death' should have no meaning for him."[18] It bestows a measure of certainty, of vitality, upon his existence. Yet this joy is rooted in the most trivial and ordinary of moments: the taste of a simple cake dipped in tea, the loss of one's balance on a stepping-stone, the ringing of a bell. And so just as I have long asked myself about the significance of synesthesia, Proust wonders, "But why had the images of Combray and of Venice, at these two different moments, given me a joy which was like a certainty and which sufficed, without any other proof, to make death a matter of indifference to me?"[19]

Indeed, if synesthesia and the resurrections are, at root, parallel experiences, then what is interesting is that my sensation of the colors in Vienna, unlike Marcel's sensation of the blue sky of Venice, was not linked to involuntary memory. Thus, the joy that so marked both experiences could not have flowed from a possession of "lost time"—not from recovery of the images of memory that preserve the past as an object for contemplation, like anamnesis. We must not turn to ordinary accounts of recollection—of the past *as past*—for the key to this experience. Proust himself questions the centrality of the past in the resurrections: "A moment of the past, did I say? Was it not perhaps very much more: something that, common both to the past and to the present, is much more essential than either of them?"[20] We must, therefore, turn to that which is "very much more" than what would be grasped within the past or present alone. In this way, looking for what is "outside time" does not reveal an eternal and frozen image of the past (as in the Platonic notion of anamnesis); it discloses the relation—the rhythm—that is "common . . . to [the sensations of] the past and of the present."[21] It is not the *past* that inspires within Marcel a feeling of joy—it is the *rhythm* of the past and present. This rhythm—as a binding relation—is not contingent on the particular sensual content of his experience, as if the madeleine were itself imbued with a magical power. Rhythm is not derived from a particular external object through the operation of the senses, nor from an interior image of the past, through recollection or imagination; it is not the object or subject that constitutes rhythm. Rather, rhythm is a structure that binds the past and present, subject and object, ideal and sensible; it holds together the "inside of the outside and the outside of the inside," through which a common vision arises as expression.[22]

At the heart of rhythm, as we know, is silence—the unheard—transcendence. Yet we must understand how this transcendence is neither far away from nor above the sensible, but works according to a membrane—a fold. "Against the doctrine of contradiction, absolute negation, the *either or*—," writes Merleau-Ponty, "Transcendence is identity within difference."[23] Transcendence acts at the very point at which difference holds through—as the interior of rhythm. It is a negativity, a fold, a silence that is operative: transcendence is an "absence [that] counts in the world."[24] It is not outside of the world. Merleau-Ponty writes that it is "not invisible in the sense of the absolute negation (or of the absolute positivity of the 'intelligible world'), but in the sense of the *other dimensionality*, as depth hollows itself out behind height and breadth, as time hollows itself out behind space."[25] Transcendence comes forth as resonance, reverberation, resurrection. It serves as the center of a dynamic unfolding through which there is not return to what was *before* (i.e., recollection); instead, a luminosity is born through which the world is held together and sustained from behind. What is essential to rhythm is this radiance—this institution of transcendence—in the movement of expression.

What then, of the power of the resurrections? Marcel had speculated that his joy was inspired by the isolation of an essence "outside time." For him, it seemed to be a joy born of the presentiment of eternity—of defeating death. Proust writes, "A minute freed from the order of time has re-created in us, to feel it, the man freed from the order of time. And one can understand that this man should have confidence in his joy, even if the simple taste of a madeleine does not seem logically to contain within it the reasons for this joy, one can understand that the word 'death' should have no meaning for him; situated outside time, why should he fear the future?"[26] What then, do we make of this joy when it is clear that what Marcel grasped through the resurrections was not a moment of the eternal past, but transcendence at the heart of rhythm?

It is not possession of the eternal that inspires the joy, but attunement with the rhythm of Being. Indeed, how could we mistake this emotion for the mere afterglow of consciousness in contemplation of the eternal idea? Surely, in synesthesia and in the resurrections, it is not the case that first we understand ourselves to have outmaneuvered finitude and only then feel glorious joy at having cheated death. Rather, one simply and immediately feels. At the steps of the Guermantes' courtyard, Marcel is awestruck. At the moment of the resurrection, it is not that he would be so removed from the sensible so as finally to grasp an eternal essence. At the moment of the resurrection, his being is disclosed as rhythm: his soul is felt in its essential movement—a movement of regeneration; his being lives as that which is born again and again.[27] How terrible and incredible is this feeling. It is only as rupture and rebirth—only through the upheaval of an opening—that such ecstasy comes forth. It is not recovery or possession, nor closure or finality. Through the resurrection, an external vision (of Venice) performs a rhythm of the present and the past in relation—performs their noncoincidence—and at the fold between Marcel's external vision and his internal memory, Being enacts being.

Is this not also the case with synesthesia? For what is certain now is that the resurrections do not in any way rely upon recovery of a fixed or "eternal" past. Proust himself makes this clear when he compares the joy of the resurrections to experiences that (like synesthesia) do not make use of memory: the twin steeples of Martinville, the sight of trees near Balbec, and the musical works of Vinteuil. These offer, for Marcel, the "same happiness" as the madeleine dipped in tea or the vision of Venice on the stepping-stones.[28] They are similar to the resurrections, "except that they concealed within them not a sensation dating from an earlier time, but a new truth."[29] They do not depend upon involuntary memory; they dispel any need to posit a realm of eternal image or idea. Here, rhythm arises through relation not to the past but to a "new truth": here we catch most explicitly the work of transcendence in the movement of expression.

Of the vision of the twin steeples of Martinville (and the third of Vieux-vicq) that inspires him as a young boy, the narrator relates: "In noticing and registering the shape of their spires, their shifting lines, the sunny warmth of their surfaces, I felt that I was not penetrating to the core of my impression, that something more lay behind that mobility, that luminosity, something which they seemed at once to contain and to conceal."[30] This "something more" that lies behind movement ("mobility") and "luminosity" is transcendence, that which is contained and concealed at the fold of being—at the chiasm. One does not grasp or possess this "something more"; one participates, performs, and brings it to expression. Marcel's intimation of the existence of "something more"—as the resonance of Being upon being—is this call to expression. Marcel is filled as if with a fire for the sight of these spires. Their luminosity pierces his senses such that they must be worked through him; as with synesthesia and as with the resurrections, the exterior and interior must be brought into play. It is just this participation in the relation—the rhythm—between the sensible and a "new truth" that is accomplished through the creation of art. Marcel, the young boy, begins to write; it is the first time that he realizes the possibility of his literary vocation. This initial attempt, for Marcel, is necessarily awkward and insufficient. He writes what amounts to only a fragment: "without admitting to myself that what lay hidden behind the steeples of Martinville must be something analogous to a pretty phrase, since it was in the form of words which gave me pleasure that it had appeared to me."[31] Only much later in life—only as narrator—is Marcel able to achieve an expression adequate to his vision. Even in this relationship (that between Marcel as a young writer and Marcel as the narrator) there is always the necessity of a double movement—a reinitiation—that would be in harmony with the nature of expression itself. As Merleau-Ponty writes, "The phenomenon of expression [is that] which gathers itself up and launches itself again."[32] Expression is instituted as the rhythm of Being.

This movement—dynamic and generative—is the reason for Marcel's conviction (much later in the novel) that music, above all, gives voice to the "quintessential character" of experiences such as the resurrections and the steeples of Martinville.[33] Marcel claims, "Nothing resembled more closely than some such phrase of Vinteuil the peculiar pleasure which I had felt at certain moments in my life, when gazing, for instance, at the steeples of Martinville, or at certain trees along a road near Balbec, or, more simply, at the beginning of this book, when I tasted a certain cup of tea."[34] Music expresses this pleasure most directly because music offers rhythm; in music, as we have seen Proust claim, "the sounds seem to follow the very movement of our being."[35] In music there is not representation or repetition, but resonance with Being. Being enacts being. We experience an increase in amplitude; we feel a singular joy. It is for this reason that music, above all, prompts Marcel to recognize the call to expression—the call to become, in effect, the narrator. But, as we have seen, the musical in this sense (that is to say, the rhythmic) does not solely belong to the domain of music; rhythm lies at the origin of all art—for the poet Mallarmé as for the painter Cézanne and the writer Proust.

⋆

If, for Merleau-Ponty, art as expression aims at ontology—at elucidating the structure of being which is itself expression—what remains for philosophy? For what we are pursuing is the depth of being: what we are after is the transformation—as with synesthesia, as with the resurrections—instituted through the rhythm of being. Proust writes, "As for the truths which the intellectual faculty—even that of the greatest minds—gathers in the open, the truths that lie in its path in full daylight, their value may be very great, but they are like drawings with a hard outline and no perspective; they have no depth because no depths have had to be traversed in order to reach them, because they have not been re-created."[36] Thus re-creation now becomes the task of philosophy. For if we are to disclose an ontology through depth and rhythm, it would have to be not grasped, but performed. How? We might, with Proust, ask, could it only be through "the creation of a work of art?"[37] For it is art that provides resonance for life.

But does not philosophy, too, participate in the call to re-creation? Philosophy, that is, not as the history of philosophy but as the work—the setting forth—of philosophy?[38] Merleau-Ponty writes, "The meaning of philosophy is the meaning of a genesis. Consequently, it could not possibly be summed up outside of time, and it is still expression."[39] It is reengagement of texts, returning to ideas, rethinking through the movement of expression itself—an expression that could never be finished. Here philosophy participates in what Merleau-Ponty sets as its true task: "the expression of what is before expression *and sustains it from behind*."[40] This work of philosophy must ever be taken up again, opened through the rhythm of thought. In this way we learn from Merleau-Ponty. "For art and philosophy *together*," he writes, "are precisely not arbitrary fabrications in the universe of the 'spiritual' (of 'culture'), but contact with Being precisely as creations. Being is *what requires creation of us* for us to experience it."[41]

Notes

Chapter One

1. Cf. Kearney, who argues that the project of phenomenology calls for precisely this kind of language. He writes, for example, "Phenomenology thus marks the surpassing of traditional dualisms between body and mind, real and ideal, subject and object. Unable to express this new model of existence in traditional philosophical language, phenomenology eclipses dualism specifically by adopting the *religious* language of the Eucharist and communion," pointing to several passages from Merleau-Ponty's work (and that of Proust, as well). See Richard Kearney, "Merleau-Ponty and the Sacramentality of the Flesh," in *Merleau-Ponty at the Limits of Art, Religion, and Perception*, ed. Kascha Semonovitch and Neal DeRoo (London: Continuum International Publishing Group, 2010), 151 (emphasis in original).

2. Maurice Merleau-Ponty, *The Visible and the Invisible*, trans. Alphonso Lingis (Evanston, IL: Northwestern University Press, 1968). Originally published as *Le visible et l'invisible*, ed. Claude Lefort (Paris: Éditions Gallimard, 1964). Hereafter cited as *Visible and Invisible*, with pagination of the English translation followed by that of the French original.

3. "The ultimate truth": these are the final words of the chapter "The Intertwining: The Chiasm." Ibid., 155/201.

4. Of particular importance are the notes on the course that Merleau-Ponty was offering at the time of his death, "L'ontologie cartésienne et l'ontologie d'aujourd'hui," in Maurice Merleau-Ponty, *Notes de cours au Collège de France, 1958–1959 et 1960–1961*, ed. Stéphanie Ménasé (Paris: Éditions Gallimard, 1996). Hereafter cited as *Notes de cours*. The precedent for the remarkable chapter in *The Visible and the Invisible* entitled "The Chiasm" is to be found largely in the section called "Le visible et l'invisible: Proust," 191–98.

5. Merleau-Ponty, *Visible and Invisible*, 102/137.

6. In "Cézanne's Doubt," Merleau-Ponty writes of the impressionists' technique: "The color of objects could not be represented simply by putting on the canvas their local tone, that is, the color they take on isolated from their surroundings; one also had to pay attention to the phenomena of contrast which modify local colors in nature. Furthermore, by a sort of reversal, every color we perceive in nature elicits the appearance of its complement; and these complementaries heighten one another. To achieve sunlit colors in a picture which will be seen in the dim light of apartments, not only must there be a green—if you are painting grass—but also the complementary red which will make it vibrate." Maurice Merleau-Ponty, "Cézanne's Doubt,"

in *The Merleau-Ponty Aesthetics Reader: Philosophy and Painting*, ed. Galen A. Johnson, trans. ed. Michael B. Smith (Evanston, IL: Northwestern University Press, 1993), 61–62. Originally published as "Le doute de Cézanne," in *Sens et non-sens* (Paris: Nagel, 1948), 16. Hereafter cited as "Cézanne's Doubt," with pagination of the English translation followed by that of the French original.

7. Merleau-Ponty, *Visible and Invisible*, 102/137.

8. Maurice Merleau-Ponty, "Resumé of the Course: Husserl at the Limits of Phenomenology," in *Husserl at the Limits of Phenomenology*, rev. trans. Leonard Lawlor (Evanston, IL: Northwestern University Press, 2002), 5. Originally published as "Husserl aux limites de la phénoménologie," in *Résumés de cours: Collège de France, 1952–1960* (Paris: Éditions Gallimard, 1968), 159–60. Hereafter cited as "Resumé Course: Husserl," with the pagination of the English translation followed by that of the French original.

9. Merleau-Ponty, "Resumé Course: Husserl," 5/159.

10. Merleau-Ponty, *Visible and Invisible*, 167/219 (emphasis in original).

11. Maurice Merleau-Ponty, *Husserl at the Limits of Phenomenology*, trans. Leonard Lawlor (Evanston, IL: Northwestern University Press, 2002), 12 (emphasis in original). Originally published as *Notes de cours sur "L'origine de la géométrie" de Husserl, suivi de recherches sur la phénoménologie de Merleau-Ponty*, ed. Franck Robert (Paris: Presses Universitaires de France, 1998), 13 (emphasis in original). Hereafter cited as *Husserl at Limits*, with pagination of the English translation followed by that of the French original.

12. Merleau-Ponty, "Resumé Course: Husserl," 5/160.

13. "But in fact I should say that there was a thing perceived and an openness upon this thing which the reflection has neutralized and transformed into perception-reflected-on and thing-perceived-within-a-perception-reflected-on." Merleau-Ponty, *Visible and Invisible*, 38/59.

14. Ibid.

15. Ibid.

16. Ibid., 38/60.

17. Ibid., 35–36/56.

18. Ibid., 38/59–60. Cf. Lawlor: "Below reflection, and as the origin of reflection, is spontaneous self- or auto-experience. For Merleau-Ponty, auto-experience takes place in the sensible itself, or, as Heidegger would say, in Being itself. More importantly, Merleau-Ponty transforms auto-affection into hetero-affection. Auto-experience is never self-adequate; it always contains latency and invisibility." Leonard Lawlor, *Early Twentieth-Century Continental Philosophy* (Bloomington: Indiana University Press, 2012), 142.

19. Merleau-Ponty, *Visible and Invisible*, 90/121.

20. Ibid., 90/122.

21. Ibid.

22. Ibid., 93/126.

23. Ibid., 94/127.

24. Ibid., 129/169.

25. Ibid., 39/60 (emphasis in original).

26. Ibid., 125/164.

27. Indeed, Merleau-Ponty explicitly connects the problem of reflective thought (as the conflation of brute perception with conscious reflection) with the poetic task of recovering the noncoincidence and bringing it to expression: "To criticize the 'little man inside the man'—perception as cognition of an ob-ject—to rediscover man finally face to face with the world *itself*, to rediscover the pre-intentional present—is to rediscover that vision of the origins, which sees itself within us, as poetry rediscovers what articulates itself within us, unbeknown to us (Max

Ernst in Charbonnier's book)." Ibid., 208/258 (emphasis in original). The editor provides the passage from Georges Charbonnier's *Le monologue du peintre I* (Paris, 1959), 34: "Just as, ever since the celebrated Letter of the Seer, the poet's role consists in writing under the dictation of what thinks itself, what articulates itself within him, the painter's role is to circumscribe and to project forth what sees itself within him." The reference is to the poet Rimbaud. An excerpt from Rimbaud's "Letter to Paul Demeny" reads: "For I is someone else. If the brass awakes as horn, it can't be to blame. This much is clear: I'm around for the hatching of my thought: I watch it, I listen to it: I release a strike from the bow: the symphony makes its rumblings in the depths, or leaps fully-formed onto the stage." Arthur Rimbaud, *Complete Works*, trans. Wyatt Mason (New York: Modern Library, 2003), 366. Merleau-Ponty mentions the connection again in the final course that he was presenting at the time of his death, "L'ontologie cartésienne et l'ontologie d'aujourd'hui," in Merleau-Ponty, *Notes de cours*, 186.

28. Merleau-Ponty, *Husserl at Limits*, 12–13/13. It should be noted that here Merleau-Ponty is speaking of Husserl's work: "His thought [of] the thing itself is not published, because his thought was aiming at making silence speak." Ibid., 12/13. Once again it is important to state that Merleau-Ponty's treatment of Husserl can be taken as a paradigm for the way in which we, ourselves, must think through the work of Merleau-Ponty.

29. Maurice Merleau-Ponty, "Indirect Language and the Voices of Silence," in *The Merleau-Ponty Aesthetics Reader: Philosophy and Painting*, ed. Galen A. Johnson, trans. ed. Michael B. Smith (Evanston, IL: Northwestern University Press, 1993), 82. Originally published as "Le langage indirect et les voix du silence," in *Signes* (Paris: Éditions Gallimard, 1960), 72. Hereafter cited as "Indirect Language," with pagination of the English translation followed by that of the French original.

30. Stéphane Mallarmé, "Crisis of Verse," in *Divagations*, trans. Barbara Johnson (Cambridge, MA: Belknap Press, 2007), 210–11. Originally published as "Crise de vers," in *Oeuvres complètes, II*, ed. Bertrand Marchal (Paris: Éditions Gallimard, 2003), 213. Hereafter cited as "Crisis of Verse," with pagination of the English translation followed by that of the French original. The poet writes:

> Je dis: une fleur! et, hors de l'oubli où ma voix relègue aucun contour, en tant que quelque chose d'autre que les calices sus, musicalement se lève, idée même et suave, l'absente de tous bouquets.
>
> Au contraire d'une fonction de numéraire facile et représentatif, comme le traite d'abord la foule, le dire, avant tout, rêve et chant, retrouve chez le Poëte, par nécessité constitutive d'un art consacré aux fictions, sa virtualité.

31. In *Signs* Merleau-Ponty writes, linking Mallarmé with Rimbaud: "As different as the ventures of Rimbaud and Mallarmé may well have been, they had this much in common: they freed language from the control of 'obvious facts' and trusted it to invent and win new relationships of meaning. Thus language ceased to be (if it ever has been) simply a tool or means the writer uses to communicate intentions given independently of language." He continues: "From now on there is no other way to comprehend language than to dwell in it and use it. As a professional of language, the writer is a professional of insecurity. His expressive operation is renewed from *oeuvre* to *oeuvre*. Each work, as it has been said of the painter, is a step constructed by the writer himself upon which he installs himself in order to construct (with the same risk) another step and what is called the *oeuvre*—the sequence of these attempts—which is always broken off, whether it be by the end of life or through the exhaustion of his speaking power." This "expressive operation" is what Merleau-Ponty will term, in his later works, the process of

institution. See chapter 5. Maurice Merleau-Ponty, *Signs*, trans. Richard McCleary (Evanston, IL: Northwestern University Press, 1964), 232–33. Originally published as *Signes* (Paris: Éditions Gallimard, 1960), 379. Hereafter cited as *Signs*, with pagination of the English translation followed by that of the French original.

32. Mallarmé, "Crisis of Verse," 205/208.

33. Ibid.

34. See, for example, the work of Diana Deutsch, professor of psychology at the University of California, San Diego. Of particular interest is the paper "The Speech-to-Song Illusion," accessible on her faculty webpage at http://deutsch.ucsd.edu/psychology/pages.php?i=101.

35. These are the opening words of the *Iliad*. Richmond Lattimore, trans., *The Iliad of Homer* (Chicago: University of Chicago Press, 1961), 59.

36. Cf. Derrida: "The sonorous source attempts to rejoin itself only by differentiating itself, dividing, differing, deferring without end. . . . Valéry, as we will verify in an instant, did describe this movement which goes back to the source and which separates from the source or simultaneously interdicts the source. . . . The source therefore is not the origin, it is neither at the departure or the arrival. Valéry marks in speech both the circle of hearing-oneself-speak, the lure of the source rejoined, and the law which makes such a return to itself an effect." Jacques Derrida, *Margins of Philosophy*, trans. Alan Bass (Chicago: University of Chicago Press, 1982), 287. Compare this movement not only to rhythm (below), but also to institution (chapter 5).

37. Letter to Edmund Grosse, January 10, 1893. Elizabeth McCombie, *Mallarmé and Debussy: Unheard Music, Unseen Text* (Oxford: Oxford University Press, 2003), 24.

38. The example provided here, of two noncoincident articulations, is perhaps the most obvious illustration of the retroactive dynamism of rhythm, but the argument applies equally to a single, sustained pitch insofar as we understand the duration of that pitch with respect to the noncoincidence of past and present. The work of rhythm behind the sound (here understood as a temporal relation and not as an implied metrical pulse or measured beat) is indeed, I would argue, what makes a single note expressive, like the resonant call of an alpenhorn.

39. Merleau-Ponty, *Visible and Invisible*, 125/164.

40. Maurice Merleau-Ponty, *The World of Perception*, trans. Oliver Davis (London: Routledge Classics, 2008), 75. Originally published as *Causeries, 1948*, ed. Stéphanie Ménasé (Paris: Éditions du Seuil, 2002), 59. Hereafter cited as *World of Perception*, with pagination of the English translation followed by that of the French original.

41. In "The Mystery in Letters," Mallarmé describes this magical work of language: "Words, all by themselves, light each other up on the sides that are known as the rarest or meaningful only for the spirit, the center of vibratory suspense; whoever perceives them independent of the usual context, projected onto cave walls so long as their mobility or principle lasts, being what is not said in speech: all eager, before they are extinguished, to exchange a reciprocity of flames, or presented obliquely as a contingency." At the conclusion of this essay, Mallarmé articulates the "Mystery in Music" that underlies poetic creation: "The melody beneath the text, conducting divination from here to there, applies its invisible floral or lamp-bottomed ornament to mark the end." Stéphane Mallarmé, "The Mystery in Letters," in *Divagations*, trans. Barbara Johnson (Cambridge, MA: Belknap Press of Harvard University Press, 2007), 234–36. Originally published as "Le mystère dans les lettres," in *Oeuvres complètes, II*, ed. Bertrand Marchal (Paris: Éditions Gallimard, 2003), 233–34. The poet writes: "Les mots, d'eux-mêmes, s'exaltent à mainte facette reconnue la plus rare ou valant pour l'esprit, centre de suspens vibratoire; qui les perçoit indépendamment de la suite ordinaire, projetés, en parois de grotte, tant que dure leur mobilité ou principe, étant ce qui ne se dit pas du discours: prompts tous, avant extinction, à une réci-

procité de feux distante ou présentée de biais comme contingence." And he concludes: "L'air ou chant sous le texte, conduisant la divination d'ici là, y applique con motif en fleuron et cul-de-lampe invisibles." This "melody beneath the text" resonates with Merleau-Ponty's course notes to "L'ontologie cartésienne et l'ontologie d'aujourd'hui," where he writes, "In the musical idea, one has an idea that is not *this that* we see, but behind it." Merleau-Ponty, *Notes de cours*, 196 (emphasis in original; my translation). See also the discussion of the musical idea in chapter 8.

42. In "Presenting the Unpresentable: The Metaphor in Merleau-Ponty's Last Writings," Vanzago writes that "a good metaphor is not good because it gives an object a new, unexpected name, but because it lets something *different* become visible. Metaphors, accordingly, are instruments of vision, in the sense that they allow one to see differently. They institute new relations, bring to light what was concealed. This is not simply to embellish the expression of what can otherwise be said more ordinarily. This means that what is visible depends on the relations that are instituted, and this in turn means that the institution of a new relation corresponds to the institution of a new entity." Luca Vanzago, "Presenting the Unpresentable: The Metaphor in Merleau-Ponty's Last Writings," *Southern Journal of Philosophy* 43 (2005): 467–68 (emphasis in original). Yet, more than "instruments of vision," metaphors arise as reverberations or rhythms (through the "center of vibratory suspense," as Mallarmé has said), for it is in this sense that we can say that they bring to presence that which is absent: "something other than the known . . . arises, *musically* . . . in other words, what is absent from every bouquet." Mallarmé, "Crisis of Verse," 210/213 (emphasis added).

43. Merleau-Ponty, "Indirect Language," 79/68.

44. McCombie, *Mallarmé and Debussy*, 24.

45. Stéphane Mallarmé, "Un coup de dés," in *Collected Poems*, trans. Henry Weinfield (Berkeley and Los Angeles: University of California Press, 1994), 122. In *Oeuvres complètes*, ed. Henri Mondor and G. Jean-Aubry (Paris: Éditions Gallimard, 1945), 455. Hereafter cited as "Un coup de dés," with pagination of the English translation followed by that of the French original.

46. Ibid., 121/455. The poet writes: "Les 'blancs' en effet, assument l'importance, frappent d'abord; la versification en exigea, comme silence alentour, ordinairement, au point qu'un morceau, lyrique ou de peu de pieds, occupe, au milieu, le tiers environ du feuillet: je ne transgresse cette mesure, seulement la disperse." For an extraordinary reading of Mallarmé, see Jacques Derrida, "The Double Session," in *Dissemination*, trans. Barbara Johnson (Chicago: University of Chicago Press, 1981), 173–286.

47. Merleau-Ponty, "Indirect Language," 80/70 (emphasis in original).

48. Merleau-Ponty, *World of Perception*, 75/59–60. A few lines later, Merleau-Ponty applies this analysis to modern literature, emphasizing the significance of movement, temporality, and rhythm: "And some of today's authors, such as Maurice Blanchot, have been asking themselves whether what Mallarmé said of poetry should not be extended to the novel and literature in general: a successful novel would thus consist not of a succession of ideas or theses but would have the same kind of existence as an object of the senses or a thing *in motion*, which must be perceived *in its temporal progression by embracing its particular rhythm*." Merleau-Ponty, *World of Perception*, 75–76/60–61 (emphases added).

49. Merleau-Ponty, *Visible and Invisible*, 153/198.

50. Merleau-Ponty's note, referring specifically to the poet Valéry, reads:

Is that still "philosophy"? Is drawing near to speech, speaking, seeing, thinking presently, rediscovering speech, vision, thoughts which are vertical (= abyssal) a "mysticism" without God (Monsieur Teste)? Coincidence?

No: it is not extraphilosophical, coincidence with an unsayable, an external ineffable. All of speculation is necessary in order to discover a sense for this prespeculative
Being.

But what we will say about it? Everything that we will say *about it* will be in principle
false. Silence?

There would really be indirect language. The one which would not try to objectify
the *Gesagte* ['the said'], but which gives it through gestures = poetry—And we could
generalize: history, life, Passions.

But then ['philosophy'] *replaced* by art, poetry, life? No, because they speak only
silently. ['Philosophy'] as the thematization of this speaking silence.

Merleau-Ponty, *Husserl at Limits*, 49/60 (emphases in original).

51. Merleau-Ponty, *Visible and Invisible*, 179/231 (emphasis in original). Σιγή translates as
"silence." The reference here is to Paul Claudel's *Poetic Art*, a work that will be more fully taken
up in chapter 9.

52. Mallarmé, "Crisis of Verse," 210/212.

Chapter Two

1. Maurice Merleau-Ponty, "Eye and Mind," in *The Merleau-Ponty Aesthetics Reader: Philosophy and Painting*, ed. Galen A. Johnson, trans. ed. Michael B. Smith (Evanston, IL: Northwestern University Press, 1993). Originally published as *L'oeil et l'esprit* (Paris: Éditions Gallimard,
1964). Hereafter cited as "Eye and Mind," with pagination of the English translation followed
by that of the French original.

2. For a subtle reading of Merleau-Ponty's relation to Descartes, see the chapter "Dwelling
in the Texture of the Visible: Merleau-Ponty's 'Eye and Mind' (1961)" in Lawlor, *Early Twentieth-
Century Continental Philosophy*, 141–73.

3. Merleau-Ponty, *Visible and Invisible*, 37/58.

4. Merleau-Ponty, "Eye and Mind," 134/47 (emphasis in original).

5. Maurice Merleau-Ponty, *Phenomenology of Perception*, trans. Colin Smith (London: Routledge & Kegan Paul, 1962), 297. Originally published as *Phénoménologie de la perception* (Paris:
Éditions Gallimard, 1945), 303. Hereafter cited as *Phenomenology of Perception*, with pagination
of the English translation followed by that of the French original. Merleau-Ponty's analysis is
made in reference to Berkeley.

6. Merleau-Ponty, *Visible and Invisible*, 113/150.

7. Merleau-Ponty, "Indirect Language," 87/81.

8. Ibid., 87/80.

9. Ibid., 87/81.

10. Merleau-Ponty, *World of Perception*, 40/20.

11. Merleau-Ponty, "Eye and Mind," 134/47.

12. Merleau-Ponty, *Phenomenology of Perception*, 310/316.

13. Ibid.

14. Ibid., 298/305.

15. Merleau-Ponty, "Eye and Mind," 140/64.

16. Ibid., 140/65 (emphasis in original).

17. Merleau-Ponty, *Visible and Invisible*, 35/56. Cf. chapter 1.

18. Merleau-Ponty, "Eye and Mind," 140/64–65.

19. Merleau-Ponty, *Visible and Invisible*, 219/268.

20. See also *Still Life with Fruit Basket*. Besides exhibiting a distortion of the breadth of the table, this painting also articulates different points of view by means of subtle shifts in aspects of the ginger jar and basket. An analysis is provided in Erle Loran, *Cézanne's Composition: Analysis of His Form with Diagrams and Photographs of His Motifs* (Berkeley and Los Angeles: University of California Press, 2006), 76–77.

21. Loran's investigation of this technique, a technique which was certainly of great consequence for the cubists, extends from the still life to landscape and is founded upon photographs that he took while traveling across Provence in search of Cézanne's views. Indeed, the comparisons between the photographs and the paintings are remarkable. In reference to *The Bibémus Quarry* (c. 1895) for example, Loran shows how Cézanne dramatically shifted points of view within his painting in order to expose certain rock configurations. But it would perhaps be misleading to draw the conclusion from Loran that the use of different points of view was Cézanne's most significant contribution to modern painting. In a very real sense, even Renaissance painters worked from different points of view within the same painting, for although the vanishing point served as a central structure of organization in the work, the physical limitations of the eye had still to be overcome: the inability of the eye to perceive images at the limits of vision with the same clarity as images within the center of vision meant that the painter, when portraying the outer regions of a canvas, would necessarily have been forced to shift his or her focus. Therefore one could make the claim that a Renaissance painting brings together on one canvas an artistic synthesis of different points of view. And thus the innovative nature of Cézanne's work cannot be reduced to this simple formula. As Merleau-Ponty writes, the enigma of depth is not the juxtaposition of these different points of view: "The enigma . . . lies in *their bond*, in what is *between* them." Merleau-Ponty, "Eye and Mind," 140/64 (emphasis added).

22. Merleau-Ponty, *World of Perception*, 41/21–22.

23. Merleau-Ponty, "Eye and Mind," 138/58–59.

24. In *Innovation and Visualization: Trajectories, Strategies, and Myths*, Amy Ione gives an account of the invention and significance of Wheatstone's stereoscope: "The instrument [was] designed to show that our two eyes merge the two slightly different images we perceive into a singular form. Wheatstone was able to convey the fusion accurately because the stereoscope's design was based on measurable distances between our eyes. This means the instrument was able to clearly accommodate for the fact that we normally converge two perceptions when we see, although we think we see one image with both of our eyes. The noteworthy feature . . . was the instrument's capacity to convincingly demonstrate how the two slightly different images formed on the retina of each eye are due to each eye's different position in space. More concisely, since Wheatstone's demonstration produced what appeared to be a 3-dimensional form to the viewer, he was able to experientially convey that the fused result we see is neither a flat image nor an exact counterpart of a physical object as the object is extended into space. . . . Instead, two slightly different visual experiences are merged to appear as a whole and the singular whole has a quality that differs from the perspectival depth of a singular form drawn on a flat surface. . . . [This] demonstrated that the way we perceive the world does not correspond to the kind of one point linear perspective artists have presented since the Renaissance. (In Renaissance perspective the sense of depth is technically created using vanishing points that are constructed using a one-eyed or monocular vantage point.)" Amy Ione, *Innovation and Visualization: Trajectories, Strategies, and Myths* (Amsterdam: Editions Rodopi, 2005), 110–11. It should be noted that the stereoscope forms a common trope in Proust's *Recherche*. See chapter 3.

25. Merleau-Ponty, *Phenomenology of Perception*, 270/279.

26. Merleau-Ponty, *Visible and Invisible*, 7/22.

27. Ibid., 135/176.

28. Merleau-Ponty writes: "The unity of binocular vision, and with it the depth without which it cannot come about is, therefore, there from the very moment at which the monocular images are presented as 'disparate.' When I look in the stereoscope, a totality presents itself in which already the possible order takes shape and the situation is foreshadowed. My motor response takes up this situation. Cézanne said that the painter in the face of his 'motif' is about 'to join the aimless hands of nature.' The act of focusing at the stereoscope is equally a response to the question put by the data, and this response is contained in the question." Merleau-Ponty, *Phenomenology of Perception*, 305/311.

29. Merleau-Ponty, *Visible and Invisible*, 135/176.

30. Merleau-Ponty, *Phenomenology of Perception*, 298/305.

31. Merleau-Ponty, *Visible and Invisible*, 123/162.

32. Ibid., 133–34/174.

33. Ibid., 133/174.

34. Ibid., 113–14/150–51.

35. Merleau-Ponty, "Eye and Mind," 129/31.

36. Ibid., 125/22.

37. Ibid., 129/31–32.

38. Merleau-Ponty, *Visible and Invisible*, 136/177. Remarking upon this passage from Merleau-Ponty, Françoise Dastur writes, "If in fact the body is indeed an *exemplar sensible*, it is because this separation between the within and the without which thus creates a being with two dimensions, with two leaves, with two lips, constitutes its 'natal secret.' This secret is the secret of the genesis of all being, which is none other than the general movement of the segregation of within and without." Françoise Dastur, "Thinking from Within," in *Merleau-Ponty in Contemporary Perspectives*, ed. Patrick Burke and Jan Van der Veken (Dordrecht: Kluwer Academic, 1993), 31.

39. Maurice Merleau-Ponty, *Themes from the Lectures at the Collège de France, 1952–1960*, trans. John O'Neill (Evanston, IL: Northwestern University Press, 1970), 91. Originally published as *Résumés de cours: Collège de France, 1952–1960* (Paris: Éditions Gallimard, 1968), 128. Hereafter cited as *Themes from Lectures*, with pagination of the English translation followed by that of the French original.

40. Merleau-Ponty, *Signs*, 166–67/271.

Chapter Three

1. Marcel Proust, *Remembrance of Things Past*, 3 vols., trans. C. K. Scott Moncrieff, Terence Kilmartin, and Andreas Mayor (New York: Vintage Books, 1981), 2:376. Originally published as *À la recherche du temps perdu*, 3 vols., ed. Pierre Clarac and André Ferré (Paris: Éditions Gallimard, 1954), 2:362. Hereafter cited with pagination of the English translation followed by that of the French original.

2. Merleau-Ponty, *Husserl at Limits*, 47/58 (emphasis in original). In this context, Merleau-Ponty speaks not of Proust specifically, but of Husserl's theory of intersubjectivity. Proust's achievement, accomplished by means of the temporal shift that he introduces between Marcel and the narrator, is to introduce an intersubjectivity that is rhythmical or auto-differentiating.

3. Merleau-Ponty, *Visible and Invisible*, 151/196.

4. Proust, *Remembrance of Things Past*, 1:195/1:179.

5. The narrator complains, "But so arduous was the task imposed on my conscience by these impressions of form or scent or color—to try to perceive what lay hidden beneath them—that I was not long in seeking an excuse which would allow me to relax so strenuous an effort and to spare myself the fatigue that it involved." Ibid.

6. Ibid., 1:195/1:178.

7. Ibid., 1:196/1:179.

8. As Merleau-Ponty writes, "The universal is not above, it is beneath." Merleau-Ponty, *Visible and Invisible*, 218/268.

9. "So the 'Méséglise way' and the 'Guermantes way' remain for me linked with many of the little incidents of the life which, of all the various lives we lead concurrently, is the most episodic, the most full of vicissitudes; I mean the life of the mind. Doubtless it progresses within us imperceptibly, and we had for a long time been preparing for the discovery of the truths which have changed its meaning and its aspect, have opened new paths for us; but that preparation was unconscious; and for us those truths date only from the day, from the minute when they become apparent. The flowers which played then among the grass, the water which rippled past in the sunshine, the whole landscape which surrounded their apparition still lingers around the memory of them with its unconscious or unheeding countenance." Proust, *Remembrance of Things Past*, 1:200/1:183–84.

10. Ibid., 1:201/1:184.

11. Ibid., 1:202/1:185.

12. Ibid., 1:201/1:184.

13. Ibid., 1:48/1:45 (emphasis in original).

14. Ibid., 1:49/1:46.

15. Ibid., 1:51/1:48.

16. Ibid., 1:50–51/1:47.

17. Plato, *Meno*, trans. W. R. M. Lamb (Cambridge, MA: Harvard University Press, 2006), 81c–d.

18. Ibid., 85d.

19. Ibid., 86.

20. "Alas! that first *matinée* was to prove a bitter disappointment," confesses Marcel regarding Berma's performance. Proust, *Remembrance of Things Past*, 1:480/1:445. Again, Marcel meets with "disappointment" when he journeys to see the Balbec Church for the first time. Ibid., 1:710/1:660. Similarly, Marcel speaks of "the disappointments of my pilgrimage to and arrival in the Faubourg Saint-Germain" because he finds it to be "so different from what I had imagined it to be." Ibid., 2:514/2:496.

21. Ibid., 1:709–10/1:659–60.

22. Ibid., 1:710/1:660.

23. Merleau-Ponty addresses the problems that arise from conceiving of memory as a representation by asking us to consider the realm of the flesh—"the body . . . as that which answers each time to the question 'Where am I and what time is it?'" (Claudel's questions in the opening of *Poetic Art*): "The problem of memory remains a dead end as long as one hesitates between the conceptions of memory as conservation and memory as construction. It is always possible to show that consciousness only finds in its 'representations' what it has put into them, and thus that memory is construction—and yet that nevertheless another memory behind the latter is needed to measure the value of its creations, in other words, a past given gratuitously and in a way quite opposite to the operation of memory as construction. Only if we abandon

the description of the problem in terms of 'representation' can we reconcile the immanence and transcendence of the past, the activity and passivity of memory. Instead of a 'representation' (*Vorstellung*), we might begin by viewing the present as a certain unique position of the index of being-in-the-world, and our relations with the present when the present slips into the past, like our relations with our surroundings, might be attributed to a postural schema which unfolds and shapes a series of positions and temporal possibilities, so that the body could be regarded as that which answers each time to the question 'Where am I and what time is it?' Then there would be no question of any alternative between conservation and construction; memory would not be the opposite of forgetfulness, and it might be seen that true memory is to be found at the intersection of the two, at the moment where memory forgotten and kept by forgetfulness returns. It might then be clear that forgetfulness and memory recalled are two modes of our oblique relation with a past that is present to us only through the determinate void that it leaves in us." Merleau-Ponty, "Themes from Lectures," 50–51/71–72.

24. Proust, *Remembrance of Things Past*, 1:47–48/1:44.

25. Ibid., 3:716/3:699. A beautiful passage from the beginning of the *Recherche* illustrates the creative power of this bodily sense, as the narrator describes the intersection between desire and physical memory (a sensation in his thigh) in the dream-state of his sleep: "Sometimes, too, as Eve was created from a rib of Adam, a woman would be born during my sleep from some strain in the position of my thighs. Conceived from the pleasure I was on the point of consummating, she it was, I imagined, who offered me that pleasure." Ibid., 1:4/1:4.

26. Merleau-Ponty, *Visible and Invisible*, 221/270 (emphasis in original). Merleau-Ponty is referring to Paul Valéry.

27. We can trace this development from the body to the flesh in Merleau-Ponty's earlier work, especially *Phenomenology of Perception*. In the following passage, it is the body as flesh that expresses existence:

> If we therefore say that the body expresses existence at every moment, this is in the sense in which a word expresses thought. Anterior to conventional means of expression, which reveal my thoughts to others only because already, for both myself and them, meanings are provided for each sign, and which in this sense do not give rise to genuine communication at all, we must, as we shall see, recognize a primary process of signification in which the thing expressed does not exist apart from the expression, and in which the signs themselves induce their significance externally. In this way the body expresses total existence, not because it is an external accompaniment to that existence, but because existence realizes itself in the body. This incarnate significance is the central phenomenon of which body and mind, sign and significance are abstract moments.
>
> Understood in this way, the relation of expression to thing expressed, or of sign to meaning is not a one-way relationship like that between original text and translation. Neither body *nor existence* can be regarded as the original of the human being, since they presuppose each other, and because the body is solidified or generalized existence, and existence a perpetual incarnation.

Merleau-Ponty, *Phenomenology of Perception*, 192/204 (emphasis in original).

28. Merleau-Ponty, *Visible and Invisible*, 146/189.

29. Ibid., 139/181.

30. Ibid., 147/191.

31. Ibid., 152/197.

32. Ibid., 137–38/179–80.

33. Ibid., 138/180.

34. Merleau-Ponty's description of this expressive space, so characteristic of the flesh, can be read even in his early work *Phenomenology of Perception*. Once again, we might read this sense of the "body" as the flesh:

> The example of instrumentalists shows even better how habit has its abode neither in thought nor in the objective body, but in the body as mediator of a world. It is known that an experienced organist is capable of playing an organ which he does not know, which has more or fewer manuals, and stops differently arranged, compared with those on the instrument he is used to playing. He needs only an hour's practice to be ready to perform his program. Such a short preparation rules out the supposition that new conditioned reflexes have here been substituted for the existing sets, except where both form a system and the change is all-embracing. . . . During the rehearsal, as during the performance, the stops, pedals and manuals are given to him as nothing more than possibilities of achieving certain emotional or musical values, and their positions are simply the places through which this value appears in the world. Between the musical essence of the piece as it is shown in the score and the notes which actually sound round the organ, so direct a relation is established that the organist's body and his instrument are merely the medium of this relationship. Henceforth the music exists by itself and through it all the rest exists. There is here no place for any "memory" of the position of the stops, and it is not in objective space that the organist in fact is playing. In reality his movements during rehearsal are consecratory gestures: they draw affective vectors, discover emotional sources, and create a space of expressiveness as the movements of the augur delimit the *templum*. . . .
>
> Now the body is essentially an expressive space. . . . The organist distributes, through "organ space," musical significances. But our body is not merely one expressive space among the rest, for that is simply the constituted body. It is the origin of the rest, expressive movement itself, that which causes them to begin to exist as things, under our hands and eyes.

Merleau-Ponty, *Phenomenology of Perception*, 167–69/180–81.

35. Merleau-Ponty, *Visible and Invisible*, 139–40/181–82 (emphases in original).

36. In this respect, *The Visible and the Invisible* cites the same Claudel quotation twice, at the end of the chapter entitled "Interrogation and Dialectic" and again in the following chapter, "Interrogation and Intuition." Merleau-Ponty quotes from Claudel's *Poetic Art*: "'From time to time, a man lifts his head, sniffs, listens, considers, recognizes his position: he thinks, he sighs, and, drawing his watch from the pocket lodged against his chest, looks at the time. *Where am I?* and, *What time is it?* such is the inexhaustible question turning from us to the world.'" Then Merleau-Ponty offers his analysis: "Inexhaustible, because the time and the place change continually, but especially because the question that arises here is not at bottom a question of knowing in what spot of a space taken as given, at what hour of a time taken as given, we are—but first what is this indestructible tie between us and hours and places, this perpetual taking of our bearing on the things, this continual installation among them, through which first it is necessary that I be at a time, at a place, whatever they be." Ibid., 121/159.

37. Ibid., 268/315.

38. Proust, *Remembrance of Things Past*, 3:1106/3:1047.

39. Merleau-Ponty seems to echo Proust when he writes: "In every focusing movement my body unites present, past and future, it secretes time, or rather it becomes that location in nature where, for the first time, events, instead of pushing each other into the realm of being, project round the present a double horizon of past and future and acquire a historical orientation. There is here indeed the summoning, but not the experience, of an eternal *natura naturans*. My body takes possession of time; it brings into existence a past and a future for a present; it is not a thing, but creates time instead of submitting to it." Merleau-Ponty, *Phenomenology of Perception*, 278–79/287.

40. Proust, *Remembrance of Things Past*, 3:1084–85/3:1029.

41. Ibid., 3:1105/3:1046.

42. Merleau-Ponty, *Visible and Invisible*, 117/155. Cf. chapter 9 on simultaneity in Claudel.

43. Ibid., 243/291–92 (emphasis in original).

44. Proust, *Remembrance of Things Past*, 1:201/1:184.

45. Merleau-Ponty, *Visible and Invisible*, 151/196.

46. Proust, *Remembrance of Things Past*, 1:201/1:184–85.

47. Merleau-Ponty, *Visible and Invisible*, 267/315 (emphasis in original).

48. The analysis draws upon an important and lengthy working note of *The Visible and the Invisible* dated April 1960. The Freudian unconscious, according to Merleau-Ponty, addresses the fundamental question that Meno (as we saw) posed to Socrates: How can one know what one has never known? Socrates proposes the notion of anamnesis—recollection that would depend upon the eternal soul having been separate from the temporal appearance of the body. The Freudian unconscious, however, could account for this possibility of knowing the unknown without having to posit the existence of a separate, eternal realm, as Merleau-Ponty points out. Yet, at the same time (as we learn from a course summary, "Nature and Logos," in which he poses this same question), it is clear that Merleau-Ponty seeks to replace this Freudian unconscious (which would dwell solely within the mind) with his own notion of flesh: "The double formula of the unconscious ('I did not know' and 'I have always known it') corresponds to two aspects of the flesh, its poetic and its oneiric powers . . . it comprises a double movement of progress and regression." Merleau-Ponty, "Themes from Lectures," 130/179 (translation modified). The note from *Visible and Invisible*, 243–44/291–93, is quoted in full here (emphases in original):

> The Freudian idea of the unconscious and the past as "indestructible," as "intemporal" = elimination of the common idea of time as a "series of *Erlebnisse*"—There is an architectonic past. cf. Proust: the *true* hawthorns are the hawthorns of the past—Restore this life without *Erlebnisse*, without interiority . . . which is, in reality, the "monumental" life, *Stiftung*, initiation.
>
> This "past" belongs to a mythical time, to the time before time, to the prior life, "farther than India and China"—
>
> What is the *intentional analysis* worth in regard to it? It gives us: every past *sinngemäss* has been present, i.e. its past being has been founded in a presence—And, certainly, that is so true [of?] it that it *is still present*. But precisely there is here something that the intentional analytic cannot grasp, for it cannot rise (Husserl) to this "simultaneity" which is meta-intentional (cf. Fink article on the *Nachlass*). The intentional analytic tacitly assumes a place of absolute contemplation *from which* the intentional explicitation [*sic*] is made, and which could embrace present, past, and even openness toward the future—It is the order of the "consciousness" of significations, and in this order there

is no past-present "simultaneity," there is the evidence of their divergence—Whereas the *Ablaufsphänomen* that Husserl describes and thematizes contains itself something quite different: it contains the "simultaneity," the *passage*, the *nunc stans*, the Proustian corporeity as guardian of the past, the immersion in a Being in transcendence not reduced to the "perspectives" of the "consciousness"—it contains an intentional reference which is not only from the past [subordinated] to the factual, empirical present, but also and inversely from the factual present to a dimensional present or *Welt* or Being, where the past is "simultaneous" with the present in the narrow sense. . . . And in fact here it is indeed the past that adheres to the present and not the *consciousness* of the past that adheres to the *consciousness* of the present: the "vertical" past contains in itself the exigency to have been perceived, far from the consciousness of having perceived bearing that of the past. . . . The whole Husserlian analysis is blocked by the framework of *acts* which imposes upon it the philosophy of *consciousness*. . . . It is necessary to take as primary, not the consciousness and its *Ablaufsphänomen* with its distinct intentional threads, but the vortex which this *Ablaufsphänomen* schematizes, the spatializing-temporalizing vortex (which is flesh and not consciousness facing a noema).

49. Merleau-Ponty, *Visible and Invisible*, 168/220.

50. Ibid., 24/42–43.

51. Ibid., 189/240.

52. Ibid., 138/179–80.

53. Indeed, Merleau-Ponty emphasizes that "movement is *carnal*." Ibid., 257/305 (emphasis in original).

54. Merleau-Ponty, "Themes from Lectures," 91/128.

55. Merleau-Ponty, *Visible and Invisible*, 115/152–53.

56. Ibid., 218/268 (emphases in original).

Chapter Four

1. McCombie, *Mallarmé and Debussy*, 24.

2. Debussy's letter of invitation to Mallarmé reads: "Dear Master, I need not say how happy I should be if you were kind enough to honor with your presence the arabesque which, by an excess of pride perhaps, I believe to have been dictated by the flute of your faun." François Lesure and Roger Nichols, eds., *Debussy Letters*, trans. Roger Nichols (Cambridge, MA: Harvard University Press, 1987), 75.

3. Ibid., 218.

4. Translation from Rosemary Lloyd, "Debussy, Mallarmé, and 'Les Mardis,'" in *Debussy and His World*, ed. Jane F. Fulcher (Princeton: Princeton University Press, 2001), 255. The poet's original inscription reads: "Sylvain d'haleine première / Si ta flûte a réussi / Ouïs toute la lumière / Qu'y soufflera Debussy." The notion of light or radiance (*la lumière*) is significant for Merleau-Ponty, as we will explore in later chapters.

5. Ibid., 256.

6. Mallarmé, "Un coup de dés," 123/456. The poet writes of "une influence . . . étrangère, celle de la Musique entendue au concert; on en retrouve plusieurs moyens m'ayant semblé appartenir aux Lettres, je les reprends."

7. Stéphane Mallarmé, "L'après-midi d'un faune," in *Divagations*, trans. Henry Weinfield (Berkeley and Los Angeles: University of California Press, 1994), 38. In *Oeuvres complètes*, ed.

Henri Mondor and G. Jean-Aubry (Paris: Éditions Gallimard, 1945), 50. As the opening line of the poem, the poet writes: "Ces nymphes, je les veux perpétuer."

8. On repetition that "cannot be explained by the form of identity in concepts or representations" but that operates, rather, according to an "internal difference," compare the classic text by Gilles Deleuze, *Difference and Repetition*, trans. Paul Patton (New York: Columbia University Press, 1994), 19–20.

9. Maurice Merleau-Ponty, *Le monde sensible et le monde de l'expression: Cours au Collège de France Notes, 1953*, ed. Emmanuel de Saint Aubert and Stefan Kristensen (Genève: MetisPresses, 2011), 116 (my translation). In his analysis of this passage, Vanzago writes, "Meaning itself is related to movement. Meaning is made possible by the distribution of movement and rest, the rhythm of translations and transformations, acceleration and deceleration, that is, time. These are not simply mechanical phenomena. They rather convey their own meaning, including an affective tone." Luca Vanzago, "The Many Faces of Movement," *Chiasmi International* 12 (2010): 118. Vanzago's analysis, although (like Merleau-Ponty's) conducted without reference to music, seems to apply quite directly to this temporal art.

10. Maurice Merleau-Ponty, "Two Unpublished Notes on Music," trans. Leonard Lawlor, *Chiasmi International* 3 (2001): 18.

11. The circle of fifths, in tonal harmony, refers to relationships between different tonal areas or key centers. The circle moves in one direction by descending fifths (by means of the addition of flats to the key signature) and in the other direction by ascending fifths (by means of the addition of sharps), so that from the top of the circle, at C major (which has no flats or sharps), the progression moves through closely related keys until it arrives at the most distant key, F♯ or G♭ major (the two are enharmonically equivalent, that is to say, they use different note names to refer to the same pitch class). Usually the circle of fifths is represented as a clock face, with keys positioned like the numerals on the clock.

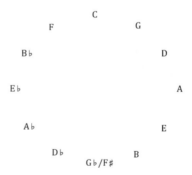

Keys that are positioned closer together on the "clock" share a multitude of common tones; for example, the key signatures of C major and G major differ by only one accidental (an F♮ in C major as opposed to an F♯ in G major). Keys that are positioned across from each other on the "clock" (separated, as one can see, by the interval of the tritone) are the most distantly related, sharing only one common tone; for example, the major scale on C and the major scale on F♯ share only the pitch B as a common tone (excluding the enharmonic respelling of F in C major as E♯ in F♯ major). Therefore, modulation to closely related keys can be relatively smooth, but modulation to the very distantly related ones can have a jarring effect, and the relationship between the most distantly related keys (at the interval of the tritone, i.e., six half steps) is the most dissonant. These harmonic conventions, which are operative in virtually all of the classical repertoire, are the very parameters against which Debussy plays.

12. Lloyd, "Debussy, Mallarmé, and 'Les Mardis,'" 265.

13. Merleau-Ponty, *Visible and Invisible*, 24/42–43.

14. Merleau-Ponty, "Two Notes on Music," 18.

Chapter Five

1. Merleau-Ponty, "Cézanne's Doubt," 65/20.

2. Ibid. (emphasis in original).

3. "There has been, for example, a prosaic conception of the line as a positive attribute and property of the object in itself. Thus, it is the outer contour of the apple or the border between the plowed field and the meadow, considered as present in the world, such that, guided by points taken from the real world, the pencil or brush would only have to pass over them. But this line has been contested by all modern painting, and probably by all painting. . . . There are no lines visible in themselves. . . . neither the contour of the apple nor the border between field and meadow is in *this* place or that. . . . they are always on the near or the far side of the point we look at. They are always between or behind whatever we fix our eyes upon; they are indicated, implicated, and even very imperiously demanded by the things, but they themselves are not things. They were thought to circumscribe the apple or the meadow, but the apple and the meadow 'form themselves' from themselves, and come into the visible as if they had come from a pre-spatial world behind the scenes." Merleau-Ponty, "Eye and Mind," 142–43/72–73 (emphasis in original).

4. Ibid., 126/22–23 (emphases in original).

5. Older than Lascaux (but not known in Merleau-Ponty's time), the cave of Chauvet–Pont-d'Arc features paintings created over thirty thousand years ago. See the website provided by the French Ministry of Culture and Communication, www.culture.gouv.fr/culture/arcnat/chauvet/en/.

6. Merleau-Ponty, *Visible and Invisible*, 152/197. It is a style that would never be completely transparent even to the painter himself, as Merleau-Ponty mentions with respect to Van Gogh: "Even when the painter has already painted, and even if he has become in some respects master of himself, what is given to him with his style is not a manner, a certain number of procedures or tics that he can inventory, but a mode of formulation that is just as recognizable for others and just as little visible to him as his silhouette or his everyday gestures." Merleau-Ponty, "Indirect Language," 90/86. This resistance of style has to do with its emergence across the process of institution (cf. the "little phrase" that Swann is unable to grasp in its temporal unfolding, chapter 8).

7. Merleau-Ponty, "Eye and Mind," 145/79.

8. Ibid., 145/78–79 (emphasis in original).

9. Jonathan Crary offers a description that evokes Merleau-Ponty's own theories on the significance of Cézanne's ability to synthesize mutually exclusive elements without effecting a conflation of differences: "Part of the strangeness of Cézanne's late work may be due, as some critics have suggested, to an attempt to grasp peripheral retinal sensation simultaneously and with the same immediacy and intensity as the central or foveal region of the eye. It would not have been a question of aspiring to a unified homogeneous field of vision but rather to having the fixed eye apprehend many disconnected areas of the visual field at once, instead of repressing the periphery as most of us do almost all the time. . . . Thus, much of his work from the mid-1890s on is a

radical rethinking of the nature of *synthesis*—synthesis in the sense of the rhythmic coexistence of radically heterogeneous and temporally dispersed elements. Cézanne's work poses the idea of an attentive fixation, a subjective immobilization that, instead of holding together the contents of the perceived world, seeks to enter into its ceaseless movements of destabilization." Jonathan Crary, *Suspensions of Perception: Attention, Spectacle, and Modern Culture* (Cambridge, MA: MIT Press, 1999), 297 (emphasis in original).

10. At the end of an essay in *Poetic Art* entitled "Knowledge of Time"—a piece often cited in the later work of Merleau-Ponty—Claudel writes, "All movement, we have stated, is *from* and not *toward* a point." He compares this movement to "the string on which the bow starts and ends its play." Claudel's essay will be more fully taken up in chapter 9. Paul Claudel, *Poetic Art*, trans. Renee Spodheim (New York: Philosophical Library, 1948), 35 (emphases in original).

11. Merleau-Ponty, *Visible and Invisible*, 152/197.

12. Neither depth nor movement can be captured through a singular image or event. Merleau-Ponty claims that "all movement is stroboscopic." Maurice Merleau-Ponty, *Le monde sensible*, 96 (my translation). This depth of movement is indeed lost, according to Merleau-Ponty, within the ordinary photograph: "Rodin said profoundly, 'It is the artist who is truthful, while the photograph lies; for, in reality, time never stops.' The photograph keeps open the instants which the onrush of time closes up forthwith; it destroys the overtaking, the overlapping, the 'metamorphosis' [Rodin] of time. This is what painting, in contrast, makes visible." Merleau-Ponty, "Eye and Mind," 145/80. For a sense of the fin-de-siècle context from which Merleau-Ponty takes his assessment of photography, consult David Halliburton on speed in Proust. David Halliburton, "Reflections on Speed," in *Between Philosophy and Poetry: Writing, Rhythm, History*, ed. Massimo Verdicchio and Robert Burch (New York and London: Continuum, 2002), 152–58.

13. Merleau-Ponty, "Eye and Mind," 144/77.

14. In his summary to the course, "The Sensible World and the World of Expression," Merleau-Ponty makes an interesting connection between this resonant movement and the rhythm of the breath in the sounding of a wind instrument: "The quality of the sound from a wind instrument bears the mark and the organic rhythm of the breath from which it came, as can be shown by the strange impression received by reversing the normal register of the sounds. Far from being a simple 'displacement,' movement is inscribed in the texture of the shapes or qualities and is, so to speak, the revelation of their being." Maurice Merleau-Ponty, "Themes from Lectures," 6/15.

15. Merleau-Ponty, "Eye and Mind," 145/81.

16. Thus Merleau-Ponty writes, "Cézanne already knew what cubism would restate: that the external form, the envelope, is secondary and derived, that it is not what makes a thing to take form, that that shell of space must be shattered—the fruit bowl must be broken. But then what should be painted instead? Cubes, spheres, and cones—as he said once? Pure forms having the solidity of what could be defined by an internal law of construction, forms which taken together, as traces or cross-sections of the thing, let it appear between them like a face in the reeds? This would be to put Being's solidity on one side and its variety on the other. Cézanne had already made an experiment of this kind in his middle period. He went directly to the solid, to space—and came to find that inside this space—this box or container too large for them—the things began to move, color against color; they began to modulate in the instability. Thus we must seek space and its content *together*. The problem becomes generalized; it is no longer solely that of distance, line, and form; it is also, and equally, the problem of color." Ibid., 140–41/65–67 (emphasis in original).

17. Ibid., 142/71 (emphases in original).

18. On the constellation of radiance, repetition, and rhythm in the work of Merleau-Ponty, Deleuze, and Nietzsche, cf. Galen A. Johnson, "Beauty, Repetition, and Difference," in *The Retrieval of the Beautiful* (Evanston, IL: Northwestern University Press, 2010), 169–208.

19. The internal quote is from Delauney. Merleau-Ponty, "Eye and Mind," 141/67.

20. In his analysis of movement and painting, Merleau-Ponty insists that "in the history of painting the category of movement develops far beyond simple local displacement." He continues, "From the simplest perception of movement to the experience of painting, we are always faced with the same paradox of a *force* legible in a form, a trace or *signature of time* in space" (emphases added). Merleau-Ponty, "Themes from Lectures," 10/19–20. In thematizing this "force" or "signature of time," Merleau-Ponty later explores the notion of institution, the effect of which he continues to describe in multiple terms (as style, carnal essence, and movement) and which we here compare to rhythm. Merleau-Ponty himself makes that comparison, in *The World of Perception*, when he describes the style of a film as "a particular overall cinematographical rhythm" and again as "a radiant image, a particular rhythm." Interestingly, he then states that "music offers too straightforward an example [of this particular rhythm] and, for this reason, we shall not dwell on it." Merleau-Ponty, *World of Perception*, 73–74/58.

21. Merleau-Ponty, *Visible and Invisible*, 218/267–68. One must caution that we cannot think of the carnal essence as a thing, not even as a painting. Carnal essence is revealed through the process of institution—through the *act* of painting. Merleau-Ponty draws our attention to this animating capacity, describing "a certain style" as "radiating about a wholly virtual center—in short, [as] a certain manner of being, in the active sense, a certain *Wesen*, in the sense that, says Heidegger, this word has when it is used as a verb." Ibid., 115/152. In a later working note, Merleau-Ponty expands upon this notion of *Wesen* in the context of color, analyzing "this active *Wesen*, coming from the red itself." Ibid., 247/296.

22. He continues, "What is proper to the sensible (as to language) is to be representative of the whole, not by a sign-signification relation, or by the immanence of the parts in one another and in the whole, but because each part is *torn up* from the whole, comes with its roots, encroaches upon the whole, transgresses the frontiers of the others. It is thus that the parts overlap (transparency), that the present does not stop at the limits of the visible (behind my back)." Ibid., 218/267 (emphases in original). There is "overlap" and the unseen ("behind my back") precisely because this universality of color is also that of movement and depth.

23. Merleau-Ponty, "Eye and Mind," 133/43.

24. Merleau-Ponty, *Visible and Invisible*, 132–33/173 (emphasis in original).

25. Philip Conisbee and Denis Coutagne, *Cézanne in Provence* (New Haven: Yale University Press, 2006), 283.

26. We are reminded, as we read in chapter 2, of Merleau-Ponty's claim in "Eye and Mind" that "inevitably the roles between the painter and the visible switch. That is why so many painters have said that things look at them. As André Marchand says, after Klee: 'In a forest, I have felt many times over that it was not I who looked at the forest. Some days I felt that the trees were looking at me, were speaking to me.... I was there, listening.... I think that the painter must be penetrated by the universe and not want to penetrate it.... I expect to be inwardly submerged, buried. Perhaps I paint to break out.'" Merleau-Ponty, "Eye and Mind," 129/31.

27. Conisbee and Coutagne, *Cézanne in Provence*, 289.

28. Lawrence Gowing writes, "Cézanne's patches do not represent materials or facets or variations of tint. In themselves they do not represent anything. It is the relationships between them—relationships of affinity and contrast, the progressions from tone to tone in a color scale,

and the modulations from scale to scale—that parallel the apprehension of the world. The sense of these color patches rests on their juxtapositions and their alignments one with another." Conisbee and Coutagne, *Cézanne in Provence*, 287.

29. Merleau-Ponty, "Cézanne's Doubt," 67/22–23.

30. Conisbee and Coutagne, *Cézanne in Provence*, 287.

31. One could compare, for example, the portrayal of the mountain in Renoir's *Montagne Sainte-Victoire* (c. 1888–89). Here, the mountain—the subject indicated by the title of the painting—has an almost insignificant presence, dwarfed by the blues of the broad, open sky that harmonize with the blues of the olive trees in the foreground.

32. Merleau-Ponty writes: "The 'world's instant' that Cézanne wanted to paint, an instant long since passed away, is still hurled toward us by his paintings. His *Mont. Sainte-Victoire* is made and remade from one end of the world to the other in a way different from but no less energetic than in the hard rock above Aix. Essence and existence, imaginary and real, visible and invisible—painting scrambles all our categories, spreading out before us its oneiric universe of carnal essences, actualized resemblances, mute meanings." Merleau-Ponty, "Eye and Mind," 130/35.

33. Merleau-Ponty, "Cézanne's Doubt," 67–68/23.

34. It is interesting to note, in this respect, that the paintings in Chauvet Cave show signs of having been traced multiple times; here, too, there was a call to reinitiation. Merleau-Ponty describes such a "call" in a passage on the creative expression of art: "[There is] motivation that comes simultaneously from colors, light, substance, movement, a call from all of that to the movement of the hand which resolves the problem while being unaware of it just as when we walk or gesture." Maurice Merleau-Ponty, *Institution and Passivity: Course Notes from the Collège de France (1954–1955)*, trans. Leonard Lawlor and Heath Massey (Evanston, IL: Northwestern University Press, 2010), 47. Originally published as *L'institution, la passivité: Notes de cours au Collège de France (1954–1955)*, ed. Dominique Darmaillacq, Claude Lefort, and Stéphanie Ménasé (Paris: Éditions Belin, 2003), 86. Hereafter cited as *Institution and Passivity*, with pagination of the English translation followed by that of the French original.

35. Merleau-Ponty, "Cézanne's Doubt," 59/13.

36. Merleau-Ponty writes: "How do we know what we are making in painting? We do not work by chance. And yet, the entire field of *the* art of painting, and, for each painter, the field of *his* painting, is not truly given. History is retrospective, metamorphoses, and in this sense painters do not know what they are making. And yet, each rediscovers the whole of painting, just as each life discovers all lives." Merleau-Ponty, *Institution and Passivity*, 41/78 (emphasis in original).

37. Merleau-Ponty, "Cézanne's Doubt," 69/25 (emphasis in original).

38. In a lengthy but important passage Merleau-Ponty writes: "A camera once recorded the work of Matisse in slow motion. The impression was prodigious, so much so that Matisse himself was moved, they say. That same brush that, seen with the naked eye, leaped from one act to another, was seen to meditate in a solemn, expanded time—in the imminence of a world's creation—to try ten possible movements, dance in front of the canvas, brush it lightly several times, and crash down finally like a lightening stroke upon the one line necessary. Of course, there is something artificial in this analysis. And Matisse would be wrong if, putting his faith in the film, he believed that he really chose between all possible lines that day and, like the God of Leibniz, solved an immense problem of maximum and minimum. He was not a demiurge; he was a human being. He did not have in his mind's eye all the gestures possible, and in making his choice he did not have to eliminate all but one. It is slow motion which enumerates the

possibilities. Matisse, set within a human's time and vision, looked at the still open whole of his work in progress and brought his brush toward the line which called for it in order that the painting might finally be that which it was in the process of becoming. By a simple gesture he resolved the problem which in retrospect seemed to imply an infinite number of data. . . . And yet, Matisse's hand did hesitate. Consequently, there was a choice, and the chosen line was chosen in such a way as to observe, scattered out over the painting, a score of conditions which were unformulated and even informulable for anyone but Matisse, since they were only defined and imposed by the intention of executing *that particular painting which did not yet exist.*" Merleau-Ponty, "Indirect Language," 82–83/73–74 (emphasis in original).

39. Merleau-Ponty, "Cézanne's Doubt," 65–66/21 (emphasis in original).

40. In the labor of artistic expression, as Merleau-Ponty tells us, "'Conception' cannot precede 'execution.' Before expression, there is nothing but a vague fever, and only the work itself, completed and understood, will prove that there was *something* rather than *nothing* to be found there. Because he has returned to the source of silent and solitary experience on which culture and the exchange of ideas have been built in order to take cognizance of it, the artist launches his work just as a man once launched the first word." Ibid., 69/24–25 (emphases in original). There is a resonance here with Rimbaud's famous letter to Paul Demeny, noted in chapter 1: "For I is someone else. If the brass awakens as horn, it can't be to blame. This much is clear: I'm around for the hatching of my thought: I watch it, I listen to it: I release a stroke from the bow: the symphony makes its rumblings in the depths, or leaps fully-formed onto the stage." Rimbaud, *Complete Works*, 366.

41. Merleau-Ponty, "Cézanne's Doubt," 69/25 (emphasis in original).

42. See, for example, chapter 4 and the discussion of the effect of the arabesque in the final measures of Debussy's *Prélude.*

43. Merleau-Ponty denies that this process of expression would be ruled entirely by chance or circumstance. "However," he cautions, "painting is not a logic of painting; the construction is retrospective (and provisional), what we have found; we do not know exactly what it is going to mean." Merleau-Ponty, *Institution and Passivity*, 44/82.

44. Ibid., 47/86.

45. Ibid., 77/124. That is to say, it is a logic of depth.

46. Merleau-Ponty describes the debt that he owes to Husserl with respect to this notion of institution: "Husserl has used the fine word *Stiftung*—foundation or establishment—to designate first of all the unlimited fecundity of each present which, precisely because it is singular and passes, can never stop having been and thus being universally; but above all to designate the fecundity of the products of a culture which continue to have value after their appearance and which open a field of investigations in which they perpetually come to life again." Merleau-Ponty, "Indirect Language," 96/95.

47. Merleau-Ponty, *Institution and Passivity*, 48–49/87.

48. Ibid., 77/124.

49. Merleau-Ponty, "Indirect Language," 105/110 (emphasis added).

50. Ibid.

51. Merleau-Ponty, *Husserl at Limits*, 29/34 (emphasis in original).

Chapter Six

1. Proust, *Remembrance of Things Past*, 3:61/3:67.

2. Ibid., 3:63/3:69.

3. Ibid., 3:63/3:68–69.

4. Ibid., 2:378–79/2:365.

5. Ibid., 2:379/2:365.

6. Ibid., 3:95/3:100.

7. The method of the *kosmotheoros*, as we saw in chapter 2, operates according to a system of ideality removed from the world. Merleau-Ponty writes, "If I am *kosmotheoros*, my sovereign gaze finds the things each in its own time, in its own place, as absolute individuals in a unique local and temporal disposition. Since they participate in the same significations each from its own place, one is led to conceive another dimension that would be a transversal to this flat multiplicity and that would be the system of significations without locality or temporality." Thus Marcel searches for this "transversal" that, "without locality or temporality," would reveal the *pure essence* of Albertine. Merleau-Ponty, *Visible and Invisible*, 113/149–50.

8. "A pure essence which would not be at all contaminated and confused with the facts could result only from an attempt at total variation. It would require a spectator himself without secrets, without latency, if we are to be certain that nothing be surreptitiously introduced into it." Ibid., 111/147.

9. On the question of eliminating all that is extraneous to essence, Merleau-Ponty asks, "But does what remain after these eliminations belong necessarily to the Being in question? In order to affirm that I should have to soar over my field, suspend or at least reactivate all the sedimented thoughts with which it is surrounded, first of all my time, my body—which is not only impossible for me to do in fact but would deprive me of that very cohesion in depth (*en épaisseur*) of the world and of Being without which the essence is subjective folly and arrogance. There is therefore for me something inessential, and there is a zone, a hollow, where what is not inessential, not impossible, assembles; there is no positive vision that would definitively give me the essentiality of the essence." Ibid., 112/148–49.

10. Proust, *Remembrance of Things Past*, 3:393/3:387.

11. "I felt at such moments that I had possessed her more completely, like an unconscious and unresisting object of dumb nature." Ibid., 3:67/3:73.

12. Ibid., 3:64/3:70.

13. Ibid., 3:64/3:69.

14. Ibid., 2:857/2:828–29.

15. See Leonard Lawlor's analysis of this rhythm as "a mirroring relation." Leonard Lawlor, " 'Benign Sexual Variation': An Essay on the Late Thought of Merleau-Ponty," *Chiasmi International* 10 (2008): 53. As the title of the article indicates, Lawlor's essay explores the greater philosophical significance of Merleau-Ponty's study of the love between Marcel and Albertine.

16. One might compare the operation of narcissism to that of reflective consciousness which "presume[s] upon what it finds and condemn[s] itself to putting into the things what it will then pretend to find in them" (as we saw in chapter 1). Merleau-Ponty, *Visible and Invisible*, 38/60.

17. Merleau-Ponty, *Institution and Passivity*, 32/68.

18. "Marry her, that's what I ought to have done long ago, that's what I must do now, that's what made her write her letter [of farewell] without meaning a word of it; it's only to bring about our marriage that she has postponed for a few hours what she must desire as keenly as I do: her return to this house." Proust, *Remembrance of Things Past*, 3:429/3:422. Merleau-Ponty remarks upon this turn of events in *Institution and Passivity*, 32–33/68.

19. Merleau-Ponty, *Institution and Passivity*, 32/68 (emphasis in original).

20. Proust, *Remembrance of Things Past*, 3:487/3:478.

21. Ibid., 3:608/3:595.

22. Ibid.

23. Ibid., 3:607/3:594.

24. Ibid., 1:636/1:591.

25. Merleau-Ponty, *Institution and Passivity*, 33/69.

26. Proust, *Remembrance of Things Past*, 2:783/2:756.

27. Ibid., 2:784/2:756.

28. Ibid., 2:783–84/2:756.

29. Merleau-Ponty, *Visible and Invisible*, 112/149 (emphasis in original).

30. Ibid., 112–13/149.

31. Merleau-Ponty writes in a working note of *The Visible and the Invisible*, "the essence, the Platonic idea, the object are the concretion of the *there is*, are *Wesen*, in the verbal sense, i.e., *ester*—." Ibid., 203/253. Cf. also ibid., 115/152. This *Wesen*, Merleau-Ponty clarifies in a working note, is "the operation of *ester*, the apparition of an *Etwas* existing by radiation—." Ibid., 206–7/257. Marc Richir undertakes a similar analysis of essence in Merleau-Ponty when he describes it as a kind of "wild *Wesen*." Marc Richir, "Phenomenological Architectonics," in *Merleau-Ponty in Contemporary Perspectives*, ed. Patrick Burke and Jan Van der Veken (Dordrecht: Kluwer Academic, 1993), 47.

32. In an essay on the significance of perception, Merleau-Ponty writes a remarkable passage on the nature of love, worth quoting in its entirety: "Nothing is more pessimistic or skeptical than the famous text in which Pascal, asking himself what it is to love, remarks that one does not love a woman for her beauty, which is perishable, or for her mind, which she can lose, and then suddenly concludes: 'One never loves anybody; one loves only qualities.' . . . But [*contra* Pascal] it is *true*, at the moment of this promise, that our love extends beyond *qualities*, beyond the body, beyond time, even though we could not love without qualities, bodies, and time. In order to safeguard the ideal unity of love, Pascal breaks human life into fragments at will and reduces the person to a discontinuous series of states. The absolute which he looks for beyond our experience is implied in it. Just as I grasp time through my present and by being present, I perceive others through my individual life, in the tension of an experience which transcends itself." In this sense, one can read Marcel as making the same mistake as Pascal, for he "reduces the person [Albertine] to a discontinuous series of states." Yet the essence of Albertine for which Marcel searches as "beyond" experience is rather, according to Merleau-Ponty, "implied in" experience: through the work of her essence as operative, for precisely the discontinuous or incompossible states cohere as the resonance or affect known as love. Maurice Merleau-Ponty, "The Primacy of Perception and Its Philosophical Consequences," trans. James M. Edie, in *The Primacy of Perception* (Evanston, IL: Northwestern University Press, 1964), 26–27 (emphases in original). Subsequently released in *Le primat de la perception et ses conséquences philosophiques* (Lagrasse: Éditions Verdier, 1996), 70–71.

33. Merleau-Ponty, *Visible and Invisible*, 110/146. Deleuze similarly writes on this problem of essence in Proust: "It is not the subject that explains essence, rather it is essence that implicates, envelops, wraps itself up in the subject." *Proust and Signs*, trans. Richard Howard (Minneapolis: University of Minnesota Press, 2000), 43.

34. Merleau-Ponty cites this quotation twice in his course notes on the relationship between Marcel and Albertine. Merleau-Ponty, *Institution and Passivity*, 35/71 and 37/74.

35. Proust, *Remembrance of Things Past*, 3:536/3:526. Again, Merleau-Ponty cites this quotation twice. Merleau-Ponty, *Institution and Passivity*, 36/72 and 38/74.

36. Merleau-Ponty, *Visible and Invisible*, 220/269.

37. As with the hawthorns, this emotion manifests through a double (see chapter 3). Proust writes, "For it was in myself that Albertine's possible actions were performed. Of every person we know we possess a double; but, being habitually situated on the horizon of our imagination, of our memory, it remains more or less extraneous to us. . . . But ever since the wound I had received at Balbec, it was deep in my heart, and very difficult to extricate, that Albertine's double was lodged." Proust, *Remembrance of Things Past*, 3:254/3:252–53.

38. Merleau-Ponty, *Institution and Passivity*, 38/74.

39. Proust, *Remembrance of Things Past*, 3:392/3:386.

40. Merleau-Ponty, *Institution and Passivity*, 32/68. Proust writes, "Anyone who wished to make a fresh drawing of things as they really were would now have had to place Albertine, not at a certain distance from me, but inside me." Proust, *Remembrance of Things Past*, 2:1154/2:1116.

41. Merleau-Ponty, *Visible and Invisible*, 113/149.

42. Merleau-Ponty, *Institution and Passivity*, 35/71 (emphasis in original).

43. Proust, *Remembrance of Things Past*, 2:858/2:829.

44. Merleau-Ponty, *Institution and Passivity*, 38/75.

45. Proust, *Remembrance of Things Past*, 3:254/3:252.

46. Ibid., 3:512/3:502. Merleau-Ponty points to this and similar passages of Proust several times, confirming in a marginal note, "The love for Albertine is as different from the ones preceding it just as the septet was from the sonata." Merleau-Ponty, *Institution and Passivity*, 94/75. It is thus that the institution of love is connected, for Merleau-Ponty, to the institution of a musical idea. Compare Mauro Carbone, "Love and Music: Theme and Variations," in *An Unprecedented Deformation: Marcel Proust and the Sensible Ideas*, trans. Niall Keane (Albany: State University of New York, 2010).

47. Merleau-Ponty, *Institution and Passivity*, 36/73.

48. Ibid., 77/124.

49. Ibid. On the peculiarity of this cause, which works through a process of institution, we might consider Claudel, who writes on cause in terms similar to those that describe the dynamic movement or reverberation of rhythm or, as we shall see in chapter 7, harmony: "A proportion, that is, a difference: a cause is fundamentally that. It is the achievement or the breaking of the equilibrium between two terms, the satisfaction of a need, the composition of an accord. It is not positive, it is not included in the subject. It is what the subject lacks most." Claudel, *Poetic Art*, 18.

50. Merleau-Ponty, *Institution and Passivity*, 38/75.

51. Marcel describes this when he confesses, after Albertine's death, "And yet how often we had expressed them, those painful, ineluctable truths which dominated us and to which we were blind, the truth of our feelings, the truth of our destiny, how often we had expressed them without knowing it, without meaning it, in words which doubtless we ourselves thought mendacious but the prophetic force of which had been established by subsequent events." Proust, *Remembrance of Things Past*, 3:517/3:507.

52. Merleau-Ponty, *Institution and Passivity*, 48–49/87.

53. This is how we might understand the distinction between Albertine and Marcel's other loves: with respect to their effect upon him. Gilberte, for example, does not enter into his heart in the same way as Albertine, thus there can be no genuine love between them because it is a one-sided love, a narcissistic love from Marcel directed toward Gilberte.

54. Proust, *Remembrance of Things Past*, 3:607/3:594.

55. One could compare this discontinuity to the individual frames of a film through which a sense of movement—cohesion of incompossibles—arises. See the discussion of movement, chapter 8.

56. Merleau-Ponty, *Institution and Passivity*, 48/87.

Chapter Seven

1. The exact spelling of the pitches in the opening measures implies a root of A♯. However, throughout the piece the A♯ is often respelled enharmonically as B♭, which would imply a root of C♯. Likewise, other enharmonic respellings suggest a root of E or a root of G. This is an ambiguity characteristic of all fully diminished seventh chords.

2. This presentation of the two ways in which a tritone can be divided (i.e., in series of either half steps or whole steps) is articulated, in fact, in an earlier moment in the piece, m. 27 (see chapter 4, ex. 4.5). Here, the melody in the flutes operates according to a sort of mirror principle: the descending line moves according to a specific intervallic pattern (whole step–whole step–half step–half step), and the ascending line simply repeats this pattern (whole step–whole step–half step–half step), presenting new pitches according to the descent or ascent. This manifests yet another example of symmetry within the piece.

3. Because of enharmonic equivalency, there are many ways that one can spell a whole-tone scale. I use Debussy's note names within the given context in an effort to facilitate comparison with the score.

4. For example, the root of the B♭ seventh chord, B♭, comes from the whole-tone collection B♭–C–D–E–G♭–A♭, and the tritone contained within the B♭ seventh chord (D–A♭) also comes from that collection. It is the same for each of the chords outlined in example 7.4.

5. It seems that the harmonies of the *Prélude* always proliferate or develop in two ways—just as, in the *Recherche*, Marcel's interior life unfolds according to the Méséglise and Guermantes ways.

6. This tritone, one could say, exerts a gravitational force upon Debussy's work that is similar to the way that Montagne Sainte-Victoire orients the effort of Cézanne's paintings or that Albertine affects Marcel. In each case, there is a repeated encounter—whether with sonority, mountain, or woman—that never inspires an identical response: such is the process of institution.

7. Merleau-Ponty, *Institution and Passivity*, 78/125.

Chapter Eight

1. Critics have long attempted to identify a specific composer, such as Franck, Wagner, or Debussy, upon whom the character of Vinteuil is modeled. However, it would be more in keeping with the spirit of Proust to consider Vinteuil not as a representation or derivation, but as a fiction—not as an imitation, but a reverberation. Vinteuil, one could say, articulates an amplification of Franck, Wagner, and Debussy. In this context it is interesting to note that what arises as a commonality between these three composers (whose works in terms of harmony, phrasing, orchestration, and genre are quite distinctive) is their commitment to forms that use repetition as a technique of difference (through cyclical motifs, leitmotifs, and variations). Compare this to Nattiez, who argues that Schopenhauerian metaphysics lies at the origin of Proust's engagement with music. Jean-Jacques Nattiez, *Proust as Musician*, trans. Derrick Puffett (Cambridge: Cambridge University Press, 1989).

2. Proust, *Remembrance of Things Past*, 1:229/1:210.

3. Ibid., 1:229–30/1:211.

4. Ibid., 1:228/1:209.

5. Ibid., 1:380/1:349.

6. Ibid., 1:379/1:349.

7. Ibid., 1:380/1:350.

8. Merleau-Ponty, *Visible and Invisible*, 149/193.

9. Merleau-Ponty, *Notes de cours*, 193 (my translation). These notes, from the course entitled "L'ontologie cartésienne et l'ontologie d'aujourd'hui," anticipate much of the later sections of the final chapter of *The Visible and the Invisible*, entitled "The Intertwining—The Chiasm," and so are helpful in elucidating the difficult material from that chapter, particularly with respect to Merleau-Ponty's engagement with Proust.

10. Proust, *Remembrance of Things Past*, 1:379–80/1:349.

11. Merleau-Ponty, *Notes de cours*, 191 (my translation).

12. Merleau-Ponty, *Visible and Invisible*, 149–50/194 (emphases in original).

13. Merleau-Ponty writes: "The musical meaning of a sonata is inseparable from the sounds which are its vehicle: before we have heard it no analysis enables us to anticipate it; once the performance is over, we shall, in our intellectual analyses of the music, be unable to do anything but carry ourselves back to the moment of experiencing it. During the performance, the notes are not only the 'signs' of the sonata, but it is there through them, it enters into them." Merleau-Ponty, *Phenomenology of Perception*, 212/223.

14. Proust, *Remembrance of Things Past*, 1:378/1:347.

15. Merleau-Ponty, *Visible and Invisible*, 151/196 (emphasis in original).

16. Proust, *Remembrance of Things Past*, 1:238/1:218. Cf. Deleuze's analysis of Swann, Wagnerian leitmotif, and style: "For Swann, the art lover, Vinteuil's little phrase often acts as a placard associated with the Bois de Boulogne and the face and character of Odette: as if it reassured Swann that the Bois de Boulogne was indeed his territory, and Odette his possession. There is already something quite artistic in this way of hearing music. Debussy criticized Wagner, comparing his leitmotifs to signposts signaling the hidden circumstances of a situation, the secret impulses of a character. The criticism is accurate, on one level or at certain moments. But as the work develops, the motifs increasingly enter into conjunction, conquer *their own plane*, become autonomous from the dramatic action, impulses, and situations, and independent of characters and landscapes; they themselves become melodic landscapes and rhythmic characters continually enriching their internal relations. . . . Proust was among the first to underscore this life of the Wagnerian motif. Instead of the motif being tied to a character who appears, the appearance of the motif itself constitutes a rhythmic character in 'the plenitude of a music that is indeed filled with so many strains, each of which is a being.' . . . The discovery of the properly melodic landscape and the properly rhythmic character marks the moment of art when it ceases to be a silent painting on a signboard. This may not be art's last word, but art went that route . . . : motifs and counterpoints that form an autodevelopment, in other words, a style." Gilles Deleuze and Félix Guattari, *A Thousand Plateaus: Capitalism and Schizophrenia*, trans. Brian Massumi (Minneapolis: University of Minnesota Press, 1987), 319 (emphasis in original).

17. Proust, *Remembrance of Things Past*, 1:380/1:349.

18. Ibid., 1:381/1:350.

19. Merleau-Ponty, *Notes de cours*, 194 (my translation).

20. Merleau-Ponty, *Visible and Invisible*, 152/196–97.

21. We cannot dismiss this sense of movement in music as mere illusion simply because we know that a melody is comprised of individual notes. By analogy, Merleau-Ponty writes, "The discontinuous images of the cinema prove nothing with regard to the phenomenal truth of the movement that connects them before the eyes of the spectator." Ibid., 157/206.

22. Merleau-Ponty, "Two Notes on Music," 18.

23. Merleau-Ponty, *Visible and Invisible*, 150–51/195.

24. Ibid., 151/195.

25. Merleau-Ponty, *Notes de cours*, 194 (my translation).

26. Merleau-Ponty, *Visible and Invisible*, 151/196.

27. Ibid., 150/194–95.

28. Ibid., 149/194.

29. Proust, *Remembrance of Things Past*, 1:380/1:349.

30. Merleau-Ponty, *Husserl at Limits*, 19/20 (translation modified). Merleau-Ponty seeks to understand this notion of ideality not only through Husserl, but also through a reading of Claudel, who writes that, "even time, meant to express existence under its fleeting aspect, implies a permanent, irresistible necessity." Claudel, *Poetic Art*, 25–26. See chapter 9 for an analysis of this passage.

31. Merleau-Ponty, "Resumé Course: Husserl," 6/161.

32. Maurice Merleau-Ponty, *Nature: Course Notes from the Collège de France*, trans. Robert Vallier (Evanston, IL: Northwestern University Press, 2003), 174. Originally published as *La nature: Notes, cours du Collège de France, 1956–57*, ed. Dominique Séglard (Paris: Éditions de Seuil, 1995), 228.

33. Merleau-Ponty, *Visible and Invisible*, 267/315.

34. Merleau-Ponty, *Notes de cours*, 65 (my translation).

35. Merleau-Ponty, *Husserl at Limits*, 55/66.

36. Ibid., 79/20.

37. Ibid., 55/66.

38. Merleau-Ponty, *Visible and Invisible*, 208/258. In remarkably similar terms Merleau-Ponty describes movement itself as a "phenomenon of autolocomotion"—an "interior flux"—and therefore as a "revelation of being" that is "clearly something other than change of place." Merleau-Ponty, *Le monde sensible*, 101–2 (my translation).

39. In an analogous passage, Merleau-Ponty explains this dynamicism in terms of the dialectic: "The dialectic is, Hegel said approximately, *a movement which itself creates its course and returns to itself*, and thus a movement which has no other guide but its own initiative and which nevertheless does not escape outside itself but doubles back to confirm itself from time to time. So the Hegelian dialectic is what we call by another name the phenomenon of expression, which gathers itself up and launches itself again through the mystery of rationality." Merleau-Ponty, "Indirect Language," 110/118 (emphasis in original).

40. Merleau-Ponty, *Visible and Invisible*, 151/195.

41. Merleau-Ponty, *Notes de cours*, 65 (my translation).

42. Ibid., 196 (emphasis in original; my translation).

43. Again, this might be understood in light of the words of Claudel (see chapter 9), who writes, "All movement, we have stated, is *from* and not *toward* a point." Claudel, *Poetic Art*, 35 (emphases in original).

44. Merleau-Ponty, *Visible and Invisible*, 208/258.

45. Rimbaud, *Complete Works*, 365.

46. Merleau-Ponty, *Visible and Invisible*, 150/194.

47. We must recall that "element" is a term that Merleau-Ponty employs to refer to the flesh: "The flesh is not matter, is not mind, is not substance. To designate it, we should need the old term 'element,' in the sense it was used to speak of water, air, earth, and fire, that is, in the sense of a *general thing*, midway between the spatio-temporal individual and the idea, a sort of incarnate principle that brings a style of being wherever there is a fragment of being. The flesh is in this sense an 'element' of Being." Ibid., 139/181–82 (emphasis in original).

48. One passage in particular is useful in elucidating the reference to Claudel: "And it is a little too much to forget that Christianity is, among other things, the recognition of a mystery in the relations of man and God, which stems precisely from the fact that the Christian God wants nothing to do with a vertical relation of subordination. He is not simply a principle of which we are the consequence, a will whose instruments we are, or even a model of which human values are only the reflection. There is a sort of impotence of God without us, and Christ attests that God would not be fully God without becoming fully human. Claudel goes so far as to say that God is not above but beneath us—meaning that we do not find Him as a suprasensible idea, but as another ourself, who dwells in and authenticates our darkness." Merleau-Ponty, "Indirect Language," 107–8/114.

49. It is helpful to read Merleau-Ponty's notion of the *Transponierbarkeit* in reference to a working note that precedes this one, on the *Gestalt*: "It is a principle of distribution, the pivot of a system of equivalencies, it is the *Etwas* of which the fragmentary phenomena will be the manifestation—But is it then an essence, an idea? The idea would be free, intemporal, aspatial. The *Gestalt* is not a spatio-temporal individual, it is ready to integrate itself into a constellation that spans space and time—but it is not free in regard to space and time, it is not aspatial, atemporal, it only escapes the time and space conceived as a series of events in themselves, it has a certain weight that doubtless fixes it not in an objective site and in a point of objective time, but in a region, a domain, which it dominates, where it reigns, where it is everywhere present without one ever being able to say: it is here. It is transcendence. This is what one expresses again in speaking of its generality, of its *Transponierbarkeit*—It is a double ground of the lived." Merleau-Ponty, *Visible and Invisible*, 205/255. Here, the *Etwas* and transcendence are significant notions that apply not only to Merleau-Ponty's understanding of the *Gestalt* but to music as well. See also chapter 10. Indeed, music, Merleau-Ponty writes, performs itself as "rolled up around an *Etwas*—inverting itself, turning the background into a figure and the figure into a background." Merleau-Ponty, "Two Notes on Music," 18.

50. Merleau-Ponty, *Visible and Invisible*, 218–19/267–68 (emphases in original).

51. Ibid., 203/253 (emphasis in original).

52. Proust, *Remembrance of Things Past*, 3:381/3:374.

53. Merleau-Ponty, *Visible and Invisible*, 150/195.

54. Proust, *Remembrance of Things Past*, 1:380/1:349–50.

55. Deleuze and Guattari also note that "Swann does not at all occupy the same position as the narrator." This, they claim, is because "Swann is always thinking and feeling in terms of subjects, forms, resemblances between subjects, and correspondences between forms," whereas, for Marcel, "Vinteuil gradually ceases to be apprehended in terms of forms and comparable subjects, and assumes incredible speeds and slownesses that combine on a plane of consistency of variation, the plane of music and of the *Recherche* (just as Wagnerian motifs abandon all fixity of form and all assignation of personages)." Deleuze and Guattari, *A Thousand Plateaus*, 271–72. It is significant to note that this passage follows directly upon a discussion of music (270–71), where the authors write: "Music has always submitted its forms and motifs to tem-

poral transformations, augmentations or diminutions, slowdowns or accelerations, which do not occur solely according to laws of organization or even of development. . . . Wagner and the post-Wagnerians free variations of speed between sound particles to an even greater extent. Ravel and Debussy retain just enough form to shatter it, affect it, modify it through speeds and slownesses." Cf. Merleau-Ponty's description of the meaning of movement as dependent upon the "realization of a certain *time* [*tempo*]. Change of meaning through change of cadence of the movement [*cadence du mouvement*], fast or slow [*accéléré ou ralenti*]." The terms "tempo," "cadence," "accelerando," and "rallentando" are, of course, commonly employed in music. Merleau-Ponty, *Le monde sensible*, 116 (my translation).

56. It is through the sonata that Marcel is able to appreciate the septet and to ascertain, according to the noncoincidence of the two compositions, the sense of Vinteuil's musical style. Marcel's encounter with the septet begins: "All of a sudden, I found myself, in the midst of this music that was new to me, right in the heart of Vinteuil's sonata; and, more marvelous than any maiden, the little phrase, enveloped, arrayed in silver, glittering with brilliant sonorities, as light and soft as silken scarves, came to me, recognizable in this new guise. My joy at having rediscovered it was enhanced by the tone, so friendly and familiar, which it adopted in addressing me, so persuasive, so simple, and yet without subduing the shimmering beauty with which it glowed. Its intention, however, this time was merely to show me the way, which was not the way of the sonata, for this was an unpublished work of Vinteuil in which he had merely amused himself, by an allusion that was explained at this point by a sentence in the program which one ought to have been reading simultaneously, by reintroducing the little phrase for a moment. No sooner was it thus recalled than it vanished, and I found myself once more in an unknown world, but I knew now, and everything that followed only confirmed my knowledge, that this world was one of those which I had never even been capable of imagining that Vinteuil could have created, for when, weary of the sonata which was to me a universe thoroughly explored, I tried to imagine others equally beautiful but different, I was merely doing what those poets do who fill their artificial paradise with meadows, flowers and streams which duplicate those existing already upon earth. What was now before me made me feel as keen a joy as the sonata would have given me if I had not already known it, and consequently, while no less beautiful, was different. Whereas the sonata opened upon a lily-white pastoral dawn, dividing its fragile purity only to hover in the delicate yet compact entanglement of a rustic bower of honeysuckle against white geraniums, it was upon flat, unbroken surfaces like those of the sea on a morning that threatens storm, in the midst of an eerie silence, in an infinite void, that this new work began, and it was into a rose-red daybreak that this unknown universe was drawn from the silence and the night to build up gradually before me. This redness, so new, so absent from the tender, pastoral, unadorned sonata, tinged all the sky, as dawn does, with a mysterious hope. And a song already pierced the air, a song on seven notes, but the strangest, the most remote from anything I had ever imagined, at once ineffable and strident, no longer the cooing of a dove as in the sonata, but rending the air, as vivid as the scarlet tint in which the opening bars had been bathed, something like a mystical cock-crow, the ineffable but ear-piercing call of eternal morning." Proust, *Remembrance of Things Past*, 3:251–52/3:249–50.

57. Ibid., 3:257–58/3:256.

58. Merleau-Ponty, *Notes de cours*, 64 (my translation).

59. It is useful to consider this quote on music in relation to Merleau-Ponty's discussion of what stands before reflection: "primordial faith" and "original opinion" (*Urdoxa*) that has not yet become knowledge (cf. chapter 10). In "The Philosopher and His Shadow," Merleau-Ponty's homage to the work of Husserl, he writes that "relative to this scientific *naturalism*, the *natural*

attitude involves a higher truth that we must regain." He continues: "In the unreflected there are 'syntheses which dwell this side of any thesis' [*en deçà de toute thèse*]. . . . The natural attitude itself emerges unscathed from the complaints which can be made about naturalism, because it is 'prior to any thesis,' because it is the mystery of a *Weltthesis* prior to all theses. It is, Husserl says in another connection, the mystery of a primordial faith and a fundamental and original opinion (*Urglaube, Urdoxa*) which are thus not even in principle translatable in terms of clear and distinct knowledge, and which—more ancient than any 'attitude' or 'point of view'—give us not a representation of the world but the world itself." Merleau-Ponty, *Signs*, 163–64/265–67 (emphases in original). It is in this sense that we must understand Merleau-Ponty's charac-terization of music as dwelling "on this side of the ambivalence and the thesis" (*en deçà de l'ambivalence et de la thèse*): that music "give[s] us not a representation of the world but the world itself." This context may also help illuminate Merleau-Ponty's comment that music "is too far on the hither side of the world [*est trop en deçà du monde*] and the designatable to depict anything but certain schemata of Being—its ebb and flow, its growth, its upheavals, its turbu-lence." Merleau-Ponty, "Eye and Mind," 123/14.

60. Merleau-Ponty, *Notes de cours*, 65 (my translation).

61. Merleau-Ponty, *Visible and Invisible*, 152/197.

62. Merleau-Ponty, *Notes de cours*, 65 (my translation).

63. Merleau-Ponty, *Visible and Invisible*, 167/219 (emphasis in original).

64. Ibid., 147/191.

65. Ibid., 151/196.

66. Ibid., 124/163.

67. Merleau-Ponty, *Notes de cours*, 64 (my translation).

68. Ibid.

69. Merleau-Ponty, *Visible and Invisible*, 151/196.

70. Ibid.

71. Ibid., 265/313 (emphasis in original).

Chapter Nine

1. Quoted from Leon Botstein, "Beyond the Illusions of Realism: Painting and Debussy's Break with Tradition," in *Debussy and His World*, ed. Jane F. Fulcher (Princeton: Princeton University Press, 2001), 160.

2. As Botstein remarks, "Louis Laloy, Debussy's friend and first biographer, pointed out (directly echoing Debussy's own self-representation) that the essence of Debussy's achieve-ment was a radically economical abandonment of artificial demarcations within musical time." Ibid., 158.

3. Claude Debussy, *Prelude to "The Afternoon of a Faun,"* ed. William W. Austin (New York: W. W. Norton, 1970), 71.

4. See, for example, Arthur Wenk, *Claude Debussy and Twentieth-Century Music* (Boston: Twayne, 1983); Roy Howat, *Debussy in Proportion: A Musical Analysis* (Cambridge: Cambridge University Press, 1983); and Jean Barraqué, *Debussy* (Paris: Éditions du Seuil, 1962); as well as Austin's critical analysis in the Norton score.

5. Austin, critical analysis, in Debussy, *Prelude to "The Afternoon of a Faun,"* 71.

6. See chapter 7 for a more detailed analysis of this section of the piece.

7. Merleau-Ponty, "Eye and Mind," 132/42.

8. For recent discussions of musical variations within the context of Merleau-Ponty's *Na-*

ture lectures and the *Umwelt* of Jakob von Uexküll, see Mauro Carbone, "Nature: Variations on the Theme," in *The Thinking of the Sensible: Merleau-Ponty's A-Philosophy* (Evanston, IL: Northwestern University Press, 2004), and Ted Toadvine, "The Melody of Life and the Motif of Philosophy," *Chiasmi International 7* (2005): 263–78. Cf. Deleuze and Guattari, "1837: Of the Refrain," in *A Thousand Plateaus*, 310–50.

9. Merleau-Ponty, *Visible and Invisible*, 208/258.

10. Merleau-Ponty, *Notes de cours*, 65 (my translation). For an analysis of this claim, see chapter 8.

11. Proust, *Remembrance of Things Past*, 1:380/1:349.

12. Merleau-Ponty, *Visible and Invisible*, 152/197.

13. Merleau-Ponty, *Notes de cours*, 194 (my translation).

14. Merleau-Ponty, *Visible and Invisible*, 151/196.

15. Ibid.

16. Merleau-Ponty writes, "It is nonetheless clear that Husserl himself never obtained one sole *Wesenschau* that he did not subsequently take up again and rework, not to disown it, but in order to make it say what at first it had not quite said." In this sense we could say that philosophical writing is musical in its form. Ibid., 116/153.

17. Ibid.

18. Maurice Merleau-Ponty, *The Structure of Behavior*, trans. Alden L. Fischer (Pittsburgh: Duquesne University Press, 2006), 87. Originally published as *La structure du comportement* (Paris: Presses Universitaires de France, 1942), 96. Merleau-Ponty's description is reminiscent of a passage in Proust, where Marcel is struck by a vision of the twin steeples of Martinville and tries to articulate his impression that "something more lay behind that mobility, that luminosity, something which they seemed at once to contain and conceal." Proust, *Remembrance of Things Past*, 1:196/1:180. This "something" might be thought with respect to rhythm. See chapter 10.

19. Merleau-Ponty, *Husserl at Limits*, 31/37.

20. Ibid., 45/54.

21. Ibid., 15/15.

22. Ibid., 16/16 (emphases in original).

23. Ibid., 27/31.

24. Botstein, "Beyond Illusions," 160.

25. Cf. Derrida's critique of this simultaneity in Claudel and Proust. Jacques Derrida, "Force and Signification," in *Writing and Difference*, trans. Alan Bass (Chicago: University of Chicago Press, 1978).

26. Merleau-Ponty, *Notes de cours*, 199 (my translation).

27. Claudel, *Poetic Art*, 25–26.

28. Merleau-Ponty, *Notes de cours*, 200 (my translation).

29. Indeed, in this respect Merleau-Ponty writes in the course notes of the "antiplatonism" of Claudel, just as he did with the musical idea of Proust. Ibid., 201.

30. Claudel, *Poetic Art*, 12.

31. Ibid., 12.

32. Ibid., 18.

33. Ibid.

34. Ibid., 27.

35. Ibid. (emphasis in original).

36. Merleau-Ponty, *Husserl at Limits*, 55/66.

37. Claudel, *Poetic Art*, 27.

38. Merleau-Ponty, *Visible and Invisible*, 179/231.

39. Ibid., 179/230 (emphasis in original).

40. The editor of *The Visible and the Invisible* points to the "Sigè" from a passage of Claudel, below.

41. Merleau-Ponty, *Visible and Invisible*, 179/230–31 (emphasis in original).

42. Merleau-Ponty, *Notes de cours*, 62 (my translation).

43. Claudel, *Poetic Art*, 35.

44. Ibid. (emphases in original).

Chapter Ten

1. Cf. Ione, "Polyphonic Chords," 55–74.

2. In *Phenomenology of Perception*, Merleau-Ponty makes a study of sense perception in general as synesthetic, rejecting a reductionist view of the senses as separate layers of perceptual experience: "Seen in the perspective of the objective world, with its opaque qualities, and the objective body with its separate organs, the phenomenon of synaesthetic experience is paradoxical. The attempt is therefore made to explain it independently of the concept of sensation: it is thought necessary, for example, to suppose that the excitations ordinarily restricted to one region of the brain—the optical or auditory zone—become capable of playing a part outside these limits, and that in this way a specific quality is associated with a non-specific one. Whether or not this explanation is supported by arguments drawn from brain physiology, this explanation does not account for synaesthetic experience, which thus becomes one more occasion for questioning the concept of sensation and objective thought. *For the subject does not say only that he has the sensation both of a sound and a color: it is the sound itself that he sees where colors are formed.*" Merleau-Ponty, *Phenomenology of Perception*, 265–66/274–75 (emphasis in original).

3. Rimbaud, letter to Paul Demeny, in *Complete Works*, 367 (emphases in original). Merleau-Ponty cites this letter in his course "L'ontologie cartésienne et l'ontologie d'aujourd'hui," commenting that "the derangement of the senses is the breaking down of the divisions between them in order to rediscover their indivision." Merleau-Ponty, *Notes de cours*, 186 (my translation).

4. Merleau-Ponty describes this notion of the seer in Rimbaud—and the vision or *voyance* of the seer—as offering the very "transcendence" that he wishes to articulate in his own ontology: "Yet this unveiling of 'voyance' in modern art—voyance that is not Cartesian thought—has perhaps [an] analogue in arts of speech. Perhaps, we should, instead of reducing vision to the reading of signs by thought, conversely rediscover in speech a transcendence of the same type as in vision. Vinci vindicates voyance *against* poetry. The moderns make of poetry also a voyance—Max Ernst compares the painter projecting forth this that *sees itself* in him and the poet. Since Rimbaud (*Lettre du voyant*) writing 'under the dictation of this that thinks itself, this that articulates itself in him.'" Ibid., 182–83 (emphases in original; my translation). See also Carbone's reading of *voyance* in *An Unprecedented Deformation*, 16–21.

5. See Plato's account of prophets and poets in the *Meno*, 81b.

6. Merleau-Ponty, *Visible and Invisible*, 196/246.

7. In a note: "Or *possibly* visible (in different degrees of possibility: the past has been, the future will be able to be seen)."

8. Ibid., 227–28/277 (emphases in original).

9. Ibid., 268/315.

10. Proust, *Remembrance of Things Past*, 3:904/3:871.

11. The importance of forgetting—of oblivion, of the unseen and unknown—in the recovery of the past must be emphasized. Proust writes: "If, owing to the work of oblivion, the returning memory can throw no bridge, form no connecting link between itself and the present minute, if it remains in the context of its own place and date, if it keeps its distance, its isolation in the hollow of a valley or upon the highest peak of a mountain summit, for this very reason it causes us suddenly to breathe a new air, an air which is new precisely because we have breathed it in the past, that purer air which the poets have vainly tried to situate in paradise and which could induce so profound a sensation of renewal only if it had been breathed before, since the true paradises are the paradises that we have lost." Ibid., 3:903/3:870. Likewise, Proust's casting of artistic production under the theme of forgetting and remembrance resonates with *Meno* insofar as creativity seems to spring from recovery of the eternal soul, as it does for the prophets and poets in *Meno*: "Each artist seems thus to be the native of an unknown country, which he himself has forgotten. . . . Composers do not actually remember this lost fatherland, but each of them remains all his life unconsciously attuned to it; he is delirious with joy when he sings in harmony with his native land, betrays it at times in his thirst for fame, but then, in seeking fame, turns his back on it, and it is only by scorning fame that he finds it when he breaks out into that distinctive strain the sameness of which—for whatever its subject it remains identical with itself—proves the permanence of the elements that compose his soul." Ibid., 3:258–59/3:257. In both of these examples it is forgetting—oblivion—that secures a double or fold of the present, either as "the paradises that we have lost" or the "elements that compose his soul."

12. The vision of the Venice sky, like *doxa*, resists Marcel's intellectual grasp, and he struggles to form an understanding of it: "Impressions such as those to which I wished to give permanence could not but vanish at the touch of a direct enjoyment which had been powerless to engender them." Ibid., 3:911/3:877. To grasp the vision of the resurrection, as to search out *doxa*, is necessarily to change it; the original sensation vanishes. Like *doxa*, which, as Socrates declares, comes to prophets and poets only as a gift of the gods, Marcel's vision of the resurrection is not an accomplishment of conscious effort. Moreover, this gift quiets Marcel's anxiety about death just as, for Socrates, recollection proves the immortality of the soul.

13. Ibid., 3:899–900/3:867.

14. Merleau-Ponty, *Visible and Invisible*, 229/278 (emphases in original).

15. Proust, *Remembrance of Things Past*, 3:899/3:867.

16. In speaking of Merleau-Ponty's work on the intertwining of the seer and the visible, Dastur emphasizes, "*There is no experience except of the metamorphosis of an inside into an outside and of an outside into an inside.*" Françoise Dastur, "Thinking from Within," in *Merleau-Ponty in Contemporary Perspectives*, ed. Patrick Burke and Jan Van der Veken (Dordrecht: Kluwer Academic, 1993), 29 (emphasis in original).

17. Proust, *Remembrance of Things Past*, 3:905/3:872 and 3:908/3:875.

18. Ibid., 3:906/3:873.

19. Ibid., 3:900/3:867.

20. Ibid., 3:905/3:872.

21. Ibid., 3:935/3:898.

22. Merleau-Ponty, "Eye and Mind," 126/23.

23. Merleau-Ponty, *Visible and Invisible*, 225/274 (emphasis in original).

24. Ibid., 228/277.

25. Ibid., 236/285 (emphasis in original).

26. Proust, *Remembrance of Things Past*, 3:906/3:873.

27. Once again, in reading *Meno*, Socrates seems simply to say that recollection is possible because the soul is immortal or undying (*athanatos*): "Then if the truth about reality is always in our soul, the soul would be immortal." Plato, *Meno*, 86b. Yet a more precise investigation shows that this "undying" is not a single prefabricated and unchanging kind of eternity, separate from the world (as in the traditional theory of forms); rather, recollection is possible because the soul is born again and again. The essence of the soul is movement: "At times it comes to an end, which they call dying, at times it is reborn, but it is never destroyed." Plato, *Meno*, 81b. (On the soul as movement, see Plato, *Phaedrus*, 245c–e.) It is not through the positing of a static, ideal- ized realm of the past that the soul "can recollect the things it knew before." Socrates tells us: "As the soul is immortal, has been born often and has seen all things here and in the underworld, there is nothing which it has not learned; so it is in no way surprising that it can recollect the things it knew before, both about virtue and other things." Plato, *Meno*, 81c–d. Indeed, from the vantage point of the poets and prophets, the soul appears to die and to be born again—to have a beginning and an end. Yet because it is the soul itself that sets the condition through which "beginning" and "ending" exist insofar as it generates the time of becoming, "it is never destroyed." (On the world soul as generating time, see Plato, *Timaeus*, 37d–38b.) Thus, the soul expresses a specific kind of eternal movement—an "undying"—that we characterize as constant renewal, as a unity of difference across all time. This reading offers a closer relation to Proust and even to Merleau-Ponty. It is interesting, in this context, to recall Merleau-Ponty's claim, in the *Notes de cours*, that the "consciousness of music is of 'always.'" Merleau-Ponty, *Notes de cours*, 65 (my translation).

28. Marcel says of his Venice resurrection: "All my discouragement vanished and in its place was that same happiness which at various epochs of my life had been given to me by the sight of trees which I had thought that I recognized in the course of a drive near Balbec, by the sight of the twin steeples of Martinville, by the flavor of a madeleine dipped in tea, and by all those other sensations of which I have spoken and of which the last works of Vinteuil had seemed to me to combine the quintessential character." Proust, *Remembrance of Things Past*, 3:899/3:866.

29. Ibid., 3:912/3:878.

30. Ibid., 1:196/1:180.

31. Ibid., 1:197/1:181.

32. Merleau-Ponty, "Indirect Language," 110/118.

33. Proust, *Remembrance of Things Past*, 3:899/3:866.

34. Ibid., 3:381/3:375.

35. Ibid., 3:381/3:374.

36. Ibid., 3:934–35/3:898.

37. Ibid., 3:912/3:879.

38. As we saw in chapter 1, Merleau-Ponty takes this as his model for engaging the works of Husserl, where "we could not define a philosopher's thought solely in terms of what he had achieved; we would have to take account of what until the very end his thought was trying to think." Merleau-Ponty, "Resumé Course: Husserl," 5/160.

39. Merleau-Ponty, "Indirect Language," 119/133.

40. Merleau-Ponty, *Visible and Invisible*, 167/219 (emphasis in original).

41. Ibid., 197/248 (emphases in original). And Proust writes, "The creation of the world did not occur at the beginning of time, it occurs every day." Proust, *Remembrance of Things Past*, 3:685–86/3:669.

Bibliography

Maurice Merleau-Ponty

Merleau-Ponty, Maurice. *Adventures of the Dialectic.* Translated by Joseph Bien. Evanston, IL: Northwestern University Press, 1973. Originally published as *Les aventures de la dialectique* (Paris: Éditions Gallimard, 1955).

———. "Cézanne's Doubt." In *The Merleau-Ponty Aesthetics Reader: Philosophy and Painting,* revised translation by Michael B. Smith, edited by Galen A. Johnson. Evanston, IL: Northwestern University Press, 1993. Originally published as "Le doute de Cézanne," in *Sens et non-sens* (Paris: Nagel, 1948).

———. "Eye and Mind." In *The Merleau-Ponty Aesthetics Reader: Philosophy and Painting,* revised translation by Michael B. Smith, edited by Galen A. Johnson. Evanston, IL: Northwestern University Press, 1993. Originally published as *L'oeil et l'esprit* (Paris: Éditions Gallimard, 1964).

———. *Husserl at the Limits of Phenomenology.* Translated by Leonard Lawlor with Bettina Bergo. Evanston, IL: Northwestern University Press, 2002. Originally published as *Notes de cours sur "L'origine de la géométrie" de Husserl, suivi de recherches sur la phénoménologie de Merleau-Ponty,* under the direction of Renaud Barbaras and edited by Franck Robert (Paris: Presses Universitaires de France, 1998).

———. "In Praise of Philosophy." In *In Praise of Philosophy and Other Essays,* translated by John Wild, James Edie, and John O'Neill. Evanston, IL: Northwestern University Press, 1963. Originally published as "Éloge de la Philosophie," collected in *Éloge de la philosophie et autres essais* (Paris: Éditions Gallimard, 1960).

———. "Indirect Language and the Voices of Silence." In *The Merleau-Ponty Aesthetics Reader: Philosophy and Painting,* revised translation by Michael B. Smith, edited by Galen A. Johnson. Evanston, IL: Northwestern University Press, 1993. Originally published as "Le langage indirect et les voix du silence," in *Signes* (Paris: Éditions Gallimard, 1960).

———. *Institution and Passivity: Course Notes from the Collège de France (1954–1955).* Translated by Leonard Lawlor and Heath Massey. Evanston, IL: Northwestern University Press, 2010. Originally published as *L'institution, la passivité: Notes de cours au Collège de France (1954–1955),* with a preface by Claude Lefort and texts established by Dominique Darmaillacq, Claude Lefort, and Stéphanie Ménasé (Paris: Éditions Belin, 2003).

———. *Le monde sensible et le monde de l'expression: Cours au Collège de France, notes, 1953.* Text established by Emmanuel de Saint Aubert and Stefan Kristensen. Genève: MetisPresses, 2011.

————. *Nature: Course Notes from the Collège de France.* Translated by Robert Vallier. Evanston, IL: Northwestern University Press, 2003. Originally published as *La nature: Notes, cours du Collège de France, 1956–57,* edited by Dominique Séglard (Paris: Éditions du Seuil, 1995).

————. *Notes de cours au Collège de France, 1958–1959 et 1960–1961.* Edited by Stéphanie Ménasé. Paris: Éditions Gallimard, 1996.

————. *Phenomenology of Perception.* Translated by Colin Smith. Revised ed. London: Routledge & Kegan Paul, 1981. Originally published as *Phénoménologie de la perception* (Paris: Éditions Gallimard, 1945).

————. "Philosophy and Non-Philosophy since Hegel." In *Philosophy and Non-Philosophy since Merleau-Ponty,* edited by Hugh J. Silverman. Evanston, IL: Northwestern University Press, 1997. Originally published as "Philosophie et non-philosophie depuis Hegel," in *Notes de cours au Collège de France, 1958–1959 et 1960–1961,* edited by Stéphanie Ménasé (Paris: Éditions Gallimard, 1996).

————. "The Primacy of Perception and Its Philosophical Consequences." Translated by James M. Edie in *The Primacy of Perception.* Evanston, IL: Northwestern University Press, 1964. Subsequently released in *Le primat de la perception et ses conséquences philosophiques* (Lagrasse: Éditions Verdier, 1996).

————. *The Prose of the World.* Translated by John O'Neill. Evanston, IL: Northwestern University Press, 1973. Originally published as *La prose du monde* (Paris: Éditions Gallimard, 1969).

————. "Resumé of the Course: Husserl at the Limits of Phenomenology." In *Husserl at the Limits of Phenomenology,* revised translation by Leonard Lawlor. Evanston, IL: Northwestern University Press, 2002. Originally published as "Husserl aux limites de la phénoménologie," in *Résumés de cours: Collège de France, 1952–1960* (Paris: Éditions Gallimard, 1968).

————. *Sense and Non-Sense.* Translated by Hubert Dreyfus and Patricia Allen Dreyfus. Evanston, IL: Northwestern University Press, 1964. Originally published as *Sens et non-sens* (Paris: Nagel, 1948).

————. *Signs.* Translated by Richard McCleary. Evanston, IL: Northwestern University Press, 1964. Originally published as *Signes* (Paris: Éditions Gallimard, 1960).

————. *The Structure of Behavior.* Translated by Alden L. Fischer. Pittsburgh: Duquesne University Press, 2006. Originally published as *La structure du comportement* (Paris: Presses Universitaires de France, 1942).

————. *Themes from the Lectures at the Collège de France, 1952–1960.* Translated by John O'Neill. Evanston, IL: Northwestern University Press, 1970. Originally published as *Résumés de cours: Collège de France, 1952–1960* (Paris: Éditions Gallimard, 1968).

————. "Two Unpublished Notes on Music." Translated by Leonard Lawlor. *Chiasmi International* 3 (2001): 18.

————. *The Visible and the Invisible.* Translated by Alphonso Lingis. Evanston, IL: Northwestern University Press, 1968. Originally published as *Le visible et l'invisible,* edited by Claude Lefort (Paris: Éditions Gallimard, 1964).

————. *The World of Perception.* Translated by Oliver Davis. London: Routledge Classics, 2008. Originally published as *Causeries, 1948,* edited by Stéphanie Ménasé (Paris: Éditions du Seuil, 2002).

Other Authors

Barbaras, Renaud. *The Being of the Phenomenon: Merleau-Ponty's Ontology.* Translated by Ted Toadvine and Leonard Lawlor. Bloomington: Indiana University Press, 2004.

Barraqué, Jean. *Debussy*. Paris: Éditions du Seuil, 1962.

Behnke, Elizabeth. "At the Service of the Sonata: Music Lessons with Merleau-Ponty." In *Merleau-Ponty: Critical Essays*, edited by Henry Pietersma. Washington, DC: University Press of America, 1989.

Bogue, Ronald. *Deleuze on Music, Painting, and the Arts*. New York: Routledge, 2003.

Botstein, Leon. "Beyond the Illusions of Realism: Painting and Debussy's Break with Tradition." In *Debussy and His World*, edited by Jane F. Fulcher. Princeton: Princeton University Press, 2001.

Brettell, Richard R. *Impression: Painting Quickly in France, 1860–1890*. New Haven: Yale University Press, 2000.

Burke, Patrick, and Jan Van der Veken, eds. *Merleau-Ponty in Contemporary Perspectives*. Dordrecht: Kluwer Academic, 1993.

Carbone, Mauro. *The Thinking of the Sensible: Merleau-Ponty's A-Philosophy*. Evanston, IL: Northwestern University Press, 2004.

———. *An Unprecedented Deformation: Marcel Proust and the Sensible Ideas*. Translated by Niall Keane. Albany: State University of New York Press, 2010.

Carman, Taylor, and Mark B. N. Hansen, eds. *The Cambridge Companion to Merleau-Ponty*. Cambridge: Cambridge University Press, 2005.

Claudel, Paul. *The Eye Listens*. Translated by Elsie Pell. New York: Philosophical Library, 1950.

———. *Poetic Art*. Translated by Renee Spodheim. New York: Philosophical Library, 1948. In *Oeuvre poétique*, introduced by Stanislas Fumet (Paris: Éditions Gallimard, 1957).

Conisbee, Philip, and Denis Coutagne. *Cézanne in Provence*. New Haven: Yale University Press, 2006.

Crary, Jonathan. *Suspensions of Perception: Attention, Spectacle, and Modern Culture*. Cambridge, MA: MIT Press, 1999.

Dastur, Françoise. "Thinking from Within." In *Merleau-Ponty in Contemporary Perspectives*, edited by Patrick Burke and Jan Van der Veken. Dordrecht: Kluwer Academic, 1993.

Debussy, Claude. *Prelude to "The Afternoon of a Faun."* Edited by William W. Austin. New York: W. W. Norton, 1970.

Deleuze, Gilles. *Difference and Repetition*. Translated by Paul Patton. New York: Columbia University Press, 1994.

———. *Proust and Signs*. Translated by Richard Howard. Minneapolis: University of Minnesota Press, 2000.

Deleuze, Gilles, and Félix Guattari. *A Thousand Plateaus: Capitalism and Schizophrenia*. Translated by Brian Massumi. Minneapolis: University of Minnesota Press, 1987.

Derrida, Jacques. *Margins of Philosophy*. Translated by Alan Bass. Chicago: University of Chicago Press, 1982.

———. "The Double Session." In *Dissemination*. Translated by Barbara Johnson. Chicago: University of Chicago Press, 1981.

———. "Force and Signification." In *Writing and Difference*. Translated by Alan Bass. Chicago: University of Chicago Press, 1978.

Doran, Michael, ed. *Conversations with Cézanne*. Translated by Julie Lawrence Cochran. Berkeley and Los Angeles: University of California Press, 2001.

Evans, Fred, and Leonard Lawlor, eds. *Chiasms: Merleau-Ponty's Notion of Flesh*. Albany: State University of New York Press, 2000.

Fóti, Véronique M. "Chiasm, Flesh, Figuration." In *Merleau-Ponty and the Possibilities of*

Philosophy: Transforming the Tradition, edited by Bernard Flynn, Wayne J. Froman, and Robert Vallier. Albany: State University of New York Press, 2009.

Fry, Roger. *Cézanne: A Study of His Development*. New York: Farrar, Straus, and Giroux, 1970.

Fulcher, Jane, ed. *Debussy and His World*. Princeton: Princeton University Press, 2001.

Gasquet, Joachim. *Joachim Gasquet's Cézanne: A Memoir with Conversations*. Translated by Christopher Pemberton. London: Thames and Hudson, 1991.

Gill, Jerry H. *Merleau-Ponty and Metaphor*. New Jersey: Humanities Press International, 1991.

Halliburton, David. "Reflections on Speed." In *Between Philosophy and Poetry: Writing, Rhythm, History*, edited by Massimo Verdicchio and Robert Burch. New York: Continuum, 2002.

Harrison, Charles and Paul Wood, eds. *Art in Theory, 1900–1990: An Anthology of Changing Ideas*. Oxford: Wiley-Blackwell, 2002.

Howat, Roy. *Debussy in Proportion: A Musical Analysis*. Cambridge: Cambridge University Press, 1983.

Ihde, Don. *Listening and Voice: Phenomenologies of Sound*. Albany: State University of New York Press, 2007.

Ione, Amy. *Innovation and Visualization: Trajectories, Strategies, and Myths*. Amsterdam: Editions Rodopi, 2005.

Johnson, Galen A. *The Retrieval of the Beautiful: Thinking Through Merleau-Ponty's Aesthetics*. Evanston, IL: Northwestern University Press, 2010.

Kearney, Richard. "Merleau-Ponty and the Sacramentality of the Flesh." In *Merleau-Ponty at the Limits of Art, Religion, and Perception*, edited by Kascha Semonovitch and Neal DeRoo. London: Continuum International, 2010.

Lattimore, Richmond, trans. *The Iliad of Homer*. Chicago: University of Chicago Press, 1961.

Lawlor, Leonard. *Early Twentieth-Century Continental Philosophy*. Bloomington: Indiana University Press, 2012.

———. *Thinking Through French Philosophy: The Being of the Question*. Bloomington: Indiana University Press, 2003.

———. " 'Benign Sexual Variation': An Essay on the Late Thought of Merleau-Ponty." *Chiasmi International* 10 (2008): 47–58.

Lefebvre, Henri. *Rhythmanalysis: Space, Time and Everyday Life*. Translated by Stuart Elden and Gerald Moore. London: Continuum, 2004.

Leo, Daniela de. "Music: The Place of A-Philosophy." *Chiasmi International* 11 (2009): 445.

Lesure, François, and Roger Nichols, eds. *Debussy Letters*. Translated by Roger Nichols. Cambridge, MA: Harvard University Press, 1987.

Lloyd, Rosemary. "Debussy, Mallarmé, and 'Les Mardis.' " In *Debussy and His World*, edited by Jane F. Fulcher. Princeton: Princeton University Press, 2001.

Loran, Erle. *Cézanne's Composition: Analysis of His Form with Diagrams and Photographs of His Motifs*. Berkeley and Los Angeles: University of California Press, 2006.

Mallarmé, Stéphane. "Un coup de dés." In *Collected Poems*, translated by Henry Weinfield. Berkeley and Los Angeles: University of California Press, 1994. In *Oeuvres complètes*, edited by Henri Mondor and G. Jean-Aubry (Paris: Éditions Gallimard, 1945).

———. "L'après-midi d'un faune." In *Collected Poems*, translated by Henry Weinfield. Berkeley and Los Angeles: University of California Press, 1994. In *Oeuvres complètes*, edited by Henri Mondor and G. Jean-Aubry (Paris: Éditions Gallimard, 1945).

———. "Crisis of Verse." In *Divagations*, translated by Barbara Johnson. Cambridge, MA: Belknap Press of Harvard University Press, 2007. Originally published as "Crise de vers," in *Oeuvres complètes, II*, edited by Bertrand Marchal (Paris: Éditions Gallimard, 2003).

———. "The Mystery in Letters." In *Divagations*, translated by Barbara Johnson. Cambridge, MA: Belknap Press of Harvard University Press, 2007. Originally published as "Le mystère dans les lettres," in *Oeuvres complètes, II*, edited by Bertrand Marchal (Paris: Éditions Gallimard, 2003).

McCombie, Elizabeth. *Mallarmé and Debussy: Unheard Music, Unseen Text*. Oxford: Oxford University Press, 2003.

Michaud, Guy. *Mallarmé*. Translated by Marie Collins and Bertha Humez. New York: New York University Press, 1965.

Nattiez, Jean-Jacques. *Proust as Musician*. Translated by Derrick Puffett. Cambridge: Cambridge University Press, 1989.

Olkowski, Dorothea, and James Morley, eds. *Merleau-Ponty: Interiority and Exteriority, Psychic Life and the World*. Albany: State University of New York Press, 1999.

Plato. *Meno*. Translated by W. R. Lamb. Cambridge, MA: Harvard University Press, 2006.

———. *Phaedrus*. Translated by Harold North Fowler. Cambridge, MA: Harvard University Press, 2005.

———. *Timaeus*. Translated by R. G. Bury. Cambridge, MA: Harvard University Press, 2005.

Proust, Marcel. *Remembrance of Things Past*. 3 vols. Translated by C. K. Scott Moncrieff, Terence Kilmartin, and Andreas Mayor. New York: Vintage Books, 1981. Originally published as *À la recherche du temps perdu*, 3 vols., edited by Pierre Clarac and André Ferré (Paris: Éditions Gallimard, 1954).

Richir, Marc. "Phenomenological Architectonics." In *Merleau-Ponty in Contemporary Perspectives*, edited by Patrick Burke and Jan Van der Veken. Dordrecht: Kluwer Academic, 1993.

Rimbaud, Arthur. *Complete Works*. Translated by Wyatt Mason. New York: Modern Library, 2003.

Saint Aubert, Emmanuel de. *Vers une ontologie indirecte: Sources et enjeux critiques de l'appel à l'ontologie chez Merleau-Ponty*. Paris: Librairie Philosophique J. Vrin, 2006.

Silverman, Hugh, ed. *Philosophy and Non-Philosophy since Merleau-Ponty*. Evanston, IL: Northwestern University Press, 1997.

Toadvine, Ted. "The Melody of Life and the Motif of Philosophy." *Chiasmi International* 7 (2005): 263–79.

Trezise, Simon. *The Cambridge Companion to Debussy*. Cambridge: Cambridge University Press, 2003.

Vanzago, Luca. "The Many Faces of Movement. Phenomenological and Ontological Questions Concerning the Relation between Perception, Expression and Movement in Merleau-Ponty's Lecture Course on *The Sensible World and the World of Expression*." *Chiasmi International* 12 (2010): 111–27.

———. "Presenting the Unpresentable: The Metaphor in Merleau-Ponty's Last Writings." *Southern Journal of Philosophy* 43 (2005): 463–74.

Vernant, Jean-Pierre, and Pierre Vidal-Naquet. *Myth and Tragedy in Ancient Greece*. Translated by Janet Lloyd. New York: Zone Books, 1988.

Waldenfels, Bernhard. "The Paradox of Expression." In *Chiasms: Merleau-Ponty's Notion of Flesh*, edited by Fred Evans and Leonard Lawlor. Albany: State University of New York Press, 2000.

Watson, Stephen. *In the Shadow of Phenomenology: Writings after Merleau-Ponty I*. London: Continuum, 2009.

———. *Phenomenology, Institution and History: Writings after Merleau-Ponty II*. London: Continuum, 2009.

Weiss, Gail, ed. *Intertwinings: Interdisciplinary Encounters with Merleau-Ponty*. Albany: State University of New York Press, 2008.

Wenk, Arthur. *Claude Debussy and the Poets*. Berkeley and Los Angeles: University of California Press, 1976.

Wiskus, Jessica. "L'Esthétique musicale et l'ouverture au Présent." In *Perspectives de l'esthétique musicale, entre théorie et histoire*, edited by Alessandro Arbo. Paris: L'Harmattan, 2007.

———. "Merleau-Ponty through Mallarmé and Debussy: On Silence, Rhythm, and Expression." *Journal of the British Society for Phenomenology* 43, no. 3 (2012): 230–49.

———. "'The Universality of the Sensible': On Plato and the Musical Idea according to Merleau-Ponty." *Epoché: A Journal for the History of Philosophy* 13, no. 1 (2008): 121–32.

Index

A page number in italics refers to an illustration or its caption.